Praise for *Hiding in Plain Sight*

"This fucking rocks."   —Tori Amos

"Sarah Kendzior, in her brilliant new book, is one of the few journalists
who grasps what is happening. Kendzior is a student of autocracy. . . .
She has been warning from the get-go that Trump is working to turn
America into one."

> —David Cay Johnston, Pulitzer Prize–winning journalist
> and *New York Times* bestselling author of
> *It's Even Worse Than You Think*

"An amazing book about our current political situation and how
we got here."   —Peter Gallagher

"It's brilliant and also terrifying. You can't look away."

> —Alex George, author of *The Paris Hours*

"[*Hiding in Plain Sight*] outlines how Trump's rise coincided with
what [Kendzior] believes is the degradation of the American political system and the continual erosion of civil liberties in the country
by foreign powers, revealing just how fragile American democracy is
right now."   —*International Business Times*
> (Top 10 Best Books About Donald Trump in 2020)

"A chilling account of how the media, government, and public have
failed to hold Trump accountable and how this has significantly im-
pacted U.S. democracy."   —*Library Journal Review*

"Dazzling."   —*Daily Herald* (Chicago)

"Impeccably researched . . . This comprehensive, page-turning account presents a stark and uncompromising indictment of the Trump presidency as the culmination of a 'decades-long erosion of American stability, integrity, and democracy.'"   —*Publishers Weekly*

"If you only read one journalistic account of Donald Trump's America, make sure it is Sarah Kendzior's *Hiding in Plain Sight*."
—*Socialist Review*

"A scathing indictment of Donald Trump . . . Kendzior offers fresh views based on her experiences living in the declining economy of the Midwest and on observations as an academic researcher studying dictatorships in the former Soviet Union. . . . A passionate call for immediate action against the 'transnational crime syndicate' that has supplanted the U.S. government."   —*Kirkus Reviews*

"Her highly readable and well-documented new narrative explains the development of an elite criminal network in America, how digital media has shaped repression and protest, and how globalization has allowed the proliferation of organized crime."   —*National Review*

"Sarah Kendzior brings her unique perspective to bear in her engaging new book."   —*The Arts Fuse*

"This is about our country. Irrelevant of whether you consider yourself to be on the right or the left. . . . Sarah has blown the whistle. The rich have gotten richer, the government has been stripped, and the powerful are ever more so. You want to believe someone is on your page. That there's someone to listen to, to inspire you. . . . That's Sarah Kendzior."   —Bob Lefsetz, *The Lefsetz Letter*

"An elegantly written, unforgiving, trenchant bit of political analysis."
—*Inside Higher Ed*

"Sarah Kendzior's *Hiding in Plain Sight* should be required reading prior to the 2020 election. It shows the decline of American politics into the corruption that inhabits the Oval Office today. . . . By giving us a clear-eyed view of what we're up against, Sarah Kendzior has given us cause to continue the fight."   —*PrimmLife*

Praise for *The View from Flyover Country*

A *New York Times* Bestseller

An NPR Best Book of the Year 2018

"Both prescient and honest . . . Seeing the roots of the arguments that now dominate cable news is both fascinating and a little bit haunting in retrospect."   —NPR

"Kendzior's prose is sharp and consistent, whether the essay is data dense or an opinion piece. She maneuvers through big issues with a pace and clarity that make unpalatable topics fascinating and, unfortunately, relatable."   —*Hyperallergic*

"The defining journalistic account of Trump's America does complain, but it isn't bestselling gossip fodder like Michael Wolff's *Fire and Fury* or James Comey's *A Higher Loyalty*. It's the book from the Midwestern journalist who barely mentions the president's name."

—*Traverse City Record-Eagle*

"Sharply written pieces about life and inequality in middle America."

—*Milwaukee Journal-Sentinel* (85 Books for Summer Reading)

"An academic, Midwesterner, and firebrand, Kendzior crafts work that looks unflinchingly at what ails the country."

—*Shelf Awareness* (starred review)

"It's a call to arms, highlighting the struggles of disenfranchised, overworked, and underpaid Americans, and urging our elected officials to recognize and address the inequalities that have become even more pronounced since when she originally wrote the essays."

—*The Village Voice*

"*The View from Flyover Country* is well worth reading. . . . Here is a thoughtful critic who knows how to sound the alarm."

—*The Arts Fuse*

"Kendzior's essays bring to light social injustice and economic inequality in Middle America from a voice that lives there."

—*Medium*

"The talented Kendzior . . . writes intelligently and with great empathy about problems faced by the Midwest." —*New York Post*

"Kendzior's writing, while often concise and clever like this, is just as often backed by statistics, attributions, or an illustrative profile. . . . Though her message is alarming, it is softened with compassion."

—*St. Louis Post-Dispatch*

"An astonishment and a challenge to convention for all sorts of reasons . . . [One of the] books devoted to where we really were not very long ago, where we are now, and where we might well be going. They don't mess around. They play rough. But then the truth almost always does." —*The Buffalo News*

"From Russia to flyover country, Sarah Kendzior might be the voice we need." —*Columbia Journalism Review*

"Hers is a crystalline voice of reason and appraisal in a world that shifts further into unrecognizable territory minute by minute."

—Carol Haggas, *Booklist*

"A collection of sharp-edged, humanistic pieces about the American heartland . . . Passionate pieces that repeatedly assail the inability of many to empathize and to humanize." —*Kirkus Reviews*

"Authoritarianism does not happen in a vacuum. Kendzior gives us valuable information about conditions in the forgotten parts of our country that provided fertile ground for the rise of Trump."

—Amy Siskind, author of *The List*

"Urgent and beautifully expressed . . . What makes Kendzior's writing so truly important [is that] it documents where the problem lies, by somebody who lives there. Read her."   —*The Wire*

"Kendzior is no psychic. She's just whip-smart and an expert on authoritarian governments. She's also that rare writer with an analyst's brain and an empath's heart. . . . Though the essays are topical and political . . . one senses they'll stand the test of time, just for the beauty of the prose and the soundness of the philosophy."

—Stefene Russell, *St. Louis Magazine*

Also by Sarah Kendzior

The View from Flyover Country

HIDING IN PLAIN SIGHT

The Invention of Donald Trump and the Erosion of America

Sarah Kendzior

FLATIRON
BOOKS
NEW YORK

www.flatironbooks.com

"It can happen here. It is: A conversation with Sarah
Kendzior, scholar of authoritarianism and vindicated
alarmist." Interviewer: Anand Giridharadas, printed in
The Ink (Jan. 29, 2020)

The Library of Congress has cataloged the hardcover
edition as follows:

Names: Kendzior, Sarah, author.
Title: Hiding in plain sight : the invention of Donald Trump and the erosion of
America / Sarah Kendzior.
Description: First edition. | New York : Flatiron Books, 2020. | Includes
bibliographical references and index.
Identifiers: LCCN 2019047907 | ISBN 9781250210715 (hardcover) |
ISBN 9781250245397 (ebook)
Subjects: LCSH: Trump, Donald, 1946– —Influence. | Authoritarianism—United
States. | Political culture—United States. | Democracy—United States. | United
States—Politics and government—1981–1989. | United States—Politics and
government—1989– | United States—Social conditions.
Classification: LCC E912 .K46 2020 | DDC 973.933092 [B]—dc23
LC record available at https://lccn.loc.gov/2019047907

ISBN 978-1-250-77940-3 (trade paperback)

First Flatiron Books Paperback Edition: 2021

10   9   8   7   6   5   4   3   2   1

To Emily, Alex, and Pete

Contents

Author's Note

I finished writing this book in the summer of 2019. More information has since emerged and will continue to emerge, but nothing will change the events that have occurred, are recorded in these pages, and will forever be a blight on America's history.

HIDING IN PLAIN SIGHT

Introduction

The story of Donald Trump's rise to power is the story of a buried American history—buried because powerful people liked it that way. It was visible without being seen, influential without being named, ubiquitous without being overt.

The Trump administration is like a reality show featuring villains from every major political scandal of the past forty years—Watergate, Iran-Contra, 9/11, the Iraq War, the 2008 financial collapse—in recurring roles and revivals, despite the widespread desire of the public for the show to be canceled. From Roger Stone to Paul Manafort to William Barr, it is a *Celebrity Apprentice* of federal felons and disgraced operatives dragged out of the shadows and thrust back into the spotlight—with Donald Trump, yet again, at the helm.

The crises of political corruption, organized crime, and endemic racism are all connected, and they shape everyday American life. But in addition to these structural problems, we contend with specific powerful individuals who have acted against the public good for their entire careers. We see the same old men, again and again, vampires feeding on a nation and draining the lifeblood from words like "treason" and "trauma" and "tragedy." They are buffered by backers who prefer to operate in silence, free from the consequences of scrutiny. There is a reason they call it a criminal underground: you walk over it every day, unaware it exists until the earth shakes below your feet.

In the eyes of autocrats and plutocrats, the future is not a right but a commodity. As climate change brings unparalleled crises, the future becomes a rare asset, meant to be hoarded like diamonds or gold. To millionaire elites, many of whom already had an apocalyptic bent, a depopulated world is not a tragedy but an opportunity—and certainly easier to manage as they insulate themselves from the ravages of a literally scorched earth. The last four decades have led to the hoarding of resources on a heretofore unimaginable scale by people who have neither baseline respect for human life nor a traditional sense of the future. Their destructive actions have programmed a desperate generation to settle for scraps instead of settling the score.

Unless we were part of the opportunity-hoarding elite—the Ivankas and Jareds of the world—my generation did not get to have choices. Instead we had reactions. We fought to hold on to what we had before it was stolen, while thieves demanded our gratitude and supplication. The opportunity-hoarding elite told us we were imagining the permanence of our plight and sold us survival as an aspiration.

This book tells the story of how they cornered that market.

It is a terrible feeling to sense a threat coming. It is worse when the threat reveals itself to be real, especially when many of those you warned still dismiss it, and you do not know whether their reaction is rooted in apathy or doubt or fear. What is a warning, in the end, if not a confession—a declaration of what you value and what you will fight to protect? To warn of a threat and be dismissed is to have your own worth questioned, along with the worth of all you strive to keep safe. But there is a price to be paid in persuasiveness, too. I used to think that the worst feeling in the world would be to tell a terrible truth and have no one believe it. I have learned it is worse when that truth falls not on deaf ears but on receptive ones. It is one thing to listen, it is another to care—and yet another to act in time.

In fall 2015, I predicted that Donald Trump would win the presidential election, and that once installed, he would decimate American democracy. It was the latest in a career of issuing unheeded warnings. For years, I had warned of the widespread erosion of American institutions and social trust. I wrote a series of essays documenting my nation's demise, many of which were later published in my first book, *The View from Flyover Country*. The essays were shaped in part by the harsh conditions of Missouri, the state I call home, a state that had long been the bellwether of American politics and now served as the bellwether of American decline.

But the crisis I documented was nationwide: rising political paranoia, opportunity-hoarding by wealthy elites, a "post-employment economy" of side hustles and unpaid labor, the weaponization of digital media by dictators and extremists, and the catastrophic consequences of unchecked corruption. These were not abstract concerns. The cumulative effect was a collective agony intensified by the all-American shame of seeing systemic breakdowns as personal failings. It had been a long time since I or anyone I knew had dreams instead of circumstances.

I had seen these conditions before in countries often presented as antitheses of my own. Prior to covering the United States, I was an academic researcher studying dictatorships in the former Soviet Union, focusing mainly on the Central Asian country of Uzbekistan. Until 2016, Uzbekistan was ruled by Islam Karimov, a former communist official who became Uzbekistan's first president in 1991 and remained its dictator until his death, constitutional term limits be damned. Like all Central Asian presidents, Karimov was a kleptocrat: a leader who abuses executive power to enhance their personal wealth. (Kleptocracy literally means "rule by thieves.") Kleptocracy usually goes hand in hand with autocracy—a system of government in which one ruler holds absolute control—and

Karimov was no exception. He began his tenure proclaiming that he would make Uzbekistan great again and plastered his catchphrase, "Uzbekistan—a future great state!," on ubiquitous signs.[1] He called independent media "the enemy of the people" and hid information about national crises from the public.[2] He persecuted political opponents, LGBT citizens, pious Muslims, and other marginalized groups.[3] He had an intense yet strange relationship with Russia. And he had a glamorous fashionista daughter who kept inserting herself into political affairs despite her utter lack of qualifications . . .[4]

You may see where I'm going here.

When I realized in 2015 that Donald Trump was likely to become the president of the United States, I began warning everyone I knew to prepare for what was long thought impossible: an American autocracy, wrapped in a tabloid veneer. This should not have been seen as far-fetched. In eras of economic decline and political chaos—like America in 2015—demagogues and dictators tend to arise. Trump was the former and seemed determined to become the latter. He ran his campaign like an autocrat-in-waiting: scapegoating immigrants and minorities, threatening journalists who refused to coddle him, vowing to repeal rights and protections, and expressing a preference for dictators over democratic allies. The media whom Trump called his enemy acted like his best friend, airing his rallies in full, letting his lies linger, and treating the prospect of his win as a joke or a ratings boon. Throughout 2016, hate crimes rose as Trump rebranded racism as populism and recruited white supremacists from the dregs of the GOP (like Jeff Sessions) and the extreme right (like Steve Bannon) to join his campaign.

All anyone needed to see Trump as a potential American autocrat were their own eyes. His desire to dismantle democracy was out in the open. He did not bother to hide his goals because he knew few believed he could achieve them. *That sort of thing does not happen here*, commentators scoffed, citing checks and balances and centuries of democratic stability. American exceptionalism— the widespread belief that America is unique among nations and impervious to autocracy—is the delusion that paved Trump's path to victory. The only honest line of Trump's campaign was that America was broken. Trump would know: he helped break it, and now he and his backers sought to capitalize off the wreckage. Trump did not strike me as stupid, like pundits kept proclaiming, but as a master manipulator who preyed on pain like a vulture.

In America, there was more pain than people in power were willing to admit, and more pain than people on the ground could bear. Trump did not feel like a novelty. He felt like a culmination.

My initial fear that Trump sought to rule like post-Soviet dictators was soon supplanted by the realization he was directly connected to said dictators through his own staff. In March 2016, Trump hired Paul Manafort as his campaign adviser. Manafort was a Republican political operative who had known Trump for over three decades, taking up residence in Trump Tower in 2006. In the 1980s and 1990s, Manafort and Roger Stone—another old Trump friend and presidential campaign adviser—partnered in a D.C. firm nicknamed "the torturers' lobby" because their clients included the most brutal dictators in the world.[5] By the mid-2000s, Manafort had left the firm to pursue his own specialty: serving oligarchs from the former Soviet Union.

Oligarchs are extraordinarily wealthy businessmen who both buffer and are protected by the Kremlin and other dictatorships in the former USSR. (The word "oligarch" is usually used in reference to Russia, but oligarchs are transnational operators.) Oligarchs and government officials have a synergistic relationship aimed at streamlining state corruption and facilitating white-collar crime. Their American analogs are plutocrats: the millionaires and billionaires who wield undue influence over the American political system, making it less democratic in the process. To see what unchecked corporate power looks like without even the pretense of law, you need look no further than Vladimir Putin's Russia. Trump views Russia's brutal hypercapitalism with envy. Putin, who stripped Russia of resources and rights, is rumored to be the wealthiest man in the world.[6]

Trump spent the early months of his campaign praising Putin. While appalling, this made sense: the two shared an affinity for corruption, extravagance, and white supremacy. What I did not know was that they also shared a history. When Manafort joined the Trump team, I began researching Trump's ties to Russia, and discovered that the connections I assumed to be aspirational were real, stretched back decades, and had been acknowledged by Trump himself. "Putin contacted me and was *so nice*," Trump bragged to Fox News in 2014, referencing his 2013 visit to Moscow to host the Miss Universe pageant. Trump added that the United States should stop "knocking Russia" because Russia was going to help ensure a future "win," the details of which Trump did not specify.[7]

Russian state media outlet RT cheered Trump's Fox appearance, part of their regular promotion of Trump as a credible American political leader.[8] In August 2015, a team of Western scholars of Russia wondered why the Kremlin was so focused on a long-shot candidate best known as the host of *The Apprentice*, but their observation flew under the radar.[9] It was not until Trump asked Russia for Hillary Clinton's emails at a July 2016 press conference that Trump's illicit ties to the Kremlin became a mainstream media topic—but even then, most of the story remained untold. Trump's reverence for Russia was framed as mere improper behavior instead of what it was: an ominous twist on a long dark-money trail. For decades, Trump had relied on oligarchs and mobsters from the former USSR for support after Wall Street blacklisted him following his bankruptcies in the 1990s.[10] The one bank that agreed to take him on—Deutsche Bank—is notorious for facilitating Russian money-laundering.[11] But Trump's illicit dealings went as far back as the mid-1980s—when the first Russian mobsters moved into Trump Tower—and his network of criminal associates has expanded ever since. By spring 2016, Republican presidential nominee Donald Trump had spent most of his adult life connected to a transnational mafia with ties to the Kremlin.

Trump's illicit foreign ties constituted a profound national security threat, but few US officials would acknowledge it during the campaign season. One exception was Senate Minority Leader Harry Reid, who wrote an open letter to FBI Director James Comey in August 2016, warning him that the election was under attack. Citing evidence of a direct connection between the Russian government and the Trump campaign, Reid wrote that Russian operatives sought to falsify election results and begged Comey to give the American people the full story before they went to the polls.[12] Comey refused, and refused again after Reid wrote a follow-up letter in October. As the evidence mounted, I grew deeply concerned that US institutions were compromised and that the election would be as well.

The summer and fall of 2016 felt like screaming into a void, as Trump played his most reliable trick—covering up crime with scandal—on a gullible punditry convinced Hillary Clinton was both "the real criminal" and a lock to win the presidency. I warned that the polls were not reliable and that demography was not destiny: the increased diversity of America was offset by repressive new voter ID laws designed to disenfranchise nonwhite voters, who tend to vote for Democrats.[13] I covered the rise of the white supremacist mob violence stoked by the Trump campaign, explaining that his conspiracy theories were an effective form of propaganda.[14] I speculated that Trump, a real estate tycoon, had essentially bought the Fourth Estate, threatening critical journalists and witnesses into silence and exploiting the click-hungry desperation of the media economy.[15] The fringes had been pulled to the center, the extreme had become mainstreamed, and no outcome should have been ruled out.

In the end I was right. Trump won. And being right felt terrible.

Once an autocrat gets into office, it is very hard to get them out. They will disregard term limits, they will purge the agencies that enforce accountability, they will rewrite the law so that they are no longer breaking it. They will take your money, they will steal your freedom, and if they are clever, they will eliminate any structural protections you had before the majority realizes the extent of the damage. That is why it is important to act early, particularly when that autocrat is backed by a crime syndicate that transcends state borders in its pursuit of power and wealth.

Most of the coverage of Trump's apparent criminal activity, particularly with regard to the 2016 election, centers around Russia. This makes sense: the Kremlin is the main actor in the hijacking of the 2016 election, and Trump's reverence toward Russia is one of his few consistent foreign policy stances. But what we are dealing with is far more insidious than an attack on the United States by a single government. Trump is part of a complex illicit network including individuals from Russia, Saudi Arabia, Israel, the United Kingdom, the United States, and more—some of whom do not have loyalty to any particular country. Their loyalty is to themselves and their money. Many are criminals without borders who have moved from hijacking businesses to hijacking nations. Some call them fascists; I avoid this term because being a fascist requires an allegiance to the state. To these operatives, the state is just something to sell.

This elite criminal network has been building for decades. It is linked to other groups: right-wing Republican extremists, apocalyptic religious movements of varied faiths, social media corporations, advocacy groups like the National Rifle Association, and parts of the mainstream media. It is pervasive but not all-encompassing. I am not arguing that every entity has been corrupted by it, but I would argue that total domination is the outcome they seek. Now that members of this network hold the reins of power in multiple nations, the goal is to strip each nation down and sell it for parts. The network is not uniform in its desires—some are in it for the money, some for territorial ambitions, some to satisfy their religious or white supremacist fanaticism. But over the course of decades, disparate parties have joined together to destroy democracy. They permeate the very institutions tasked to stop them. How that transpired—and what it means for ordinary Americans—is the subject of this book.

Nations have faced autocracy before and recovered. It is not easy, but it is possible: witness the peaceful revolutions that preceded the collapse of the USSR, the dissolution of apartheid in South Africa, and the fall of tyrants throughout history, from Hitler to Milosevic to Mubarak. But the crisis we face now is new. Its transnational nature and reliance on non–state actors who can use digital media to override borders—Julian Assange, the founder of WikiLeaks, is a prime example—means it lacks true historic precedent. Climate change is another factor that makes our current crisis distinct from any other. It is doubtful that this group of roving criminals and kleptocrats are the climate skeptics they purport to be. It is far more likely that they are, as Naomi Klein phrases it, "disaster capitalists" who see opportunity in a dying planet, and who will spare no expense in pursuit of their own preservation.[16]

Throughout this book, I describe how digital media has transformed state repression and citizen protest, and how globalization allowed organized crime to proliferate on an unparalleled scale. I explain that mafia networks have long been accomplices of dictatorships (and sometimes democracies). But now the state has become a proxy for the mafia, an arrangement overt in Russia but present to various degrees in countries worldwide. Trump is a node in a sadistic network whose ambitions extend beyond borders, and whose ties go back decades. This book explains how America went from a flawed democracy to a burgeoning autocracy, and how the refusal to render consequences for elite criminality allowed us to get there.

The election of the first anti-American president was caused neither by electoral whim nor by the good fortune of a charismatic madman. His rise was made possible by a coterie of criminals who do not want to be punished but delight in being caught. Flaunting their criminal impunity is part of the thrill. Their belief that they would never be held accountable is logical since they had never faced serious consequences despite spending decades committing illegal acts. In fact, they had reaped ample rewards. Now, finally, they had the greatest reward of all: the power to rewrite law itself.

In 2016, the same phenomena took place all over the Western world. Demagogic white nationalists rose, elites falsely played down their loss or the ramifications of their win, and hate crimes exploded when victory was achieved. It was all predictable, but now there was no clear organized process to stop it. Instead, vulnerable people waited for responsible officials to intervene. They are still waiting.

I was not the only one to predict the election results or the reshaping of American political culture under Trump. Pundits and politicians like to say that "No one saw it coming," but what they mean is that they consider the people who saw it coming to be no one. The category of "no one" includes the people smeared by Trump in his propaganda: immigrants, black Americans, Muslim Americans, Native Americans, Latino Americans, LGBT Americans, disabled Americans, and others long maligned and marginalized—groups for whom legally sanctioned American autocracy was not an unfathomable horror, but a personal backstory.

"No one" also included a slew of scholars of authoritarian states who saw parallels to Trump in figures like Hitler, Milosevic, and, of course, Putin, but who were dismissed as alarmist despite their expertise. These scholars are a mix of liberals and conservatives from across the political spectrum—scholars who otherwise rarely agree. But we all saw the same danger: that is how predictable autocracy is and how reliably Trump meets its criteria. Our shared insistence that, yes, American democracy is destined for destruction unless we radically change course should disconcert you.

The category of "no one" is diverse and savvy and I'm glad to be in its ranks. The category of "no one" does not include the many pundits and politicians whose failure to grasp reality has created a national security threat, and whose lack of empathy toward the targeted proves even more dangerous.

.   .   .

In November 2016, I still hoped we could avoid catastrophe. We had two and a half months to get US officials to grasp the severity of the situation and to prepare Americans for the horror and chaos ahead. Alongside many others, I organized, researched, and wrote articles. One article was called "We Are Heading Into Dark Times—This Is How to Be Your Own Light."[17] It was an open letter to the people of the country I love.

I've included excerpts of this letter here to capture what I felt and what I understood at this specific time right after the election, free of the revelations and ramifications that I describe in later chapters. I want people to understand that our political plight was, in fact, predictable, and therefore to some extent preventable—and to question why those in power either denied the extent of the rot or came to embrace and embody it.

> My fellow Americans, I have a favor to ask you.
>
> Today is November 18, 2016. I want you to write about who you are, what you have experienced, and what you have endured.
>
> Write down what you value; what standards you hold for yourself and for others. Write about your dreams for the future and your hopes for your children. Write about the struggle of your ancestors and how the hardship they overcame shaped the person you are today.
>
> Write your biography, write down your memories. Because if you do not do it now, you may forget.
>
> Write a list of things you would never do. Because it is possible that in the next year, you will do them.
>
> Write a list of things you would never believe. Because it is possible that in the next year, you will either believe them or be forced to say you believe them.
>
> It is increasingly clear, as Donald Trump appoints his cabinet of white supremacists and war-mongers, as hate

crimes rise, as the institutions that are supposed to protect us cower, as international norms are shattered, that his ascendency to power is not normal.

This is an American authoritarian kleptocracy, backed by millionaire white nationalists both in the United States and abroad, meant to strip our country down for parts, often using ethnic violence to do so.

This is not a win for anyone except them. This is a moral loss and a dangerous threat for everyone in the United States, and by extension, everyone abroad.

I have been studying authoritarian states for over a decade, and I would never exaggerate the severity of this threat. Others who study or have lived in authoritarian states have come to the same conclusion as me.

And the plight is beyond party politics: it is not a matter of having a president-elect whom many dislike, but having a president-elect whose explicit goal is to destroy the nation.

I am writing this not for those who oppose him, but for those who support him, because Trump and his backers are going to hurt you too . . .

You can look to the president-elect himself for a vision of what is to come. He has told you his plans all along, though most chose to downplay or deny them. You can even look back to before his candidacy, when in February 2014, he went on Fox News to defend Russia. Why a reality TV host was on Fox News defending Russia is its own story, but here is what he said about his desired outcome for the United States: "You know what solves it? When the economy crashes, when the country goes to total hell and everything is a disaster. Then you'll have a [chuckles], you know, you'll have riots to go back to where we used to be when we were great."

This is what "Make America Great Again" means to Donald Trump. It is how he has operated his businesses, taking advantage of economic disasters like the housing market crash for personal gain. It is why, during a long and painful recession, he made "You're fired" a national catch-phrase, because he understands that sometimes it feels good to know that the person getting fired, for once, is not you. He said he could shoot someone on 5th Avenue and people would still vote for him, and he said he could grab women "by the pussy" because "When you're a star, they let you do it. You can do anything."

He is right about that last part. No one holds Trump accountable, because he is exactly what he claimed to be railing against: an elite billionaire with no concern for the average person, a kleptocrat who enjoys taunting people less powerful than him with threats. When you have that kind of money, which Trump was given at birth and further gained through fraud, there are few limitations to the ways you can hurt people.

He is right that the system is rigged: it is rigged in his favor. And now it is rigged against you, unless we find a way to stop it . . .

I will rearrange my life so I can fight this fight, because I am fighting for my country, and I never give up on my country or on my countrymen.

But I need you to fight too, in the way that matters most, which is inside. Authoritarianism is not merely a matter of state control, it is something that eats away at who you are. It makes you afraid, and fear can make you cruel. It compels you to conform and to comply and accept things that you would never accept, to do things you never thought you would do.

You do it because everyone else is doing it, because the institutions you trust are doing it and telling you to do it, because you are afraid of what will happen if you do not do it, and because the voice in your head crying out that something is wrong grows fainter and fainter until it dies.

That voice is your conscience, your morals, your individuality. No one can take that from you unless you let them.

They can take everything from you in material terms—your house, your job, your ability to speak and move freely. They cannot take away who you truly are. They can never truly know you, and that is your power.

But to protect and wield this power, you need to know yourself—right now, before their methods permeate, before you accept the obscene and unthinkable as normal.

My heart breaks for the United States of America. It breaks for those who think they are my enemies as much as it does for my friends. You still have your freedom, so use it. There are many groups organizing for both resistance and subsistence, but we are heading into dark times, and you need to be your own light. Do not accept brutality and cruelty as normal even if it is sanctioned. Protect the vulnerable and encourage the afraid. If you are brave, stand up for others. If you cannot be brave—and it is often hard to be brave—be kind.

But most of all, never lose sight of who you are and what you value. If you find yourself doing something that feels questionable or wrong a few months or years from now, find that essay you wrote on who you are and read it. Ask if that version of yourself would have done the same thing.

And if the answer is no? Don't do it.

I have followed my own advice in terms of staying true to what I value and how I treat people. But despite my best efforts, this administration changed me. I had spent my professional life studying authoritarian regimes with the luxury of being able to leave them. My studies had been voluntary; I could stop at any time. When I went abroad to authoritarian states, I faced certain risks, but I took them knowing I could always return to the relative security of American life. Now the horror had come home.

The knowledge that the political transition is not yet complete, that we are still in the process of protections being stripped, speech being suppressed, and rule of law being annihilated shakes me, because I know how much worse it can get. I don't have longing for the past. I have nostalgia for the future, because I am a mother, and whatever system wins will be the one my children inherit. When I allow myself to picture the world in ten years or twenty years, I have to force myself to stop because the pain is too much. I remind myself that the future is not set in stone, that I still have some ability to shape it. I cling to what cannot be predicted or controlled: love, imagination, originality. I try to live in a way that would break an algorithm. I pray to the unexpected.

We have lost a lot over the last few years, but one of the most disorienting losses is our sense of time. This is a common experience for people living in a democratic country that is transitioning into an autocracy. The last three years have been as much about deciphering the truth of the past as they are about debunking the lies of the present or fighting for the freedom of the future.

When I was a child, my baby boomer relatives would tell me the story of where they were when JFK was shot—the day their illusion of safety ended. That moment was crystalized: the location, the shock, the grief, the demarcation between one era and the next. In Trump's America of nonstop crises, every day brings a soul-crushing development or an earth-shattering revelation. But I can rarely pinpoint where I was for any of them without a struggle, the way the details of a nightmare fade when you awaken but your body stays tense with fright. Everyone I know who follows the news closely experiences the same exhausting disorientation. We are trapped in a reality TV autocrat's funhouse mirror, a blurred continuum of shock and sorrow that exhausts our capacity for clarity of thought.

There is a difference between expecting autocracy and accepting autocracy. It is necessary to expect it so that you can plan how you will fight. But the battle lines change, and you often end up changing with them, no matter how hard you try to resist. It is impossible not to change inside when children are snatched from their parents and held in concentration camps at the Texas border; when there is a sociopathic commander in chief with a nuke fetish threatening the world at whim; when the American government operates against the American people in collaboration with hostile states; and when you learn that men carried out horrific acts for decades without repercussions. It is impossible not to be shaken when you realize how many people knew of these crimes for so long and did nothing to help the victims. You feel haunted by the alternative America that could have existed had people told the truth.

For certain twenty-first-century elites, criminal impunity has turned into criminal immunity. Public leverage is disappearing along with the concept of the public good as a priority of the powerful. You live knowing that if you aren't a propagandist or protector of the perpetrators, you are the prey. You watch as victims of decades-old atrocities stand up and speak out, hoping for resolution in our era of reevaluation, only to be reduced to a fleeting headline or a cautionary tale. You watch as crimes become "solved" by not being called "crimes" at all. You listen to the administration lay out the road map for future horrors—an acceleration of the existential threat of climate change, an entrenchment of autocratic measures—and to pundits proclaiming that these are mere fantasies. Everyone says it can't happen here, until it does.

When I was pregnant with my second child, I remember wondering how it could be possible to love my second as much as my firstborn. A friend told me that love for your children is infinite; your heart expands to hold it, and she was right. What I did not realize until the last few years was that the same is true of grief. Whatever well exists inside us to capture the magnitude of loss—of lives, of expectations, of freedom—is vaster than I knew or wanted to know.

There's a kind of horror that shakes you to your core, when you start believing in the devil because of what you witness and in hell because you want comfort. Sometimes all you are left with is anguish, and the desire for others to find the strength to survive and fight. People say that history will be on your side, but these days history is an endangered commodity. In autocracies this is always the case: history can be erased, history can be rewritten. But our era is different: the present cannot become history unless there is still a future, and a future is no longer guaranteed.

People ask me how I find hope. I answer that I don't believe in hope, and I don't believe in hopelessness. I believe in compassion and pragmatism, in doing what is right for its own sake. Hope can be lethal when you are fighting an autocracy because hope is inextricable from time. An enduring strategy of autocrats is to simply run out the clock.

While I was a graduate student in anthropology studying post-Soviet dictatorships, the Russian journalist Anna Politkovskaya was murdered by Putin's henchmen. I grieved for Politkovskaya, and I understood why she wrote what she did, despite the risks. At the time of her death in 2006, I had just published an exposé on a state massacre in the city of Andijon, Uzbekistan, that angered the Uzbek government. This was the first time I had written a work that had consequences in terms of my safety and also in terms of public policy. My article was used by the UN High Commissioner for Refugees, as well as other international organizations, and helped enable Uzbeks from the Andijon region to receive asylum abroad.

I understood Politkovskaya's moral imperative to tell the truth no matter the cost. But it is one thing to write about the plight of another country and voluntarily make oneself vulnerable; it is another to experience the hijacking of your own nation firsthand. In 2006, living as a white woman in a flawed but relatively stable democracy, I could not comprehend on an emotional level how Politkovskaya processed Putin's brutal consolidation of power. In her 2003 book *A Small Corner of Hell*, a compendium of her reporting in the war-torn region of Chechnya, she wrote:

I have a calendar like this for the 2002 Nord-Ost year, which has passed so quickly, and for the beginning of 2003.

This calendar has no chronology and no external logic. It has nothing but images tied together by the logic of feelings surrounding this tragedy.

"Feelings?" someone might ask, dragging the word out disappointedly. "What about analysis? Practical conclusions? A sober prognosis?"

I'm not very good at prognosticating. Besides, we live in the time of Putin, when it is once again permissible to sacrifice thousands of lives "in the name of a bright non-terrorist future." There are people who can analyze this, but few who can sympathize. And since feelings are so rare now, they are the most important thing in my calendar.[18]

I am not comparing my situation to Politkovskaya's, who braved brutal conditions in both Russia and Chechnya and paid for it with her life. Nor am I proposing that America is an analog of Russia. America's history of constitutional democracy is distinct from Russia's history of entrenched autocracy, and while I've dealt with death threats for several years—a more common situation for political writers in the United States than most realize—I am not yet facing anything close to the dangers Russian independent journalists do.

Where common ground exists is in our kleptocratic leaders, in the cruel financiers who prop up our corrupt governments, and in the endless blitz of propaganda that seeks to erode the very concept of truth. Russian scholars have been discussing this phenomenon for decades, but it now dominates American discourse too. As I explained on MSNBC's *AM Joy* on January 22, 2017, days after Trump's inauguration, when the concept of "alternative facts" had first entered the vernacular: "What they're trying to do is establish power: they are lying to flaunt power. They are saying to us: 'We know that you know that this is a lie, and we don't care, because there is absolutely nothing you can do about it.'"

Over years, ceaseless propaganda and spectacle, exacerbated by corrections and retractions, can destroy your sense of reality.

Time spirals forward and lurches backward. Your memories of political events become blurred when you try to reconcile your initial reactions with the revelatory backstories behind them, forcing you to process your country's history—and your own—in new and painful ways. As you do this, you have to live your life, which in the United States means struggling to survive in a gutted economy under a brutal regime that either seems to be collapsing or consolidating, depending on the day.

Like that of Politkovskaya, my own internal calendar now lacks a clear chronology. My memories are often reduced to "images tied together by the logic of feelings." I knew this was likely to happen, and not only to me but to everyone. This is why I wrote that open letter encouraging people to write down who they were before autocratic consolidation took hold. I wanted Americans to have a way to remember what we thought of as normal and acceptable and track how far we have deviated. While many of us retained our integrity, there is no denying that we have become inured to the Trump administration and its cruelty and chaos—not accepting of it, but accustomed to it. Our expectations shifted, our standards fell, and our memories of the time before faded.

This book is an attempt to tell the truth about the time before, the story most people missed the first time around, and how the refusal to tell it led us into our current plight. It is a history of crime and corruption that ran underground for decades only to emerge in ways that are stark and unavoidable, like bedrock jutting out in a fallow field. Trump's path to power parallels a decades-long erosion of American stability, integrity, and democracy. I tell some of this American story through the lens of my own life and reporting, as I tend to be in the wrong place at the wrong time; or the right place at the right time, depending on how you see it. Trump's rise in the late 1970s coincided with my birth, and as I grew up I watched the consolidation of that corruption not so much shape my future as steal it.

I don't remember a time when I felt safe in America, but I remember when I thought it was possible I would be, someday. The nostalgia for what never was is a familiar feeling for those born in the opening salvo in the symphony of American decline.

Whether as a scholar covering authoritarian regimes abroad, a journalist covering the decline of the United States, or an involuntary dissident in my own country, my recourse has been to write things down: to try to find clarity through words and give the madness meaning. The last three years forced me to not only reevaluate my nation but my place within it. I don't believe in hope. I believe in facts and history. I believe my own eyes and ears. I believe the American people deserve the truth about what happened to their country.

To understand the truth you need to understand the history of America—the raw, mean version. I will begin in the center: in Missouri, the bellwether state turned corruption capital, the broken heartland that got the sneak preview to the national shitshow.

1

The Bellwether of American Decline

live in Missouri, a state in the center of America, a state that sits halfway down the Mississippi River and whose northern border parallels the Mason-Dixon line. In the twentieth century, Missouri was proclaimed "the bellwether state" due to the uncanny ability of its residents to vote for the winner of presidential elections. From 1904 to 2008, Missouri voted for the winning presidential candidate in every year except 1956. For over a century, Missouri was where you looked to discover what direction America would go. It's now where to look if you want to know how the country went to hell.

To understand the rise of Trump, you need to understand the history of America. To understand the history of America, you need to understand Missouri. You may blanch at this, given Missouri's presumed Midwestern irrelevance as well as the simplistic descriptions of "red states" churned out since the 2016 election. Prior to Trump taking office, the Midwest tended to be ignored by the national press unless there was a tornado, a riot, or another camera-ready disaster. But Trump's win made the heartland intriguing to coastal reporters, who dropped into a diverse and complex region with their prewritten narratives, needing only a white man or two to embody the clichés. Midwesterners were transformed into MAGA-hat-wearing retired manufacturing workers who sit in diners reciting platitudes about their unshaking loyalty to a New York City tycoon.

A media makeover is a peculiar wound. It is a terrible feeling to be in pain and to be ignored—as a place, as a person. It is worse to be given a mask and told it's your face.

I am telling you the story of Missouri because what happened to people here matters in its own right—a radical notion in a media era defined by coastal domination—but also because Missouri is a national litmus test for corruption and injustice. We show how low America can go, and while some of our wounds may be self-inflicted, they are also contagious. We live under the tyranny of the minority on a state level, which is subject to the tyranny of the minority on a national level, which is subject to the tyranny of the elite on an international level.

After the 2016 election, a journalist wrote a profile of me called "A Cassandra in Trumpland." Cassandra was a Greek goddess cursed to see the future but never be believed.[1] That article was about my book *The View from Flyover Country*, a collection of essays written between 2012 and 2014 that was once viewed as pessimistic but is now heralded as prescient. I wrote about all of America, but I saw America through Missouri's eyes, which means I saw hell and I saw it in advance. I have concluded that the surreal quality of Missouri life has prompted people to doubt my assertions even when I am simply listing the facts. The facts no longer add up, the facts make you wish they were fiction, but that is all the more reason we need to hear them.

Missouri has two nicknames. The first is "the Show Me State," which allegedly came from a congressman named Willard Duncan Vandiver, who, in 1899, displeased with a blowhard politician's response, proclaimed: "I come from a state that raises corn and

cotton and cockleburs and Democrats, and frothy eloquence neither convinces nor satisfies me. I am from Missouri. You have got
to show me!"[2]

In twenty-first-century Missouri the cornfields are contaminated
with floodwater and the Blue Dog Democrats have turned into
radical Republicans, but the dissatisfaction and demand for proof
from Vandiver's era remains. Missourians are locked in a battle
against their representatives for accountability in government. In
2018, voters across the political spectrum overwhelmingly passed
Clean Missouri, a ballot initiative aimed at ending partisan redis-
tricting, limiting lobbying, and forcing officials to reveal financial
records. Today the very legislators that Clean Missouri targeted
are attempting to overturn the initiative in defiance of public will,
leaving the Show Me State cloaked in secrecy.[3]

The other nickname of Missouri is "the Cave State." This is my
preferred nickname. It's a motto for the Trump era, where to survive you need to see in the dark.

Missouri is known as flatland, but a system of over five thousand caves, filled with million-year-old geological wonders, lurks
underground. You can't drive through Missouri without a bill-
board or barn roof beckoning you to one of the caverns: a Route
66 throwback site featuring red, white, and blue laser beams
bouncing off stalactites as "God Bless America" blares, or a drive-
through Jeep tour of an underground Civil War sanctuary, or caves
renowned for their bizarre formations alone. Nearly all caverns
proclaim to be the long-lost hideout of Jesse James, because I live
in a state that venerates a murderous bank robber.

Questionable advertising aside, there is a sanctity to Missouri
caves that's incomparable to anything else I've seen. The caverns
are a visual distillation of time—a constancy that keeps me steady
when everything else seems to be crashing down. *This took millions of years to form*, I'd think; *this will stay the same no matter
what hell we create on earth*. They are the underground heart of
a dismissed heartland, a monument to beauty and intricacy that
reveals itself only to those willing to plunge into the void.

I have a map of the Missouri cave system on my wall. When Trump won, I began visiting the caverns and crossing them off, treating each like a reprieve, a reward. I like that their twisted beauty exists in the dark, indifferent to whether it is appreciated. I like that their depth blocks out the internet along with the sun. I like that Missouri has the home-court advantage in knockout fallout shelters.

Missouri was born in sin, the centerpiece of America's bad bargain with itself. Its entry into statehood in 1821—the notorious "Missouri Compromise"—was predicated on a national agreement to keep black Missourians enslaved so that Maine could call itself free. At the time, black Americans in slaveholding states were labeled three-fifths of a person. The chroniclers of this time unironically referred to it as "the Era of Good Feelings."

Six years after Missouri became a state, a journalist named Elijah Lovejoy moved from Maine to St. Louis, Missouri. A preacher and an abolitionist, Lovejoy printed article after article railing against Andrew Jackson, the favorite president of Donald Trump, and calling for slaves to be freed. His editorials made him the target of racist white mobs and in 1836, he crossed the Mississippi River into Alton, Illinois, to continue his journalism in a free state. This made no difference to the mobs, who followed him into Alton, ransacked his office, and threw his printing press into the Mississippi River.

By 1837, Lovejoy knew he would be killed. "If the laws of my country fail to protect me," he wrote shortly before he was murdered, "I appeal to God, and with him I cheerfully rest my cause. I can die at my post, but I cannot desert it."

On November 7, 1837, Elijah Lovejoy received his fourth press and hid it in a warehouse, but the mob figured out his location and set the building ablaze. He was shot to death as he attempted to escape, and the white mob bypassed his bullet-ridden corpse to seize his printing press, which they smashed and threw into the river for the final time.

Today a monument to Elijah Lovejoy sits on the top of a hill in Alton, near the cemetery where his grave lies. In the weeks before the 2016 election, I would drive across the Mississippi and visit it, my own death threats saved on a phone I could put in my pocket.

One day in October 2016 I stood beside the monument and looked out at the town—Alton, where Abraham Lincoln, influenced by Lovejoy, debated slavery; Alton, where James Earl Ray, the killer of Martin Luther King Jr., was born; Alton, where the Underground Railroad thrived, symbolic of a region divided not only between whites and blacks, but between whites who would fight for black rights and whites who opposed them. Lovejoy's headstone said he was born on November 9, 1802, and died on November 7, 1837. In between his murder and birth was November 8—that year's Election Day.

I thought about my children and my country as I drove out of Alton, skirting East St. Louis, Illinois, where in 1917 white mob violence against black laborers was so catastrophic that terrified locals mistook the trampling hordes for a natural disaster; across the river to the downtown St. Louis courthouse where in 1847 the slave Dred Scott unsuccessfully made a case for his freedom; then on to the faded grandeur of St. Louis's Page Boulevard, whose long-abandoned homes local black activists had covered with paintings of notable black St. Louisans, in a gesture some deemed inspiring and some deemed depressing; past the inhabited neighborhoods with signs that plead WE MUST STOP KILLING EACH OTHER planted on the lawns; and then to my home, a century-old house in a neighborhood located between a Dollar General store and an abandoned lot—a ruin of my own.

I checked Twitter and saw more white supremacists had endorsed Donald Trump, and he did not reject their approval. I turned on the TV and watched cable news reporters marvel over one of Trump's hotels before declaring the inevitable win of the scandalous Hillary Clinton. I checked my email, I sorted my death threats, I waited for November and its foregone conclusions.

I have lived in St. Louis for almost my entire adult life. But in my early twenties, I briefly lived in two former imperial capitals: Vienna, Austria, where the Hapsburgs held sway over Europe and where Hitler was rejected from art school; and Istanbul, Turkey, where countless empires rose and fell. Those are cities where history feels palpable, in palaces and plague columns, museums and mosques. The triumph and tragedy of the imperial past is their calling card, dealt into a new hand, one that beckons tourists to contemplate their own time and the way the world comes undone.

St. Louis is not dissimilar, though few recognize it. Imperial grandeur lurks in every building left behind by the 1904 World's Fair, held when St. Louis was the place to be, the fourth-largest city in America. It also haunts the city in less sought-out relics. If visitors follow the standard recommendations, they see the Arch and the zoo and the Cardinals. If they turn off the tourist trail, they stumble into what looks like an urban war zone of gutted nineteenth- and early-twentieth-century buildings. They wonder what happened to make our city look this way, failing to grasp that what happened in St. Louis was nothing. Our war wasn't lost, but *loss*. There was no attack, just abandonment and apathy. Here the world ended, as St. Louis–raised poet T. S. Eliot wrote, "not with a bang but a whimper."[4]

St. Louis's history, and Missouri's history, is not well known outside the state. Perhaps that's how gatekeepers want it: an empire, even a fallen one, should have some glamour, some command, not be rooted in the region disparagingly called flyover country. But it was in St. Charles, Missouri, where explorers Lewis and Clark set off on their quest of westward imperialism; Hannibal, Missouri, where Mark Twain's trenchant tales of racism were conceived and set; Marceline, Missouri, where a young Walt Disney envisioned his fantasy empire in a backyard farmhouse; and

St. Louis, Missouri, where black musicians like Scott Joplin and Chuck Berry pioneered quintessentially American genres like ragtime and blues and rock.

There is no such thing as a "real" or "fake" America, but it is hard to ignore the significance of Missouri in shaping national culture, national dialects, national expectations, and real and fictional national icons—and the significance of its significance being ignored. You have to reconcile with an awful lot if you dare to reconcile with Missouri: Missouri, with its "Little Dixie" slavery relics sprawling across the upper half; Missouri, where Native Americans trod the Trail of Tears across the lower half; Missouri, which is so conflicted about whether it is northern or southern that residents cannot agree on whether to pronounce the state "Missouri" or "Missourah," prompting state politicians to engage in the quintessential Missouri act: the compromise that satisfies no one.

Today, Missouri lives the legacy of that compromise. The state remains divided by race, class, and a rural versus urban landscape. But what most folks agree on, regardless of their background, is the pervasiveness of pain. We are held together by the recognition that we are being torn apart.

This feeling is particularly acute in St. Louis. You see the residue of decades of white flight—first from the city to the suburbs, then from the suburbs to the exurbs—and the attempts of activists to undo the poverty and unrest left in its wake. You see teddy bears and balloons tied to trees on street corners and know it's not an invitation to a birthday party but the marking of a murder. You are no longer shocked by the violence but you always feel the grief, and the perverse way it forms bonds: a region of three million can feel like a small town when you're all six degrees of separation from a shooting victim. You live near a silver arch towering over a river of mud, the waters of which have long hidden bodies along with printing presses.

You are surrounded by the sense that everything can come undone at any time and no one will fix it when it falls. It's baked into the geology, the history, the culture. At the southernmost point of Missouri, there is a city called New Madrid. In 1811, New Madrid had a 7.9 earthquake: the worst one east of the Rocky Mountains in recorded history. The New Madrid quake caused the Mississippi River to flow backwards and church bells to ring in Washington, D.C., and Americans all over the Midwest to declare that the apocalypse had arrived. "The screams of the affrighted inhabitants running to and fro, not knowing where to go, or what to do," settler Eliza Bryan wrote in 1812, "the cries of the fowls and beasts of every species—the cracking of trees falling, and the roaring of the Mississippi . . . formed a scene truly horrible."[5]

Today the New Madrid Fault lies in wait. Seismologists say we are overdue for a sequel. When the earthquake happens, they say—and it's a when, not an if—America will be torn asunder in Missouri, causing death and destruction so severe that the National Guard has preemptively declared there is nothing that they will be able to do to help us.[6]

People often ask how I ended up in Missouri. The answer, as usual, has to do with lack of money. In 2006, Washington University in St. Louis offered me a generous scholarship to get a Ph.D. in anthropology, and I accepted. I knew St. Louis well because my in-laws lived there, and we visited them often. By the time I arrived, the city had climbed out of its 1980s and 1990s wreckage and even had moments of pop culture glory, with St. Louis rappers like Nelly topping the charts and the Rams winning the Super Bowl. St. Louis was run-down, but affordable and full of free amenities. It seemed like a good place to have children, which I proceeded to do. I haven't moved since.

In many ways, St. Louis felt like a larger, more functional version of where I grew up—Meriden, Connecticut, a postindustrial midsized city whose glory days my grandparents would tell me about with a kind of reverent disbelief. Meriden had deteriorated before I was born, but I could not mourn what I didn't remember.

I embraced what was left: strip malls and fast food and the low-key hustle of a New England gang hub. As a kid I would walk past the gun store and the porn shop to get to the pharmacy, which had a magazine rack where I could read undisturbed for hours while people from the projects nearby came and went. I loved that pharmacy, and the palatial Burger King arcade, and the mall that had replaced what used to be called "downtown." I did not notice that Meriden lacked museums or cafés or cultural institutions. I did not realize that the street violence I witnessed was unusual, unless I was reading kids' books that took place in Connecticut, which depicted a world of white suburban prosperity alien to everything around me.

I grew up in a struggling city and saw beauty in ordinary things. People only corrected me later in life, but by then it was too late: I had become hardwired to appreciate the heart of the hellholes I call home. The similarities between my original and adopted hometowns made me skeptical of the perceived divide between the coasts and the center. The real divide is between a few exorbitant cities and everywhere else, a few exorbitant individuals and everyone else—a fracture that widened into a chasm during my lifetime.

In the late 1970s, when I was born, people in St. Louis and New York made roughly the same salaries and had a similar cost of living[7]—which meant life in both cities was cheap and low-down. When John Carpenter filmed his 1981 postapocalyptic thriller *Escape from New York*—a commentary on Manhattan's shattered state—he chose to do it in St. Louis because he did not need to build a set. St. Louis's natural end-times look filled in just fine.

New York and St. Louis were brothers in blight—until they weren't. The rapacious greed of the Reagan 1980s marked the rise of New York corporate raiders like Carl Icahn, who bought out St. Louis companies like Trans World Airlines (TWA), draining St. Louis of its money and resources and pride. TWA was "a broken-winged bird helpless before the pounce of the ultimate corporate predator," wrote *St. Louis* magazine, describing the shock of Missourians that an out-of-state tycoon had bought something

as essential as an airline purely to destroy it and pocket the prof-
its.[8] By the late 1980s, New York and St. Louis were no longer
carrying a shared American burden of lost opportunity. Wall Street
predators had devised a zero-sum game and deemed the Midwest
expendable. In 2017, Icahn, a long-time friend of Donald Trump
who had helped Trump recover from his financial disasters in
the casino industry, constructed a cabinet of corrupt Wall Street
multimillionaires including himself, Steven Mnuchin, and Wilbur
Ross[9]—while Trump flew to Missouri and assured down-and-out
Missourians he was making their lives great again. In the 1980s,
Missouri was the background of a fictional New York–born nightmare. Now its people are props in a real one.

This is not to say that all corruption was imported. Missouri
has its own long history of high-end dirty dealers. Some, like early
twentieth-century Kansas City political fixer Tom Pendergast, constructed such elaborate nexuses of politics and business and crime
that they gained national notoriety. What changed in the 1980s
was that income inequality became coupled with geographical inequality in a way that would transform the American economy,
culture, and media for decades to come. The once thriving cities of the Midwest became known as "the Rust Belt," Midwest
family farms went bankrupt, and coastal elites—both liberal and
conservative—came to view the region as an object of pity or prey.

That is, when they thought about the Midwest at all. Starting
in the 2000s, Midwesterners largely disappeared from American
pop culture. This may sound trivial, but it's not: compare it to the
1980s and 1990s, with Prince, Michael Jackson, Madonna, Axl
Rose, and John Mellencamp all hailing from the Midwest, while
popular family sitcoms like *Family Ties* and *Roseanne* were set in
states like Ohio and Illinois. There was no uniform representation
of the Midwest and one did not need an excuse to set a movie or
a show there—it was simply considered as relevant a region of
America as any other. Back then, the Midwest had representation
beyond red swaths carved out on an electoral map. When a region
loses both cultural representation and economic clout, it becomes

easy for politicians to exploit the resentment of its residents, especially when that resentment stems not from envy but grief.

The story of the Midwest in the twenty-first century is the story of a narrative hijacking. This narrative began with the 2000 election, which introduced the concept of "red" and "blue" Americas—a concept partisans were eager to employ. The idea of a bifurcated America reduces a complex set of differences to an innate divide. The assumption that a state has a fixed identity gives cover to the gerrymandering, influence peddling, and general corruption of the political process that arose over the past twenty years.

As the bellwether, Missouri was the ultimate purple state, swinging with the times. In the 2000s, that began to change with the increased influence of GOP donors—both national actors, like the conservative-megadonor Koch brothers, and Missourians like Rex Sinquefield, a wealthy conservative ideologue who has been accused of trying to buy the state government.[10] In a damning study for the *Missouri Law Review*, scholar Dan Schnurbusch dubbed Missouri "the Wild Midwest" and described how dark money and loose laws had drained the state of representative democracy. Missouri's rot ran so deep, he noted, that "ethical and campaign finance laws are ill equipped to protect against even the most basic form of corruption—that which the Supreme Court of the United States has identified as 'quid pro quo corruption.'"[11]

In 2006, Missouri governor Matt Blunt signed into law a bill that eliminated all limits on direct campaign contributions. It was struck down by the Missouri Supreme Court, only to be resurrected in 2008.[12] As usual, Missouri was a preview to a national crisis. In 2010, the Supreme Court ruled in favor of *Citizens United*, which redefined campaign cash as free speech and allowed it to flow without restriction from corporations to candidates. Among the side effects of *Citizens United* was an exponential rise in dark money—money spent by organizations who are not required to disclose the identities of their donors. Between 2006 and

2012, the amount of dark money in national campaigns increased from $5.2 million to over $300 million.[13] The influence of domestic dark money was compounded by an increase in foreign money given through lobbying groups and organizations like the NRA or the American Israel Public Affairs Committee.

For Missouri, the *Citizens United* ruling exacerbated an already out of control situation. "Missouri finds itself in a bubbling mire of unlimited direct campaign contributions and lobbyist gifts, unimpeded independent electioneering expenditures, and unstoppable tycoons of monetary political persuasion," wrote Schnurbusch. He recommended that the Missouri electorate become more informed about corruption so they can catch bad actors—solid advice, but hard to implement when the local media economy is dying, which it has been since the millennium. The demise of local media not only made corruption less likely to be documented, it left Missourians scrambling for alternative sources of information. They found it in national outlets like Fox News, which provided a narrative to mask the new graft. Fox News presented the Midwest as the home of "real Americans," by which they meant white conservatives, who were portrayed as victims of evil liberal machinations. The network offered a sense of belonging that exploited the sense of abandonment brewing for decades while dodging GOP complicity in that exploitation. It offered scapegoats—immigrants, Muslims, and in 2008, a presidential candidate.

In 2008, the political mood in St. Louis, especially in my majority black neighborhood, was unusually upbeat thanks to candidate Barack Obama and his promises of hope and change—which included a vow to unite "red" and "blue" America. By this time, Missouri resembled a miniature version of the United States. Two large, racially diverse, and liberal metro areas, St. Louis and Kansas City, sat at the eastern and western state lines, together comprising roughly half the population. More sparsely inhabited regions made up much of the rest of the state, populated almost entirely by white people, with the south more conservative than the north. Mixed suburbs and college towns dotted the landscape in between.

Missouri seemed a reliable bellwether for the nation per usual. As it turned out, we were, for all the wrong reasons.

On Election Day, my husband and I voted for Obama alongside ecstatic black voters in St. Louis, then drove out to get dinner in the rural countryside, where we sat in a bar and listened to a group of white men say they could not believe that a n—— was going to become the president.

For the first time since 1956, Missouri did not vote for the winner. Obama lost by 3,900 votes, and he likely lost those votes because he's black. Centuries of Missouri racism could not be eradicated by a charismatic black candidate; instead, the Obama effect meant that white Missouri officials began saying the un-speakable aloud. In 2009, Roy Blunt, the father of governor Matt Blunt and a Republican congressman who would go on to become Missouri's US senator in 2011, compared Obama to a monkey at a D.C. conference.[14]

Obama was so perplexed by his narrow loss that he visited Missouri repeatedly during his first two years in office, taking the lay of the land and attempting to win over its residents. He could not comprehend why he was the president who had broken the bellwether. "I think the complexity of the state intrigues him, too, as a microcosm of the country," Governor Jay Nixon explained in 2010.[15] Both Obama and Nixon were confident it was a blip and that Obama would win back Missouri in 2012. Both underesti-mated the state's economic pain, anti-black racism, and the abil-ity of conservative propagandists to exploit both. Missouri was indeed a microcosm of a new America—one marked by paranoia and fear, one that pundits and politicos, with their "postracial" fantasies, were desperate to deny existed.

On Election Day 2008, Missouri began to turn a little redder. And then Missouri began to bleed.

Missouri bled cash and it bled bodies. The economic crash of 2008 shattered St. Louis's tenuous comeback, obliterating retail and office jobs while decimating the agricultural and manufacturing sectors across the rest of the state. The abandoned lots and hollowed-out houses from earlier decades of hardship were joined by foreclosed homes and empty offices. Workers were laid off in droves, long-standing malls closed, and payday-loan outlets multiplied. Some outlets combined pawn shops with gun shops, allowing Missourians to trade in their jewels for weapons. People wanted weapons because they felt afraid.

I watched as St. Louis's storefronts shuttered while Manhattan's bankers walked free. I watched as people on television, none of them from around here, assured Americans that the economy was cyclical, a line that smacked of spin. The combination of a massive recession and the first black president unleashed anger that had lurked under the surface since Obama's candidacy started gaining steam. Right-wing power brokers were ready to exploit it. In February 2009, about a thousand right-wing protesters gathered under the Gateway Arch to air their grievances, which included a sudden obsession with the national debt. They called themselves the Tea Party. Today the St. Louis Tea Party's early participants continue to flourish in extreme right-wing politics—for example, local activist Dana Loesch became a national NRA advocate, trotted out to defend the organization's dirty money scandals in the 2016 race.

That some of the Tea Party's biggest national influencers came out of Missouri is not surprising. The state's perennial swing state status was rooted in ideological diversity, indicating to both parties that Missouri voters can always be swayed. Though heavily Democratic, St. Louis had long been home to influential right-wing ideologues like antifeminist activist Phyllis Schlafly. The Tea Party capitalized on that preexisting conservative base and pushed it into populism, both manufactured and genuine, as wealthy backers like the Koch brothers stayed quiet while homegrown stars, like Loesch, rose to the fore.[16] The Tea Party's rhetoric became more racist over time, with black Missouri lawmakers among the targets of their wrath.[17]

The St. Louis white mob—the mob that chased Elijah Lovejoy, the mob that fled the city following the desegregation of schools—was not back, exactly. It had never really gone away, never even gone underground. What was new was the structure of the national media, now dominated by cable news anchors who used heartlanders to parade bigoted ideologies they did not want to overtly claim themselves.

In 2012, Missouri's official bellwether status—the one defined by citizens voting for the presidential winner—was finally eliminated, as Mitt Romney beat Obama 54 percent to 44 percent, a stark departure from Obama's narrow loss four years earlier. It was the first time since 1900 that the loser of the election won the state by a margin larger than 1 percent.[18] It was also the first race held after the *Citizens United* ruling changed the rules about corporate money in politics, resulting in a dark money spending spree on ads whose conspiratorial sentiments were amplified by outlets like Fox. Within two years, Missouri had become the only state that allowed unlimited donations from unnamed sources, and the result was a Republican sweep and an emergence of Missouri as the dark money capital of America.[19]

But the GOP sweep had a notable exception, showing there were some things dirty money could not buy—at least, not yet. 2012 was the year Democrat Claire McCaskill ran a Senate campaign against Republican Todd Akin and became the target of a dark money campaign then unrivaled in US history.[20] McCaskill was losing in the polls until one August day when Akin, asked on TV whether abortion is justified in cases of rape, proclaimed: "It seems to be, first of all, from what I understand from doctors, it's really rare. If it's a legitimate rape, the female body has ways to try to shut the whole thing down."[21]

At the time I never imagined I would have nostalgia for this moment in Missouri history, but I do. Akin's comments sparked statewide bipartisan condemnation and inspired rape survivors to speak out. Some Missouri Republican women were so offended they did ads for McCaskill, explaining that while they disliked her, they found Akin's remarks so offensive they could not abide him on moral grounds. Several of them were survivors of sexual assault themselves.[22] At the polls, women outnumbered men 55 percent to 45 percent. McCaskill won Missouri 54 percent to 39 percent, with 64 percent of voters saying Akin's remarks were either the deciding factor or one of the deciding factors of their vote.[23]

Missouri had taken a unified position: rape victims were not to be slandered, and a man making such brutal and baseless claims was to be rejected, regardless of party affiliation. It was a heartfelt moral stance, one of the last we shared. Nowadays, Akin's words would barely stoke controversy. The news cycle would last a few hours, with pundits "both-sidesing" whether his comment was offensive and debating whether the female body does, indeed "try to shut the whole thing down." We know this—we saw it happen with Trump and allegations of sexual assault, we saw it with Brett Kavanaugh and allegations of attempted rape.

Today, the ability of Akin's comments to stoke months of controversy seems almost quaint, an indication of how far both Missouri and the United States have fallen. But the pain of rape survivors did not disappear—only public standards of how to treat them did. When McCaskill won in 2012, I felt relief, as a woman and a voter. It was the last time I would feel that after a Missouri election. Misogyny once limited to rhetoric is now codified in law: in May 2019, the Missouri legislature passed a law banning abortion after eight weeks even in the case of rape or incest. The day this was passed, I woke up to learn that my husband now had more rights than me—and that any man who chose to rape me in Missouri did too.

In August 2014, I was with my friend and sometimes cowriter Umar Lee—probably the only person in America to cash a check from Politico at a corner store—in a restaurant in Ferguson, Missouri. Down the block, the staff of a major cable network had barricaded itself in a giant steel cage from black protesters, among them St. Louisans who were close friends of mine and Umar's. The brutal killing of eighteen-year-old Michael Brown by police officer Darren Wilson had happened two weeks before, and the nightly gassing of protesters by the police had begun. The world that had once ignored St. Louis—media, NGOs, public officials— had converged on it in droves.

I started covering Ferguson the day Brown was killed, and I never stopped, because it is impossible to live in St. Louis and cover politics—both local and national—without Ferguson shaping your perception. The story never stopped for us because it never had a beginning and it can never have an end. It is a continuum of pain, punctuated by reminders both brutal—like the ongoing deaths of activists—and banal—like the bureaucratic morass that still plagues St. Louis regional government. In chapter 6, I describe Ferguson and its aftermath in greater detail; for now, I mention it because the 2014 uprising and its chaotic aftermath is key to understanding Trump's 2016 Missouri win.

My friend Umar is a St. Louis native, with family going back many generations. Born in the mid-1970s, he has witnessed the St. Louis region's slow-motion collapse with his own eyes, and he came from a multiracial family whose members had long dealt with St. Louis's racism, violence, and police brutality. He had also been involved with the Ferguson protests from the start, both participating in and covering them, ending up in jail on several occasions. I remember expressing tenuous hope in August 2014 that some of St. Louis's structural problems might be remedied, because the sheer force of attention might prompt accountability.

"You know what's going to happen?" Umar said. "Write this down, to remember I said this, because no one is going to believe me. People don't know how this shit works. I guarantee you that in 2016, you are going to see the return of Richard Nixon. Not just in Missouri, but on a national level. You are going to see a hard move to the right, and a Nixon-style presidential candidate come out, only slicker, more of a demagogue, someone who can work the media, and we will be living in a new kind of hell. The people who vote for whoever it is, they'll be living in hell too, only they won't even know it. The rest of us? We'll know it. We'll know it every fucking day."

In March 2016, Umar and I drove to the Peabody Opera House to cover the campaign rally of presidential candidate Donald Trump. This was Trump's first visit to St. Louis, and it would be his last, because St. Louis was the first city to kick him out. As is usual with St. Louis, this claim to fame was forgotten, with Chicago taking credit, having booted Trump later that evening to greater fanfare. But St. Louis, which had been holding protests centered around race for nearly two years straight by the time Trump arrived, was ready for battle, and as usual in St. Louis, the battle was bloody. Pro- and anti-Trump factions brawled on the opera house steps in what would be the most violent protest until after his election.

I did not go to the rally as an official journalist, to be credentialed and put in Trump's press pen. Instead I got a ticket and stood in line with the Trump supporters. While I never lied to anyone about who I was, I never told anyone that I was a writer or that I found Trump repugnant. I did not share my views at all, and so I was assumed to be a supporter too, and I talked for hours with the Trump voters about their views.

Since I live in a state that Trump won, I am often asked to describe what "the Trump voter" is thinking, but this is an inane question. The Trump voters are no more a monolith than any other group of voters. There is also a difference between the voters— who were at times reluctant or one-issue voters focused on topics like abortion or guns—and the base, for whom Trump's most hateful and destructive qualities are the core appeal. Rally-goers tend to be the base, but in March 2016, they were simply the curious.

Some people were there to see the host of *The Apprentice* in person. Some thought he would create jobs and ease their economic misery. Some were open racists and xenophobes thrilled that a candidate would speak hateful rhetoric so freely. Almost everyone in line was white, the main quality they shared along with an intense, almost conspiratorial feeling of betrayal. Some people looked well-off, but many spoke of a struggle to find full-time jobs and affordable health care. One of the reasons the line to see Trump was so long is that Missouri had enough unemployed people to make an overbooked rally, at noon on a weekday, feasible.

The violence of the rally did not scare me, nor did the feelings of betrayal I heard expressed—I was used to the former, and shared the latter, albeit with different solutions in mind. That day, it was not cruelty but kindness that left me shaken. In line, the Trump fans at the St. Louis rally were polite and respectful. They went out of their way to help children, the sick, and the elderly. They made cheerful small talk and had thoughtful conversations with me and Umar, rarely expressing hateful sentiment outright.

This changed once we arrived at the actual rally. As Trump bellowed conspiracy theories and insults, I watched a crowd become a mob. I watched a process I had studied my whole life in history books play out in real time. As a demagogue screamed "Build the wall" in an opera house, the rally-goers who had greeted me with kindness hailed his calls for violence. I saw mothers and fathers put their children and elderly parents aside to engage in fistfights with protesters. I saw preppy white men jeeringly announce they were going to Tactical Shit, a notorious gun store in the exurbs, to load up on weapons for future rallies. I saw activists forced one by one down the opera house steps like characters in Shirley Jackson's "The Lottery"—the lone target moving toward a vicious crowd tensed to pounce. The obedience of the line had become the compliance of the mob.

I took a picture of an anti-Trump protester holding a sign that said THE BANALITY OF EVIL—a reference to Hannah Arendt, the philosopher who said of life under the Nazi regime: "The sad truth is that most evil is done by people who never make up their minds to be good or evil."[24] The Trump rally was a study in how people capable of compassion can turn cruel in response to the rhetoric of their chosen leader or in retaliation to those who dare oppose him.

By March 2016, I was pretty sure Trump would win the primary and the general, and that when he won, he would attempt to govern in a way similar to the Central Asian autocrats I had been studying for decades. But there is a difference between studying or even visiting an authoritarian state and seeing an aspiring autocrat in practice—hearing the promises yet to be broken, watching the faux-populism pitched and sold. I remember turning to Umar and saying, "You were right two years ago, but this isn't going to be Nixon. This is American authoritarianism, and they are going to tell us 'That's not possible' until nothing else is."

Trump's ascendance wasn't the only alarming political phenomenon gripping Missouri in 2016. Over and over, out-of-towners asked me, "Did you see that ad for your election? The crazy one with the candidate holding a machine gun?" To which my response was "Which one? There's one running for senator and one running for governor, you know!"

The Senate candidate was Jason Kander, a Democrat, Missouri secretary of state, and veteran of the war in Afghanistan, who in his ad assembled an AR-15 while blindfolded and challenged his opponent, Roy Blunt, to do the same. The gubernatorial candidate was Eric Greitens, a former Navy SEAL who in his ad fired a machine gun into an empty field while a narrator proclaimed him to be "a conservative warrior." Kander was pushing for sensible gun control and demonstrating he was speaking from a place of experience; Greitens was playacting as a vigilante. Neither approach seemed remarkable in Missouri: violence and turmoil had overwhelmed the election long before the gun-toting candidates arrived.

In 2015, the presumed gubernatorial front-runner, state auditor and Republican Tom Schweich, known for his harsh critiques of state corruption and megadonors like Rex Sinquefield, shot himself to death after being the subject of a nasty political whisper campaign with anti-Semitic undertones.[25] Shortly after Schweich's suicide, Schweich's spokesman, Spence Jackson, shot *himself* to death, leaving a note saying that he could not take being unemployed again.[26] The combined incidents were both tragic on a personal level and an indictment of the hardships, particularly unemployment and suicide by gun, that so many Missouri families experience.

With the race now wide open, Greitens, a former Democrat, decided to run as a Republican—going "full Missourah" and taking on a contrived redneck persona, despite being a Rhodes Scholar living in a mansion. Greitens's opponent, former Missouri attorney general Chris Koster, had switched in 2007 from Republican to Democrat, meaning that both candidates were now running in each other's former party. This party-switching is one reason why the "red" and "blue" fallacy falls so short in Missouri—party lines become fluid when disillusionment and opportunism both run so high.

And in 2016, it had become easier than ever to manipulate an election. "The problem is that so little is against the law," remarked Sean Nicholson, executive director of the advocacy organization Progress Missouri, in 2015. "Things that are standard in other states don't exist here."[27] Lobbying had ballooned, with $1.85 million spent on gifts to state officials between 2012 and 2014.[28] Despite campaign finance law being so loose that almost nothing counted as illegal, Greitens still managed to break the law. He illegally used a donor list from The Mission Continues, his nonprofit for veterans, to fundraise for his campaign.

More concerningly, Greitens was connected to a shadowy nonprofit group called A New Missouri, which was created by Greitens's campaign treasurer and his campaign attorney, and run by Austin Chambers, his senior political adviser.[29] Most of its donors were anonymous, and under Missouri law, A New Missouri was not required to disclose who was behind it or how much money was flowing in and out, even though local reporters kept asking. The group had been accused of using shell companies to funnel money into Greitens's campaign and then diverting that money into fighting progressive causes, like labor rights.[30] Ironically, Greitens had campaigned on a platform of transparency: "I've been very proud to tell people, 'I'm stepping forward and you can see every single one of our donors, because we are proud of our donors and we are proud of the campaign we are running,'" he said, and proceeded to do none of that.[31]

In 2016, Missouri regained its bellwether status, voting for the winner, Trump, as part of a GOP sweep. In stark contrast to any other point in Missouri history, all but one statewide elected official was a Republican. The election remains controversial. Greitens won in a campaign that remains suspicious due not only to the aforementioned scandals[32] but also to ethical violations he committed in office, including using apps that delete government records. Kander suffered a surprising loss to Republican Roy Blunt and went on to start Let America Vote, an organization committed to transparency and election integrity, before taking time off to get treatment for PTSD. Purged of progressives and cloaked in dark money, the GOP Missouri legislature went on to implement a radical right-wing agenda in defiance of the voters' will.

Some of the most extreme positions promoted by the new Republican legislature relate to guns. In Missouri, gun permits or background checks are no longer required if you're over nineteen years old, and the "stand your ground" law has essentially made it legal to shoot someone to death if you can prove you felt threatened at the time. New laws proposed by the GOP legislature include a measure to make it illegal for schools, hospitals, and other public facilities to prevent a person from carrying a gun inside. Another proposed law *requires* that every Missourian between the ages of eighteen and thirty-five own an AR-15 assault rifle.[33] Our state government is not only failing to protect us from gun violence but is trying to rewrite the law to force us to participate in it.

Many Missourians like guns, but to conflate a desire to hunt or protect oneself with abidance for the violence that results from lax laws is an absurd propaganda trick. As restrictions on regulations have loosened, the casualties have soared: gun homicides rose 43 percent between 2014 and 2016, the most recent statistic available.[34] When I wake up to stories of slaughter, it is with increased alarm—because the gun deaths speak to a more frightening problem, a lack of oversight that is literally murderous. It is mirrored in the opioid epidemic, which has also grabbed disproportionate hold of Missouri and has devastated communities.[35] It's the sense of having a government that seems to welcome death; a government that has abdicated even the pretense of working for its citizens or caring if they live or die.

I live in Missouri, a state plunged into darkness: dark money, dead bodies, disappearing information, and disputed votes.

We are the state with the loosest restrictions on both money and guns. Those with fantasies of a lawless world need look no further than Missouri to have a sudden longing for regulation. Missouri is not a state of free spirits reveling in anarchic dissolution of the power structure. We are citizens held captive by politicians beholden to corrupt donors whose names we do not know, and we are people who leave our homes every day assuming we might not make it back alive.

In Missouri, multiple top officials—among them Greitens and St. Louis County executive Steve Stenger, a Democrat who was arrested in April 2019 on corruption charges accusing him of trading political favors for campaign donations—are implicated in political crimes, and the integrity of state elections has fallen into question.[36] Missouri has become a petri dish for the end of the American experiment, combining the worst qualities of the states that border it: the indicted officials of Illinois and the notorious dysfunction of Kansas.

In April 2018, I went on a book tour for my essay collection *The View from Flyover Country*, and found myself constantly having to insist to people outside my state that the conditions I describe are real.

"What's it like where you live?" interviewers would ask, and I would reply:

"I live in St. Louis, Missouri, near an underground fire that has been making its way toward buried nuclear waste at a site called the West Lake Landfill.[37] This has been going on for several decades and has spawned nothing except documentaries and cancer clusters.

"In 2017, St. Louis—recently named number one in the country for both STDs and murder—became the first city in the United States to *lower* the minimum wage from $10 an hour down to $7.70, with Missouri Republicans in Jefferson City overriding a hard-fought victory by labor activists that was passed two years ago by St. Louis voters and officials . . .

"Racism is so rampant in Missouri that in 2017, three years after the Ferguson uprising, the NAACP issued a travel warning for the state, telling black people not to come here because they'll be profiled and threatened.[38] It's so misogynist that in 2017, the Republicans also attempted to make it legal for women who use birth control to be fired,[39] which didn't work. Meanwhile, our state's legislature was one of very few to give personal voting information to the Trump administration when the latter requested it after making a fatuous claim of a voter fraud crisis. To this day no one knows what happened to our data . . ."[40]

At this point the listener couldn't take it any more and would interrupt, asking, "Who is in charge of this place?!"

"Great question—we don't know! In January 2018, we found out that the governor, Eric Greitens, who campaigned closely with Mike Pence on a 'family values' platform, allegedly tied a half-naked and blindfolded woman to a piece of exercise equipment in his basement and took her picture, threatening to release the photos if she told anyone they had had an affair. He was indicted on felony invasion of privacy, but that's not why the Republicans want him to resign.[41]

"Greitens was then indicted for a *second* felony—tampering with a computer and taking donor lists from his own veterans' charity for fundraising purposes. That's the one the GOP cares about because an investigation opens the door into dark money in Missouri,[42] and Greitens was already in trouble for using an illegal app that made his texts and emails disappear. Even the Missouri Republicans want him to step down, but he won't leave . . ."

I remember telling these stories on the radio and TV in the spring of 2018, and the host would laugh, and I would laugh back, like these were simply low-key absurdities and not conditions that structured my life and filled me with dread for my children and my country. Corruption is like a weight that you never shed because no one will recognize you are carrying it. You are battling ghosts, following trails of disappearing cash and deleted data, hoping that local media (which has been gutted) will do the job of officials (who long ago surrendered their duties to their donors).

In May 2018, when the Missouri House subpoenaed Greitens for New Missouri documents, he chose to resign as governor rather than comply: even the prospect of revealing his true backers made the Greitens team panic.[43] Greitens had been indicted in February, and his three-month tenure as governor postindictment became a referendum on power versus law. Law eventually won, but only in the sense that we no longer had an indicted official governing us, not in the sense of justice being served. When Greitens resigned, the remaining charges against him were dropped. Rumors spread that he had agreed to leave office if he was guaranteed to avoid prison time, and that a desire to protect his secretive backers was key to the decision. Whereas once mere publicity about his scandals would have prompted resignation, Greitens proved that hanging on to executive power to dodge or manipulate prosecution remains a viable option in an era of unfettered corruption—a lesson the Trump administration knows well. One of the most awful things about the Greitens case is that Missourians felt *lucky* he left, like peasants relieved at the passing of an evil king. There was never accountability, there was never transparency—there was just luck, otherwise known as dead expectations.

In St. Louis there is a notorious jail nicknamed "the Workhouse," a mold-infested pit where citizens who often haven't been formally charged with a crime live in horrific conditions, suffering through extreme heat and cold, denied adequate food and water. People end up in the Workhouse after being suspected of offenses like possessing marijuana or failing to pay child support. The Workhouse keeps its captives for months on end, threatening to hold them indefinitely if they cannot pay $10,000 bond. Sometimes the guards make the prisoners fight each other for their own amusement.[44] The Workhouse sits a few miles from the mansion where Eric Greitens, the governor who was charged with two felonies and served not a day of time, is rumored to be planning his comeback.

In November 2018, Missouri had an election that put to bed the "red state" and "blue state" fallacy once and for all. Citizens were asked to vote on a series of progressive ballot initiatives, including medical marijuana and raising the minimum wage. The initiatives passed overwhelmingly, continuing a trend that had begun with the approval of a pro–labor union law that had passed in an August special election. Among the amendments that passed in November was Clean Missouri, which was seen as the road to cleaning up election corruption once and for all. But voters faced an unlikely roadblock: themselves.

When asked to vote on a specific issue, Missourians chose the most progressive options. But when asked to vote for a politician, over half of Missourians chose Republicans who sought to strike down the very ballot initiatives for which they had voted. There are many factors that may explain this discrepancy, and if we had a thriving local news infrastructure, we might have a clearer idea of the answers, but local media were gutted along with the rest of our economy.

In 2018, Claire McCaskill, the conservative Democrat who handily beat Todd Akin after his "legitimate rape" comments six years before, lost her Senate race to Missouri attorney general

Josh Hawley after Hawley was endorsed by Donald Trump, who is, among other things, a self-proclaimed sexual assaulter who in 2016 paid off a porn star he slept with a decade before while his wife was caring for their baby son. McCaskill, a conservative Democrat, had been the target of a dark money propaganda campaign that labeled her a dangerous left-wing radical.[45] A 2019 investigation indicated that many of the 2018 ads for Hawley had been illegally coordinated by the NRA.[46]

Within months of being elected, Hawley was being investigated for violating many of the same laws he had cited as reasons for Greitens to resign during his time as attorney general, including using apps to make documents disappear and hiding state information from the public.[47] He has also been accused of engaging in "an elaborate scheme designed to evade detection" of campaign finance violations involving the NRA.[48] (The NRA gave more to Hawley than to any other Senate candidate, and the organization has been accused of funneling money from Kremlin-affiliated oligarchs to the GOP.)[49] Calls have begun for Hawley's resignation. In response, the Missouri GOP is striking down the voter-backed Clean Missouri, which would have forced political misdeeds involving finances into the open, in an attempt to ensure the longevity of their own corrupt rule.

Missouri is not a red state, but it is becoming a one-party state—a party ruled by mysterious megadonors, a party that openly disregards the will of its electorate. In the most damning of ways, we are the bellwether for the United States. We are losing not only our freedom but our sovereignty to forces we do not fully understand, but which understand our own vulnerabilities all too well.

Why don't you move? people ask. They ask me both about Missouri, and about America—and in many ways, it's the same question, for they share the same sins. I always answer: *Where is there to go?* Missouri is a symptom of the American disease, and America a symptom of an international disease.

There is nowhere left to go, but I also do not want to leave. All that differentiates Missouri from other states is the scale of our corruption, and the layers of tragedy, and that citizens have been fighting these battles so long we tend to see things clearly, even if we do not see a way out.

There's a park I drive to when I just can't take it anymore, a state park that, like all parks in Missouri, charges no admission. When I go there I am almost always alone, a luxury of living in a state few want to visit. The park was created by Don Robinson, a St. Louis businessman who made a fortune selling stain removal products on late-night TV infomercials. For decades, Robinson bought up parcels of rocky land—sandstone caves and dolomite glades, land about which a farmer warned "all you can raise up there is hell."[50] The trees there look like their vines will reach out and strangle you; at random intervals, billion-year-old boulders jut out of the earth. Robinson lived on the land in a wooden shack and would let children explore his 843 acres undisturbed.

When Robinson died, he left his land to the Missouri state park system. His grave sits on a small hill at the park entrance, a slab surrounded by a swirl of pebbles. Don Robinson had bought the exact number of acres as New York City's Central Park, and he never said why he did it, but we know why he did it. You can *feel* why as you climb deep into wild and unkempt terrain marked only by two narrow dirt trails. The entire site is a rebuke to consumerism and conformity, a rejection of everything manicured and slick and tame. It is Missouri in the best way—defiant, eccentric, unexpectedly generous. He left the greatest gift of all: the audacity of alternatives, a Missouri that refused to compromise.

2

The 1980s: Roy Cohn's Orwellian America

When 1983 was about to turn into 1984, my mother decided to tell me about fascism. I was five years old.

"This is a year everyone has been waiting for, Sarah," she said. "A long time ago, a guy named George Orwell wrote a book called *1984* that was about a society where everyone lied, where people would tell you that two plus two equaled five and you had to believe it, and no one had freedom except for the people in charge, who were called Big Brother, and Big Brother was always spying on you to make sure you didn't think for yourself. This is a really famous book! It's older than I am. And now I can't believe it's really going to be 1984."

"What do you mean, *it's really going to be 1984?*" I asked, horrified. "All the stuff in that book is going to happen?"

"No, it's just a book," said my mother, a public school English teacher with a dubious sense of appropriate topics for small children. "It's a made-up story about what he imagined the future would be like, because George Orwell lived during a terrible time, and he wanted to make sure we didn't live in a terrible time. So he warned everyone about what could happen in 1984 if people didn't watch out."

I took this in like I had taken in all the other political information I picked up from adult conversations, including my belief that Ronald Reagan was *literally* a puppet, which I found both alarming and cool. The idea that a dead famous writer had fantasized about this year of 1984, the very year I was about to start writing as the date at the top of my kindergarten homework, seemed incredible.

When you are a young child, you have no sense of anything that happened before you existed unless it is explicitly spelled out. Even then, your grasp of time is tenuous. I remember when my own daughter was five and she asked me whether any of the Harry Potter books had come out before she was born and was shocked to hear nearly all of them had.

"Did any *other* books come out before I was born?" she asked. "Books that aren't Harry Potter?"

"Um . . . yes."

"How many?"

"Like . . . millions. Tens of millions of books came out before you were born."

"Wait, so you're telling me that *all this stuff* was just happening in the world *without me in it*?!" my daughter exclaimed, amazed and appalled.

I felt the same sense of wonder about *1984*, and I wanted to read it so that I could see if any of this Orwell guy's predictions panned out. (My mother did not let me read *1984* as a five-year-old, and I remain grateful that the internet did not yet exist.) I was intrigued that someone had worried enough about the future to invent his own fictional version. I wondered what had happened in the past that was so horrific that it compelled him to imagine a world of lies and control. I remember writing "$2+2 = 5$" on my kindergarten homework, below where I had written "1984," to see if anything would happen.

On November 15, 1984, *The Washington Post* published an article called DONALD TRUMP, HOLDING ALL THE CARDS: THE TOWER!

THE TEAM! THE MONEY! THE FUTURE![1] It described the thirty-eight-year-old real estate tycoon as having ambitions far beyond business. He was destined for politics, the article claimed, and sought to determine the fate of the world.

> This morning, Trump has a new idea. He wants to talk about the threat of nuclear war. He wants to talk about how the United States should negotiate with the Soviets. He wants to be the negotiator. He says he has never acted on his nuclear concern. But he says that his good friend Roy Cohn, the flamboyant Republican lawyer, has told him this interview is a perfect time to start.
>
> "Some people have an ability to negotiate," he says. "It's an art you're basically born with. You either have it or you don't."
>
> He would know what to ask the Russians for, he says. But he would rather not tip his hand publicly. "In the event anything happens with respect to me, I wouldn't want to make my opinions public," he says. "I'd rather keep those thoughts to myself or save them for whoever else is chosen . . .
>
> "It's something that somebody should do that knows how to negotiate and not the kind of representatives that I have seen in the past."
>
> He could learn about missiles, quickly, he says.
>
> "It would take an hour-and-a-half to learn everything there is to learn about missiles . . . I think I know most of it anyway. You're talking about just getting updated on a situation . . . You know who really wants me to do this? Roy . . . I'd do it in a second."

The 1984 *Washington Post* piece is the first mention of Trump's desire to build an alliance with Russia, a goal that would structure his next thirty years. While the author appears to regard this scenario as an amusing fantasy, it has now become a dangerous reality, and the piece prompts questions about how Trump's interests were propelled in this direction. The answer lies in Roy Cohn, one of the most notorious figures in US political history: a vicious Republican operative who had worked as an adviser for Joseph McCarthy, Richard Nixon, and New York City crime families while insinuating himself into and manipulating national media.[2] Before becoming Trump's mentor, Cohn was best known for prompting lawyer Joseph Welch to utter the famous phrase "Have you no sense of decency, sir?" to McCarthy in response to Cohn's ceaseless slander.

Cohn had long ago shunned the mantle of decency, viewing it as an obstacle to power. Power was information—its closed-door accumulation, its careful release—and information was different than truth. Cohn took Trump under his wing in 1973 when he defended Trump and his real estate developer father, Fred, in a lawsuit filed by the Department of Justice after they discovered the Trump Organization had refused to rent thirty-nine properties to black New Yorkers.[3] With Cohn's aid, Trump countersued the US government for $100 million, asserting that the charges were "irresponsible and baseless"[4]—a ploy the judge of the case called "a media gimmick done for local consumption."[5] The countersuit was dismissed and the Trumps were ordered to change their discriminatory housing practices (which they did not) but Trump remained drawn to Cohn's shamelessness. Cohn trained him in the strategy he refined under McCarthy and Nixon: counterattack, lie, threaten, sue, and never back down.

Cohn understood the power of the court of public opinion to outweigh the court of law. Media was a weapon: a well-timed bomb, a scalpel to carve a façade. In 1976, Trump got his first profile in *The New York Times*. They described him in glowing terms:

> He is tall, lean and blond, with dazzling white teeth, and he looks ever so much like Robert Redford. He rides around town in a chauffeured silver Cadillac with his initials, DJT, on the plates. He dates slinky fashion models, belongs to the

most elegant clubs and, at only 30 years of age, estimates
that he is worth "more than $200 million."

Flair. It's one of Donald J. Trump's favorite words, and
both he, his friends and his enemies use it when describing
his way of life as well as his business style as New York's
No. 1 real estate promoter of the middle 1970's.[6]

The 1973 discrimination lawsuit that had once dominated
headlines got only a passing mention in the piece, which is so
rapturous it feels like it was written *by* Donald Trump. This, too,
shows Cohn's sway. By the 1970s, Cohn had established a close relationship with New York's leading gossip columnists and reporters,
leaking newspapers information to humiliate and smear his foes.
When journalists deviated from his desires, he threatened them
with litigation and violence.[7] Often the threats arrived in the form
of nondisclosure agreements (NDAs), which can silence targets for
decades. Over the next thirty years, Trump would use these tactics
himself or order his new lawyers—lackluster litigators whom he
bemoaned could never compare to his beloved Roy Cohn, who
died in 1986[8]—to employ them.

Trump's connection to Cohn ran deep, comprising a rare relationship of trust outside his family circle. Why Trump, whose inherited fortune opened the door to an array of social possibilities,
chose arguably the worst person in America to be his best friend
remains unknown. Renowned *Village Voice* journalist Wayne Barrett, the foremost chronicler of Trump's corruption in the 1980s
and 1990s, described Cohn in July 2016 as "incandescent evil . . .
enough to make you rush back to church, the Satanic feeling that
he would give you . . . he was a chicken hawk after little boys, and
yet he was the most virulently anti-gay guy you could imagine.
And so, that was Donald's mentor and constant sidekick, who represented all five of the organized crime families in the City of New
York."[9]

In December 2016, Barrett, alarmed by Trump's win, elaborated on Cohn's influence: "Roy Cohn was the most satanic figure I ever met in my life. He was almost reptilian. I think he's going to handle the swearing-in at the inauguration. They're not going to bring a judge, they're going to have Roy. And then Roy's going to go back to the White House and fuck a 12-year-old. In the Oval Office."[10] Barrett died the night before Trump's inauguration.

Cohn's cousin, David Marcus, says that Cohn was sexually attracted to Trump, though there is no public indication that the attraction was mutual.[11] What is not disputed is their closeness: Trump and Cohn would call each other fifteen to twenty times a day. They were inseparable in New York work and nightlife, and Cohn widened Trump's political horizons.[12] In the early 1980s, Cohn introduced Trump to two of his protégés, a pair of GOP operatives who would become both lifelong colleagues of Trump and indicted subjects in the Russian influence investigation: Roger Stone, a Nixon acolyte who managed Trump's 2000, 2012, and 2016 presidential campaigns; and Paul Manafort, a GOP operative who in 1980, with Stone and Charles Black, started a D.C. lobbying firm that represented the world's most brutal dictators and guerilla groups.

That in 1984 Roy Cohn sought to have Donald Trump discuss nuclear weapons policy with the USSR—America's primary adversary—should have prompted alarm at the time and still should today. As a principal architect of the 1950s Red Scare, Cohn had built his reputation as an opponent of the Soviet Union, and his ambitions for Trump seemed to belie his lifelong opposition to what President Reagan called "the Evil Empire." But Cohn—a Jewish anti-Semite, a gay homophobe, and a debt-laden power broker—was often not what he seemed.[13]

Aside from the mention of his lust for a nuclear arsenal, the *Washington Post* piece was typical of 1980s articles on Trump, emphasizing his real estate deals, his model wife, and his alleged internal struggle over socialites labeling him "nouveau riche." The glittery press profiles served to mask darker deeds, as did the gleaming exterior of his landmark building, Trump Tower, which had become a fledgling dorm for the Russian mafia. In 1984, one year after the tower's completion, Soviet army veteran David Bogatin purchased five luxury condos for six million dollars—a purchase so substantial that Trump made sure to personally oversee the closing.[14] In 1987, Bogatin admitted he had purchased the Trump Tower condos "to launder money, to shelter and hide assets," and a Senate investigation revealed him to be a leading figure in the Russian mafia.[15] The Russian mafia had been growing in New York City due to a wave of Soviet émigrés and a crackdown on the Italian mob by then prosecutor and Trump friend Rudy Giuliani. Giuliani, who became the U.S. attorney for the southern district of New York in 1983, waged a tactical war against New York's five organized crime families so successful that even the Italian government gave him a medal.[16] But the near elimination of the Italian mafia only cleared the way for Russian criminal domination. Among the émigré mobsters hovering in Trump's orbit was Bogatin's brother, Jacob, a partner of Semion Mogilevich, a Russian money launderer who soon became—and likely remains—the most powerful criminal in the world.

There was no mention of Trump's criminal ties in the *Washington Post* puff piece, a pattern of omission that is blinding in hindsight. Maybe the paper did not know about them, despite his mentor, Cohn, being a well-known mafia fixer. Maybe they did not want to find out.

There is a photo of Roy Cohn in 1984, sitting cross-legged on his apartment floor, cradling a framed picture of himself with Donald Trump while surrounded by his vast collection of frogs, many of which, like Cohn himself, have faces that resemble Pepe, the cartoon frog plastered on websites by Roger Stone and other Trump backers in the 2016 election.[17] Trump grins out from Cohn's golden frame, caressed by the spin master tied to the mafia, to the GOP, to the media, to the Soviets. Who knew 1984 would feel so Orwellian thirty-five years later? Very likely, Roy Cohn did.

. . .

On January 27, 2011, Robert Mueller, the head of the FBI, gave a speech to the Citizens Crime Commission of New York City. He warned of an unprecedented menace that threatened to end democracy in the United States and destabilize the entire world. He called it "The Evolving Organized Crime Threat":

> The playing field has changed. We have seen a shift from regional families with a clear structure, to flat, fluid networks with global reach. These international enterprises are more anonymous and more sophisticated. Rather than running discrete operations, on their own turf, they are running multi-national, multi-billion dollar schemes from start to finish.
>
> We are investigating groups in Asia, Eastern Europe, West Africa, and the Middle East. And we are seeing cross-pollination between groups that historically have not worked together. Criminals who may never meet, but who share one thing in common: greed.
>
> They may be former members of nation-state governments, security services, or the military. These individuals know who and what to target, and how best to do it. They are capitalists and entrepreneurs. But they are also master criminals who move easily between the licit and illicit worlds. And in some cases, these organizations are as forward-leaning as Fortune 500 companies.
>
> This is not "The Sopranos," with six guys sitting in a diner, shaking down a local business owner for 50 dollars a week. These criminal enterprises are making billions of dollars from human trafficking, health care fraud, computer intrusions, and copyright infringement. They are cornering the market on natural gas, oil, and precious metals, and selling to the highest bidder.
>
> These crimes are not easily categorized. Nor can the damage, the dollar loss, or the ripple effects be easily cal-

culated. It is much like a Venn diagram, where one crime intersects with another, in different jurisdictions, and with different groups.

How does this impact you? You may not recognize the source, but you will feel the effects. You might pay more for a gallon of gas. You might pay more for a luxury car from overseas. You will pay more for health care, mortgages, clothes, and food.

Yet we are concerned with more than just the financial impact. These groups may infiltrate our businesses. They may provide logistical support to hostile foreign powers. They may try to manipulate those at the highest levels of government. Indeed, these so-called "iron triangles" of organized criminals, corrupt government officials, and business leaders pose a significant national security threat . . .

Last year, we set up two units, called Threat Focus Cells, to target Eurasian organized crime. The first focuses on the Semion Mogilevich Organization; the second on the Brother's Circle enterprise.

For those of you not familiar with either group, their memberships are large, their reach is global, and their scope of operations is broad, from weapons and drug trafficking to high-stakes fraud and global prostitution. If left unchecked, the resulting impact to our economy and our security will be significant. Indeed, Semion Mogilevich is on the FBI Top Ten Most Wanted List, and he will remain so until he is captured.[18]

"The Evolving Organized Crime Threat" is the kind of speech that would give you great confidence in Mueller's abilities were you not reading it about a decade after his predictions became a fixture of American reality. Members of the mob that had taken up residence in Trump Tower in the 1980s—the Semion Mogilevich Organization—are now tied to the White House. This development belies any claim of surprise from federal law enforcement about the threat posed by Trump's campaign. Instead we are left with institutional failures and unanswered questions.

Mueller's speech is a blueprint laying out how the Trump team, backed by an organized crime syndicate, and abetted by transnational alliances that would have been unthinkable a decade before, rose to power by blurring the lines between white-collar crime, mafia activity, and state corruption. It describes with uncanny accuracy the economic devastation ordinary Americans experienced from 2008 onward, and attributes it to unfettered criminal corruption that Mueller promised the FBI would combat—but it did not. Under the leadership of James Comey, who replaced Mueller as FBI head in 2013, the FBI removed Mogilevich—the dangerous Russian mafia head who had been ancillary to Trump since the 1980s—from the Ten Most Wanted list in December 2015 and replaced him with a bank robber.[19] Comey never explained why Mogilevich's removal was warranted when Mogilevich was still participating in the same extreme criminal activity that had compelled Mueller to name him a threat so profound "he will remain [on the Ten Most Wanted list] until he is captured" just four years before. The removal of Mogilevich was highly unorthodox: he was only the seventh top-ten fugitive since 1950 to be removed from the list prior to apprehension, death, or dismissal of charges.[20] The FBI's official explanation was that Mogilevich "no longer poses an immediate threat to the public" and that he is residing in a country without an extradition treaty. Yet when the FBI originally placed Mogilevich on the list in October 2009, they noted that "what makes him so dangerous is that he operates without borders."[21] The FBI did not name Mogilevich's current location, but his unnerving power is that, in many ways, it no longer matters.

Writing Trump's history is a bizarre exercise in parsing layers of propaganda. There is the propaganda written in real time by Trump's press lackeys (sometimes with anonymous quotes that were later revealed to be from Trump himself, often made under the alias "John Barron";[22] a real John Barron was the author of a 1974 bestselling book about the KGB). There is the investigative journalism written in real time on Trump's nefarious financial affairs by journalists who mostly have since died. And there is the media morass of 2015 and 2016, when investigative journalists from Trump's past were censored, threatened, or generally kept out of the news—while journalists of Trump's present ignored blatant crimes in favor of an obsessive focus on Hillary Clinton's emails, a misalignment of priorities that was stoked by the FBI itself.

I remember in 2016 thinking that this parsing of spectacle and propaganda and searching for documentation of the obvious is, ironically, the exact exercise I had to perform as a doctoral student examining materials from the former Soviet Union. It doesn't feel ironic anymore: American and former Soviet operatives are a linked entity, and prestigious institutions manufacture history in a way that would make George Orwell shudder and Roy Cohn proud. In 2017, *The New York Times* published an article insinuating that Trump and Manafort had no real relationship until 2016, when Manafort fortuitously appeared in the Trump Tower elevator to charm him, like characters in a rom-com from hell.[23] The article did not mention that Manafort had known Trump since the 1980s, had lived in Trump Tower since 2006, and was linked to Trump through Cohn, Stone, and a mafia syndicate intertwined with the Kremlin. To grasp why a Pulitzer Prize–winning paper would cover up *that* story—an accurate and far more interesting story—in favor of bland falsehoods is key to understanding how Trump operates.

Trump spent 2016 incriminating himself by doing things like asking Russia for Hillary Clinton's emails at a press conference or getting sued for child rape by a woman who claimed to be a victim of a global trafficking network. But still most of the press did not bite, writing fawning portraits despite the enticement of Trump checking every box of classic tabloid fodder: mafia ties, sex crimes, spies, secret meetings with global elites. Any one of these stories would be ratings gold. When the press works against its own financial interest—as it did by rejecting the harrowing truth of Trump—there is a deeper problem. As described throughout this book, the tactics Cohn devised to tame the press worked all too well.

Roy Cohn died of complications from AIDS in 1986. Trump, true to form, abandoned Cohn when he fell ill, prompting Cohn to proclaim in an interview with Barrett that Trump "pisses ice water."[24] Cohn, true to form, died after being disbarred for "dishonesty, fraud, deceit, and misrepresentation" and being convicted of fraud, fulfilling his dream of dying while owing the US government vast amounts of money.[25] He was feted at his funeral by the New York and D.C. celebrities who had legitimized him much in the way future New York and D.C. celebrities would legitimize his protégé, Trump. They didn't talk about the mafia ties, about the shakedowns, about the political persecution, about the pain Cohn caused his country. He was one of them, of their social class, so he had to be soft-pedaled to the status of loveable goon, much as Roger Stone would go on to be called a "dirty trickster," or Trump would be embraced as a tabloid amusement.

Before Cohn passed, he managed to teach Trump three key skills: how to swindle money, how to get married for maximum benefit, and—though the purpose behind this agenda was never publicly revealed—how to cozy up to America's enemies, the greatest one at that time being the Soviets. But most of all, he taught Trump how to construct a new American reality out of the wreckage of the American Dream.

From 1946 until 1974—the first twenty-eight years of Trump's life—the US economy experienced a period of unparalleled stability and prosperity.[26] This was the era in which "the American Dream"—once thought to be a permanent condition of American life, now increasingly recognized as a historical blip—seemed feasible. The American Dream included having a steady job and getting a raise, owning a home, not needing an advanced degree for a career, and if you did, being able to afford one without being saddled with decades of debt.

It was an era when President Harry Truman, then regarded as a moderate Democrat, could put forward an economic "Fair Deal" advocating a widened social safety net that resembles the platform of representatives like Alexandria Ocasio-Cortez, who is today maligned as a dangerous radical. It was an era when President Dwight Eisenhower could rail against the military-industrial complex and say things like "This world in arms is not spending money alone; it is spending the sweat of its laborers, the genius of its scientists, the hopes of its children" and be thought of as a patriotic, sensible member of the Republican Party.[27]

It was an era of morality in plans and in speeches, and immorality in laws and practice. The civil rights movement combatted laws denying black Americans their basic rights as whites pursued their precious ambitions. The antiwar movement exposed the rapacious military-industrial complex about which Eisenhower warned. Journalistic exposés and hearings brought down corrupt actors like Richard Nixon, despite the efforts of future Trump lackeys like Stone to save him.

Economic stability helped make these social movements possible. It gave freedom and fluidity to everyday American life. You could tune in, drop out, and drop back in. You could work, uncredentialed, in a job, and cover the basic cost of living. You could move from place to place and reinvent yourself each time. Meanwhile, regulations curbed the rich from buying politicians and policies like they had in the Gilded Age. This is not to say that 1946 to 1974 was a paradise: especially in the 1960s, it was a time of trauma and hardship on both an individual and structural level, particularly for Americans of color. But it was a time of possibility. It was a time when progress seemed propelled forward—with sacrifice and loss, but onward nonetheless. The lessons of that era were that good ultimately won over evil, that the strength and persistence of the everyday American mattered.

By the mid-1970s, this mind-set had begun to change. FORD TO CITY: DROP DEAD blared a famous *New York Daily News* cover from 1975, describing President Gerald Ford's refusal to give bottomed-out New York a federal bailout. Urban poverty and crime had begun to soar, but the most pernicious development was the one no one knew had started: the structural transformation of income and wages. Until 1979, US worker pay rose with productivity. Starting in 1980, the incomes of the very rich began growing faster than the entire economy, while the poor and middle class began to fall dramatically behind. Growth in worker productivity between 1979 and 2017 grew by 70.3 percent while hourly compensation grew by 11.1 percent.[28] (Earnings of the top 0.1 percent of Americas grew 343.2 percent by comparison.)

The extreme stratification of income and wealth that began in the late 1970s has now outdone that of the Gilded Age of robber barons. In addition to stripping Americans of opportunities and resources—and shifting expectations, casting survival as an aspiration—it has severely curtailed political movements. Foreigners ask me why American citizens are not out in the streets protesting around the clock, like people did in Hong Kong and South Korea. The answer is that protest is more of a financial risk than a political one, and financial risks form the backbone of modern American terror.

We cannot afford to overcome. We are too busy doing GoFundMe's for the funerals of our friends whose previous GoFundMe failed to cover their health care. Much as the American Dream is dead, the methods of protest that it enabled are no longer effective—the leverage and fluidity of that era is gone. This does not mean that *protest* itself is dead, that standing up and fighting back is futile, but that the "iron triangles" about which Mueller warned have strangled our traditional means of self-protection.

We live in the era of the masses versus the mob: but people

do not recognize the mob as the mob. In the twenty-first century, the mob both wears suits and files them. The mob is tasteful, and presidential, and—worst of all—legal. We are living in Roy Cohn's America, directed by his apt pupil, with the aid of a crime syndicate that does not recognize law, freedom, or the sanctity of human life.

In the late 1970s, as Ford told New York to drop dead, Cohn and Trump picked at the city's corpse like vultures. Manhattan was ready to be torn down and bludgeoned and remade with blood money in concrete: Trump Tower, the Plaza, the many, many casinos. Corporate raiders who would later aid the Trump administration—Carl Icahn, Wilbur Ross, Rupert Murdoch—commenced a national shakedown disguised as economic revival. Scams stretched from Atlantic City to Gary, Indiana, to St. Louis and beyond, to international waters where moguls parked their stolen assets.[29] Critical regulations were tossed—the fairness doctrine that had protected media; the labor laws that had protected unions. While there were objections, few recognized the long-term agenda to profit off the damage.

Trump arrived on the national scene right as the nation began to crumble.

In 2016, shortly after Trump was deemed president of the United States, the German publication *Bild* published a series of documents showing that Trump had not paid federal taxes since 1977—an allegation that echoed a vague claim Hillary Clinton had made during a debate but never fully explained.[30] The files came from the Czech security services—essentially, the Stasi of the Czechoslovak Socialist Republic (CSSR), which had been monitoring Donald Trump and his Czech wife, Ivana, since they married in 1977. It was typical of the CSSR to monitor Americans who came onto their radar—particularly rich, powerful, and connected Americans like Donald Trump—and to pass along information to their counterparts in the Soviet Union and in other communist states of the Eastern Bloc. The private information they procured for blackmail purposes is called *kompromat*.

During the Cold War, Soviet and Soviet-adjacent intelligence services routinely created dossiers on Westerners and used this information to manipulate individuals and influence world affairs.[31] US intelligence agencies employed similar tactics, though they deployed them in the USSR in a less aggressive (and arguably less effective) way. When the Soviet Union collapsed in 1991, states that remained authoritarian—including Russia—gave their security services new names while employing the same brutal practices, while states that embraced democracy, like the Czech Republic, began reforms.

Surveillance is to be expected; kompromat is not unique. What is not typical, however, is for documents to claim that, beginning in 1977, Trump would remain "completely tax-exempt for the next 30 years" thanks to a mysterious arrangement between his company and the American government; that he was contractually bound to have three children with Ivana (which he did); and that he was being groomed to run for president in 1988 (which he nearly did).[32] Despite repeated demands from officials, Trump has still not released his taxes to the American public. The head of the IRS has not complied with congressional requests.

No member of the US government has commented on the CSSR files, despite the perplexing nature of the claims inside them. The only journalist who did a follow-up on the files' existence was British reporter Luke Harding. Harding tracked down Czech officials who affirmed that the files were real and told him, "It wasn't only us who paid attention to him. The first department of the StB (Státní bezpečnost, or Czech security services) were interested in him. I don't know if the first directorate shared information on Trump with the KGB. I can't verify or deny."[33]

The question of whether Trump, in 1977—at the height of his tutelage under tax-dodger Cohn—struck up some incredible agreement where he would pay no taxes to the United States until

2007 is not just unanswered but unexamined. The answers could be found: the IRS should know. Given the number of times Trump business dealings have fallen under investigation by federal agencies, including the Department of Justice and the Treasury, other government agencies may know too. But the American people do not. And the question of *why* we do not know remains as enormous—and as disconcerting—as the information in the Czech files themselves.

The late 1970s ushered in an era in which the rich paid less and less to the government and the poor worked and suffered more. Trump was introduced into the corrupt world he now inhabits and developed the tactics he now employs to evade consequences, just as the world itself was changing to reward white-collar criminals like himself. In the 1980s, he became symbolic of this era and its rapacious greed, but the extent to which he showcases wealth as raw power is distressingly *literal*. He was not merely an outcome of the economic restructuring ushered in by Reagan's union-busting and trickle-down economics, and he was not merely a brazen player in the corporate raiding and glitzy rebuilding of New York City. Trump may have been involved in an unparalleled and inexplicable pact with the US government to remain above the law, one that was likely buffered by criminal actors and hostile foreign states. This disturbingly parallels his present-day actions as president.

The Trump administration has been notable for its reverence for criminals and dictators. While designating Canada, Mexico, and the EU to be enemies of the United States, Trump—aided by daughter Ivanka and son-in-law Jared Kushner—sought out an axis of autocrats to take their place. This axis includes Saudi prince Muhammad bin Salman (MBS), Israeli prime minister Benjamin Netanyahu, Turkish dictator Recep Tayyip Erdoğan, millennial murderer Kim Jong Un, and, of course, Vladimir Putin. Trump rehabilitated domestic criminals as well, using the power of the presidential pardon as a lure and a reward for loyalty, as he did for Republican criminals Joe Arpaio and Scooter Libby.

This ongoing image rehab of the worst people in the world mirrors the ethos of the "torturers' lobby" run by Manafort and Stone in the 1980s—who represented the Philippines' Marcos family and Congolese leader Mobutu Sese Seko while moonlighting as operatives for Republican campaigns. It also parallels Trump's 1980s social network, which included people like billionaire Saudi arms smuggler Adnan Khashoggi, whom Trump befriended and from whom he bought a "surveillance yacht" filled with hidden cameras.[34] (In fall 2018, Khashoggi's nephew, *Washington Post* writer Jamal Khashoggi, was hacked into pieces with a bone saw by aides of the Saudi government in their Turkish embassy, allegedly under the orders of MBS with information supplied by MBS's friend, Kushner, after Khashoggi had criticized Trump.[35] Adnan Khashoggi is also dead, having passed on in 2017 due to unknown causes.) The same names recur over and over in the sordid Trump saga, indicative of an interconnected web of relationships between politicians, spies, and crime lords that were built in the 1980s and continue to the present day.

Throughout his 2016 campaign, Trump insisted that he had nothing to do with Russia, had no ties to the Russian government, and had never made any business deals with Russians. This flew in the face of recent interviews—such as his claim on Fox News in 2014 that Putin had reached out to him during the Miss Universe pageant in Moscow in 2013—but also in the face of his 1987 autobiography *The Art of the Deal*. Cowritten with Tony Schwartz—a ghostwriter who later warned during the 2016 campaign that Trump was a sociopath who would likely bring forth the end of the world if elected—*The Art of the Deal* could have been subtitled *How I Became a Russian Asset*.[36]

"A prominent businessman who does a lot of business with the Soviet Union calls me to keep me posted on a construction project I'm interested in undertaking in Moscow," Trump wrote in

The Art of the Deal when explaining the origins of his first trip to Russia. "The idea got off the ground after I sat next to the Soviet ambassador, Yuri Dubinin, at a luncheon held by Leonard Lauder, a great businessman who is the son of Estee Lauder. Dubinin's daughter, it turned out, had read about Trump Tower and knew all about it. One thing led to another, and now I'm talking about a large luxury hotel, across the street from the Kremlin, in partnership with the Soviet government. They have asked me to go to Moscow in July."[37]

To be clear, doing business with the Russians was not a crime, and there was nothing illegal about visiting the USSR during the glasnost era, when Russia was opening up to the world. Many celebrities did so. Mr. Rogers, for example, also went to the USSR in 1987. The difference is that Mr. Rogers did not then propose plans for Russia and the United States to team up in nuclear arms deals for the purpose of making people suffer, as well as write op-eds decrying the government of the United States upon his return. What Mr. Rogers did in Moscow was unlikely to become a source of rich kompromat, and Mr. Rogers did not spend the rest of his life solidifying his relationships with Russian oligarchs and mafias attempting to sell the neighborhood to the highest bidder.

But that's getting ahead of the story. *The Art of the Deal* omitted an important piece of information: Trump was invited to the USSR not only by Dubinin, who died in 2013. He was also invited by Vitaly Churkin, a bureaucrat who rose through the Soviet ranks, strengthened his position as a diplomat in independent Russia, and became Russia's ambassador to the United Nations in 2006.[38] Churkin met again with Trump in 2013 and spent 2016 stridently defending Trump at the United Nations, despite Trump not having been actually criticized by anyone there, in an incident that baffled international observers.[39] The details of Trump and Churkin's relationship, their meetings, and why Churkin defended Trump remain a mystery, because on February 20, 2017, one month after Trump's inauguration, Churkin died suddenly at the age of sixty-four.

On February 21, 2017, the New York City medical examiner's office announced that Churkin's autopsy suggested the need for a toxicology test. Trump's State Department, with Russia's backing, immediately issued a gag order and prevented public disclosure of the cause and manner of death.[40] Churkin had been the fifth Russian diplomat to die unexpectedly and in an unexplained fashion since Trump won the election.[41] There has been no follow-up reporting or official investigation of his death, and the documents remain sealed. On the occasions that I have published anything on Churkin—in which I limited my commentary to noting that he had known Trump for decades and had accompanied Dubinin to the initial meeting with Trump—I was besieged with death threats and hit pieces, including from Russian state media, who falsely claimed I said Churkin was murdered by Putin.[42]

According to *The Art of the Deal*, on July 4, 1987, Trump flew to Moscow with Ivana, was housed by the Soviet government in Lenin's suite across from the Kremlin, and began talking deals with the Politburo. (The date is notable; since his inauguration, Russian officials have chosen sentimental American dates—like July 4 and September 11—to fly Trump and his GOP lackeys to Russia.) Journalist Luke Harding notes that the suite Trump stayed in had long been under KGB control and would have been bugged.[43] We do not know the details of Trump's discussions with Soviet officials, but he returned to the United States more determined to form a geopolitical alliance with Russia than ever.[44] Later in 1987, he told journalist Ron Rosenbaum that he sought to partner with Russia on nuclear weapons with the aim of threatening other countries into compliance. His dream targets included Pakistan and France.[45] Initially skeptical, Rosenbaum was shocked that Trump did seem indeed to have high-level international contacts facilitating his Soviet partnerships. In September, Trump also showcased the anti-American and xenophobic streak that remains part of his politics to this day, taking out full-page ads condemning US policies and claiming that "the world is laughing at America's politicians."[46] In October, he called America a "failure" in a speech he gave at a rally in pursuit of his new goal: becoming the president of the United States of America.[47]

In recent years, both the Trump campaign and the mainstream media have portrayed Trump as a political neophyte or outsider, but nothing could be further from the truth. Trump sought elected office for thirty years. He ran for president in 2000, 2012, and 2016, and he nearly ran in 1988 and 1996. His 1988 bid began with a rally held in late 1987 by Republican activist Michael Dunbar and was guided by Roger Stone, who began his first go-round as a Trump presidential adviser. Stone was involved in every Trump presidential run thereafter as well as in Trump's near-run for New York governor in 2014.[48]

Trump had one condition for entering a race: his win needed to be preordained. A 1987 *Newsweek* cover story on Trump paints a damning portrait of Trump's newly announced presidential ambitions. "He'd love to be president, but only if he were appointed," one friend told the magazine. John Moore, an attorney who fought a tenant dispute with Trump, warned of the consequences: "He is a dangerous man . . . he's the type who'd make the trains run on time." A friend of Trump's accurately forecast Trump's ceaseless ambition: "No achievement can satisfy what he wants. What he wants still is acceptance from his father. He is playing out his insecurities on an incredibly large canvas."[49] By winter 1988, Trump had decided to put his electoral aims on hold.[50] Perhaps the win he demanded was not yet assured. Pundits have claimed that Trump ran for president in 2016 with the intention to lose: the real goal being to boost his brand and income. Putting aside the patent ridiculousness of Trump agreeing to lose to a woman, and a Clinton at that, this view also misapprehends Trump's deep need for pre-determined outcomes. Trump's brand may be risk: the high-stakes deal, the bold venture. But for most of his life, Trump has only taken a risk when the reward is guaranteed by others.

Born rich, Trump followed his father, Fred Trump, into the family business to become richer. He remained in his hometown his whole life. His inner circle has been tightly controlled and contained, consisting mainly of his family and his lawyers. His lawyers salvage his businesses not only by exploiting loopholes and requiring NDAs, but by threatening perceived enemies. Trump functions best in scripted reality—supplying his own tabloid fodder, playing a successful version of himself on *The Apprentice*. He demands attention but shuns scrutiny. Trump needs to be a brand because he's terrified of being a person.

Much like I do not remember the era of the American Dream, I do not remember a time before Donald Trump. In this respect, I am like most Americans: he has inhabited our collective consciousness for my entire life, which means he has been committing crimes, unpunished, for my entire life. He has been profiting off American pain for my entire life, and American elites—the elites he pretends to condemn—have been enabling him for my entire life. That is the template of expectations for my generation and all that followed: crime committed brazenly is over time redefined as something other than crime. It is entertainment, and then it is autocracy, and then it is too late.

My mother, like other bored thirtysomethings of her generation, was fascinated with the Trumps, and hate-watched them as a hobby. She subscribed to *Spy* magazine, a publication dedicated to mocking and exposing the hypocrisies and crimes of elites. *Spy* ran in-depth investigatory pieces on Trump's financial shakedowns, international circle of corruption, and marital abuses. Despite the snarkiness of *Spy*, these were serious articles, and they traveled to an unlikely audience due to the popularity of the magazine, which my mom saw as *Mad* magazine for adults. You did not need to be a media insider or a political operative to know the dirt on Trump in the 1980s. I grew up in a house where the most fought-over magazine was *TV Guide*; we were ordinary people. But because of *Spy*, my family knew all about Trump's filthy lucre. "Sarah, what the fuck," my mother texted me in 2016, "why is no one reporting all the shit we knew about him when you were little? I need to find my *Spys*!"

Once a year, when I was a child, my mom would drive my sister and me to New York City to go sightseeing. This was a big deal, as we rarely ventured more than twenty minutes from our home, much less to places other people went for pleasure. Every time we would go to New York City, my mom would park the car near Trump Tower so we could walk in and use the public bathroom and "show Trump what we think of him!" Trump was synonymous with all that was terrible about America: greed, cruelty, stupidity, rich people. I remember giggling at the glitzy restrooms, an enthusiastic participant in my mom's immature defiance of a world we could never enter.

There's a bizarre tendency in New York media to, even now, position Trump as a "man of the people": to posit that because he grew up as a mere millionaire real estate scion in Queens, he should be viewed as downtrodden because he was not raised as an even richer scion in Manhattan. No ordinary person has this view. By "ordinary people," I mean people like my mom—a public school English teacher who enjoyed mocking a decadent asshole. By "ordinary," I mean people like the innocent teenagers in the Central Park Five, whose reputation and lives Trump worked to destroy. By "ordinary," I mean pretty much anyone in the tristate area who read *Spy*, or the New York City tabloids, or who watched *Lifestyles of the Rich and Famous* and thought he was both a jackass and a joke—which meant basically all Americans by the time his bankruptcies and first divorce hit in the early 1990s. By "ordinary," I mean everyone who did not know Trump personally and therefore could not be bribed or blackmailed by him or his inner circle. We were the useless people, the free people.

That a significant number of today's high-profile journalists *did* know the Trump family personally is cause for concern. We now live in a world where products of nepotism inundate industries like journalism, a field often reporting on other products of nepotism in business and politics. These powerful sectors of society have been overtaken by connections rather than merit, and dynasties rather than unbiased workforces. These conditions do not guarantee that coverage must be terrible. While wealth does not indicate merit, it also does not inherently destroy it. Any person can choose to do a good job and tell the truth. But the domination of nepotistic elites in national media over the past two decades has warped public perception of what "ordinary people" thought of Trump, and of what information about his corruption is thought fit to print. The transformation of the media into an industry for elites who may not recognize white-collar corruption as abnormal—or who may be reluctant to upset their family or social circles by revealing a crime—is described in depth over the next few chapters.

The late 1980s brought a flurry of accountability for Wall Street criminals and dirty Republicans—Michael Milken, Ivan Boesky, Leona Helmsley, the felons of the Iran Contra cases—but Trump was not among the indicted. However, he did not escape the bottoming out of the greed decade unscathed. By the end of the 1980s, Trump properties had gone bankrupt, and some were tarnished by their connection to tragedies and crimes—such as the 1989 freak helicopter crash that killed top executives running his dying Taj Mahal casino. (Trump callously blamed his financial ruin on their deaths.)[51] In 1990, Wall Street bond house Salomon Brothers advised clients to bail on Trump Castle. In 1991, Trump declared bankruptcy, and by 1992, he had lost all his signature properties, with the exception of Trump Tower. He sold Khashoggi's surveillance yacht, which he had renamed the *Trump Princess*.

Trump's marital life imploded at the same time he lost his fortune, and his divorce from Ivana prompted a tide of tabloid tales. The media coverage of this era is notable because of the sense of profound relief that emerges from mainstream publications, which, unlike *Spy* and Wayne Barrett's reporting at *The Village Voice*, had been functioning as flacks for reasons yet to be entirely discerned.

A 1990 *New York* magazine profile confesses that media coverage stemmed from both laziness and the ceaseless drive of both Donald and Ivana to make themselves available, even if the reporting was unflattering and the ratings were low:

"The deep secret of all Trump coverage is that it is cost-effective news—Nielsen ratings and newsstand sales aside. Everything is easily available: the lawyers' statements by fax, the PR quote for the day, the file footage of all the principals, the photo opportunities at convenient midtown locations—near news offices and TV studios. *Trump vs Trump* is accessible. That's why it may run forever," wrote Edwin Diamond in a March 1990 column titled "Bonfire of the Inanities."

That was 1990. Now transpose this internal logic into a world where national media is conglomerated in elite coastal cities like New York, digital and cable stories must be produced in a frenzied 24/7 cycle, fact-checking is on the wane, and the lines between news and entertainment—and truth and reality—have blurred, creating an infotainment nexus driven as much by the need to fill space and kill time as it is by the desire to make money. That is the media world that Trump inhabited in later decades, one whose vulnerabilities he understood intimately, for he had helped create them.

In later chapters, I describe how this loss of leverage in the media occurred, and how Trump capitalized on it, but it is critical to observe how early the seeds of destruction were planted—and that the media reaped the harvest of its own demise. One of the most striking examples is the coverage of the divorce itself. In 1990, Trump was brought low after decades of flagrant highs, and journalists pounced. Roy Cohn was dead and no longer a threat, and so Trump exposés abounded as Ivana opened up her own world to the press. These included scathing early 1990s *Vanity Fair* profiles, including one in which twelve-year-old Donald Trump Jr. told a reporter that Trump did not love him, did not love himself, but only loved his money;[52] to the 1993 book *Lost Tycoon* by Harry Hurt III, which declared that Trump did not know how to have sex with women and describes Ivana purchasing a book on female orgasms and announcing "I have to give this to The Donald; he can never find the spots."[53] From the start of the marriage, their terrible sex life, wrote Hurt, had sent Trump running back to Roy Cohn, who was forced to write a new prenup to placate the sexually unsatisfied Ivana. Hurt's book paints a disturbing picture of Trump's conception of love and consensual sexual relations.

The worst revelation of Hurt's book is one that was made in Ivana's 1990 divorce deposition and reemerged during the 2016 campaign: Ivana had said at the time of her divorce that Trump, angered by a painful scalp reduction surgery to remove a bald spot conducted by a doctor Ivana recommended, grabbed her, pulled out hair from her own scalp, bellowed, "Your fucking doctor has ruined me!," and raped her. The deposition papers describe a terrified Ivana hiding in a closet in the hours after the rape, emerging in the morning to find Trump sneering at her, asking: "Does it hurt?" (Before Hurt's book was published, Ivana had retracted her testimony, saying she was not raped "in a literal or criminal sense.")

When Trump's 2016 campaign began to pick up steam, making Hurt worry he may become the candidate, Hurt asked his publisher, Norton, to reissue *Lost Tycoon*. But they told him the thirty-three-year-old book was now "too dangerous to publish."[54] Hurt ended up republishing it himself on Kindle to try to get the word out. In 2015, a *Daily Beast* reporter wrote a piece detailing the alleged rape of Ivana and was threatened by Trump's aspiring Roy Cohn replacement, lawyer and future felon Michael Cohen.[55]

"What I'm going to do to you is going to be fucking disgusting. You understand me?" Cohen told the *Daily Beast* reporter. "You write a story that has Mr. Trump's name in it, with the word 'rape,' and I'm going to mess your life up . . . for as long as you're on this frickin' planet . . . you're going to have judgments against you, so much money. You'll never know how to get out from underneath it."[56]

These threats were reported in *The Daily Beast* along with details of the rape. But they did not make it into most mainstream coverage of Trump. Hurt tried to get the story of Trump's history of sexual assault on cable news, only to have CNN cancel on him multiple times—until the *Access Hollywood* "grab 'em by the pussy" tape forced the topic into the public eye. In winter 2019, in his federal testimony, Michael Cohen admitted to making at least five hundred threats under Trump's orders for over a decade, describing him as akin to a mafia boss—without using the word "mafia" itself.[57]

Other reporters who had covered Trump's early criminal history were silenced. Acclaimed journalist David Cay Johnston, author of multiple bestsellers about Trump, noted that in addition to refusing to cover the rape of Ivana, the 2016 press would not report on Trump's documented ties to organized crime:

"If people knew more of the truth about Trump and what he's doing to our government, we'd be seeing more protests," he told *The Nation*.[58] "For example, they have no idea about his years of dealings with a confessed drug trafficker. [The trafficker is Joseph Weichselbaum, indicted in 1985 for running a cocaine ring, who lived in Trump Plaza and was defended to the judge by Trump as a character witness in court; after serving a minor sentence, Weichselbaum moved into Trump Tower, purchasing a $2.4 million apartment in cash.] And my fellow journalists didn't report that; I offered them all the documents and they wouldn't print it."

Trump covers up crime with scandal. That is his main propaganda tactic, the one few seem to be able to discern. He would rather be seen as a married man who had an affair than a man who raped his wife and assaulted countless women and girls. He would rather be seen as an overconfident tycoon racking up bankruptcies than a skilled and powerful man associated with the mafia running a series of shakedowns for foreign backers. He would rather be a president mocked as an idiot in a "Make America Great Again" cap than be known as a vindictive traitor who seeks to strip America down and sell it for parts. The crimes are much worse than the scandals, but the media will always take the scandal bait.

The public, having been assured that it's just scandal, it's just Trump being Trump, will then surrender its own demands for accountability. This is called "normalcy bias": the idea that if a situation is truly dangerous, if massive crimes are being committed in plain sight, someone will intervene and stop them. "Normalcy bias" is the psychological counterpart to "American exceptionalism." You can see these dual myths at play in every massive American oversight turned tragedy, from 9/11 to the war in Iraq to the 2008 financial crisis. (Notably, you see many of the same elite scammers, men who profit off the good faith that informs normalcy bias, in each of these atrocities as well.)

But no one held Trump accountable—not in the 1980s, not now. That is to say, no one held Trump accountable in a meaningful way, the only way he and his criminal kind recognize: indictment and imprisonment. He remained a distant folk villain, a TV and tabloid monster, a threat outside my orbit. I could walk in and out of Trump Tower as a little girl and not feel afraid. It never crossed my mind that, thirty years later, this man would endanger my life.

"Who controls the past, controls the future: who controls the present, controls the past," Orwell wrote in *1984*. "Past events, it is argued, have no objective existence, but survive only in written records and in human memories. The past is whatever the records and the memories agree upon. And since the Party is in full control of all records, and in equally full control of the minds of its members, it follows that the past is whatever the Party chooses to make it."[59]

We are living in the future Orwell warned about; I am living in the 1984 my mother laughingly assured me did not exist. I am writing this book to report the past in its full truth, in the hope that an understanding of the past will impact the future. That is the hope of every journalist who documents abuses of power. But I write under the rule of a tabloid tyrant. I write about a New York past from a Missouri present; I write with a memory that it is my own job to doubt, because I have seen how the media is made. I have seen how this monster is fed. I remember absorbing its myths as a child. I have found the crimes under the scandal and struggled to bring them to public light—to make them part of "whatever the records and the memories agree upon," so that we at least know what we are fighting.

I wrote in the beginning of this chapter: "When you are a young child, you have no sense of anything that happened before you existed unless it is explicitly spelled out." The horror of the present is realizing that many adults had no sense of what was really going on during my 1980s childhood either—and that those who did know, and lived to tell the tale, are the ones who stole the future.

3

The 1990s: Elite Exploits of the New World Order

The early 1990s ushered in an anomalous period of account-ability. This was the era after the Iran-Contra criminals were sentenced but before future Trump attorney general William Barr helped pardon them; when the Berlin Wall fell and the So-viet Union soon followed; when dissidents like Nelson Mandela, Lech Walesa, and Václav Havel went from prisons to presidencies; when America had a war and a recession and both of them came to a seemingly definitive end. This was an actual era of hope and change, and it did not last long.

At the time, I was too young to appreciate the novelty of this reversal of fortune—or to appreciate that political and economic fortunes could be reversed at all. I took global shifts in stride like a preteen Francis Fukuyama, lumping "the USSR" in with "gang-ster rap" in the category of "things only adults are dumb enough to fear." My parents had been ridiculous to hide under their desks in the 1950s and 1960s, I thought, waiting for bombs that never dropped and invaders that never came. My main resource on the end of the Cold War may have been the Scorpions' "Wind of Change" video, but my casual conviction that America was in-domitable put me in the mainstream. Adults told me I lived in the last superpower and I believed them. I wondered what it would be like to live in a country torn apart from within, like the USSR, and have your whole life upended. I don't wonder about that anymore.

Throughout the early 1990s, public intellectuals proclaimed that American-style democracy and capitalism had begun their ceaseless triumph across the globe. Peace and prosperity were not mere aspirations, but the permanent condition of the new world order. The contention that we were on a brand-new geopolitical path, free from age-old travails, was discussed in bestsellers like Fukuyama's *The End of History and the Last Man*. This idea reflected the doctrine of American exceptionalism that post–Cold War US presidents pushed citizens to embrace. The rest of the world had to fall in line with America because America no longer had a rival of equal might—a position US officials marketed as civic-minded benevolence rather than de facto domination. When I was a teenager, I started reading newspapers like *The New York Times*, which told me no two countries would ever go to war so long as both of them had a McDonald's.[1]

The biggest worry for my generation, I was told, would be how to cope with the dazzling array of options the forthcoming utopia would present. The Silicon Valley gold rush of the late 1990s further boosted the belief that the future was limitless. In 1997, *Wired* magazine journalists Peter Schwartz and Peter Leyden wrote in a popular piece called "The Long Boom":

We are watching the beginnings of a global economic boom on a scale never experienced before. We have entered a period of sustained growth that could eventually double the world's economy every dozen years and bring increasing prosperity for—quite literally—billions of people on the planet. We are riding the early waves of a 25-year run of a greatly expanding economy that will do much to solve seemingly intractable problems like poverty and to ease tensions throughout the world. And we'll do it without blowing the lid off the environment.

If this holds true, historians will look back on our era as

an extraordinary moment. They will chronicle the 40-year period from 1980 to 2020 as the key years of a remarkable transformation. In the developed countries of the West, new technology will lead to big productivity increases that will cause high economic growth—actually, waves of technology will continue to roll out through the early part of the 21st century. And then the relentless process of globalization, the opening up of national economies and the integration of markets, will drive the growth through much of the rest of the world. An unprecedented alignment of an ascendant Asia, a revitalized America, and a reintegrated greater Europe—including a recovered Russia—together will create an economic juggernaut that pulls along most other regions of the planet.[2]

This was a fantasy that became accepted as conventional wisdom—first by elites, and then by the masses, who mortgaged their futures on the assurances of those who had already won. This was the mind-set that set the expectations of my generation, making the impending reality of economic rot and forever wars seem all the more brutal when it arrived. The forty years from 1980 to 2020 were indeed a period of remarkable transformation, just not in the way *Wired* predicted.

In retrospect, the danger was evident. Lurking behind the dreams of a history-less future was the unsatisfied underclass of the 1990s present, whose inconvenient existence became fodder for new forms of enmity and exploitation. With the Soviet Union no more, political elites deemed America the new problem. Not the America of wealthy men like Trump, who had allegedly been shamed or sentenced into submission, but the America of ordinary people. The America of black Los Angelenos outraged by police brutality; the America of abused women like Tonya Harding and Lorena Bobbitt and Anita Hill who were pilloried on a national scale; the

America of mythical child "super-predators"—teenagers like the Central Park Five, whose exoneration can never compensate for the brutality they endured. With no external enemy left to fight, America focused on fighting itself—and exploiting the casualties.

Transformation in media law made new forms of exploitation possible. In 1987, the FCC repealed the Fairness Doctrine, a 1949 policy that had required broadcast networks to present controversial issues of public importance in a manner that was—in the FCC's view—fair and balanced. Republicans successfully argued that the Fairness Doctrine was an attack on journalistic freedom, and both Reagan and Bush thwarted efforts by Congress to keep the doctrine intact. This repeal happened as 24-hour cable news arrived, and foreign behemoths, like Rupert Murdoch's Fox, landed in the United States. Fox TV was formed in 1986, one year before the Fairness Doctrine was repealed, and Fox News launched a decade later in 1996. According to *New Yorker* journalist Jane Mayer, Fox News founder Roger Ailes created the network to ensure Watergate-style accountability would not happen again to a president he supported.[3]

The Fairness Doctrine was repealed just as television news was being transformed in both pace and purpose. In many respects, the pace became the purpose; the truth, an afterthought. I have no memory of what it was like to watch TV news under the Fairness Doctrine, but it's hard to fathom the widespread assumption of faith in network integrity required to make "fair and balanced" anything more than a bitter joke. Even when I envision a world in which its precepts are deployed, I imagine it being exploited in cynical "both sides" debates over hard facts, like the existence of climate change, or dehumanizing myths about ethnic groups. ("Are Muslims violent? Are migrants criminal?—We report, you decide!") But the Fairness Doctrine still has an allure due to its now quaint stipulation that the TV news industry exists to serve ordinary Americans, as opposed to ordinary Americans existing to serve the TV news industry.

The public's fate as camera fodder was cast in the 1990s, when news met entertainment, never to part, and the infotainment complex of cable media and reality TV was born. Its primary locus was crime: birthed with *Cops* in 1990, reaching its apex with the OJ Simpson trial in 1994 and 1995, and continuing with this format into the new millennium—as witnessed by the criminal reality TV star currently inhabiting the White House. When there wasn't crime, cruelty would suffice. Abusive relationships were packaged as entertainment: Amy and Joey, Lorena and John Wayne, Clarence and Anita, OJ and Nicole, Pamela and Tommy, and, capping off the decade, Bill and Monica. At the time, the incessant focus on villains and victims seemed tawdry but not dangerous. After all, America's big battles had allegedly been won. What was wrong with a circus of pain, when the stakes were so low and the protagonists so low-down that sympathy for the players could be an admission of your own struggle, and disdain a form of self-validation?

You could turn away from the ritualized humiliation, or you could look at it straight on and say, "I would never let that happen to me." You could tell yourself that later, when something you saw on tabloid TV struck too close to home—a rape or a beating or a breakdown or another hell sold as a commodity; you could repeat this refrain with a fervency to mask your fear. You would know on a gut level that your story would never be viewed with sympathy, because sympathy was for suckers now. Sympathy was a junk bond emotion. Sympathy was reserved for only the most virtuous victims—and even then, they always implied, it must have been the victim's fault.

Occasionally a great horror would shake Americans out of their smug voyeurism, a tragedy so awful it could not be sold as spectacle—the Oklahoma City bombing, the Columbine massacre—but these were dismissed as anomalies instead of sparks for future flames. Their predecessors—Ruby Ridge and the school shootings that first emerged in the early 1990s—were minimized outside the fringes, where they were immortalized with a cult-like intensity.

The 1990s was a paranoid era, relentlessly unsentimental.

Comedies like *Seinfeld* proudly proclaimed to be about nothing, because nothing was what mattered now. Dramas like *The X-Files* warned us to trust no one and we agreed with a smirk, unaware that the truth that was out there in the 1990s was more disturbing than the wildest fictional government conspiracies. On daytime TV, talk shows metastasized into showdowns, as hosts like Jerry Springer got ordinary Americans to smack each other down in front of a live studio audience. But it was 24-hour cable news where this cynical view of humanity took on a far more dangerous form. Lurid tales are as old as American media itself, but cable news, which kept birthing new channels, was ceaseless. Cable news made fame for fame's sake a valid aspiration, even if you were, for example, the houseguest of a murderer.

In the 1990s, to guest star in someone else's tragedy was regarded as a worthy pursuit, amusing and potentially profitable. You could offer yourself up to the cameras, you could be the prize in a new kind of human game show—as long as you weren't there to make friends, as long as the monetary payoff outweighed the moral loss, as long as you could live like a caricature. As long as you could adopt the ethos, perfected in 1980s tabloid culture, of Donald Trump.

Where was Donald Trump during the mid-1990s, an era whose tabloid frenzy seemed designed to both reflect and amplify his appeal? In the official story—the one Ivanka and Donald Jr. tell to create the illusion of everyman relatability, the one that he told on the debut of *The Apprentice*—he was humbled by his humiliation and retreated to a simple life in his golden tower, planning his comeback. He had left Ivana for Marla Maples, a beauty queen from Georgia, who, according to Trump biographer Wayne Barrett, was selected to enhance Trump's political viability among southerners in preparation for another presidential run.[4] Barrett's claim in his 1992 Trump biography—which was not rereleased until 2016—is in direct contrast to the "Trump is a political neophyte" myth often spread by a credulous mainstream media.

Where was Donald Trump in the summer of 1994? That's a question that should have been answered well before the election. In June 2016, an anonymous plaintiff, using the pseudonym Katie Johnson and later Jane Doe, filed a lawsuit accusing Trump of raping her when she was thirteen years old—the same age that Ivanka was that year. Jane Doe's claim was consistent with verifiable facts from the court case against convicted billionaire underage sex trafficker Jeffrey Epstein, for whom Jane Doe was forced to work. In 2002, Trump told *New York* magazine that he had known Epstein, a financier with a mysterious past, for fifteen years and thought he was a "terrific guy."[5]

The story of Jeffrey Epstein is one that will define our era, and one that may clear up a lot of incongruities if it is ever fully told. But it is also one that was relentlessly suppressed for decades. In July 2019, Epstein was arrested after a series of exposés by Julie K. Brown of the *Miami Herald* prompted more of his victims to come forward. In August 2019, he allegedly hung himself in a Manhattan prison, under circumstances that raise reasonable suspicion that he did not die of suicide but strangulation.[6] The guards who were supposed to be watching Epstein both fell asleep when he allegedly killed himself, and no cameras recorded his death.[7] Meanwhile, prompted both by the flurry of coverage and by his arrest and death, Epstein's accusers continue to reveal the horror of his operation. By the end of summer 2019, over eighty women said they were recruited by Epstein and sexually abused or exploited.[8]

I am updating this chapter one week after Epstein's mysterious death, with new information confirming my worst suspicions by the hour. I hope that by the time you read it, the women who were brave enough to tell their stories will have seen some justice. I anticipate that what people learn about Epstein in the years to come will have significant geopolitical implications if the full extent of his illicit activity is revealed and accomplices brought to trial. This has never been the case for Epstein or for the circle of elites who sheltered Epstein from repercussions with the understanding that he would return the favor.

Epstein's life in the underworld of the global elite begins and ends with the family of William Barr, Trump's attorney general. As a twenty-year-old college dropout, Epstein was hired by Barr's father, Donald Barr, to teach math at Dalton, the New York private all-girls high school where the elder Barr served as headmaster. Donald Barr, a former OSS officer who had a side gig as a writer of science-fiction books depicting intergalactic sex slaves living under a dictatorship, never explained his decision to hire the unqualified Epstein.[9] His son, who joined the CIA one year before Epstein arrived in Dalton, has also offered no explanation. The younger Barr initially recused himself from the case when Epstein was arrested. But after Epstein's death, he announced that he was launching an extensive federal investigation. Barr's career of cover-ups (Iran-Contra) and lies (his Mueller Report summary) are detailed in later chapters, but for now, it is worth noting that an investigation conducted with integrity seems unlikely.

Epstein's obsession with underage girls was evident from the start: while at Dalton, he allegedly had inappropriate relationships with students.[10] He left Dalton in 1976 to work at Bear Stearns and then struck out on his own as a financial adviser for clients who were not named—with the exception of Les Wexner, the billionaire CEO of L Brands, which owns Victoria's Secret and other major companies. In the rare public examinations of Epstein's finances prior to 2019, Wexner was often listed as Epstein's closest partner.[11] Wexner is a dedicated Zionist activist who has spent a great deal of money seeking to shape global policy toward Israel through what he describes as philanthropic initiatives.[12] But for decades, Epstein allegedly controlled much of Wexner's money after Wexner gave him power of attorney, depositing millions into mysterious "charities" and running his sex-trafficking operation from one of Wexner's homes.[13] After Epstein's arrest, Wexner accused Epstein of misappropriating his funds.[14] For decades, none of the stories on Epstein specified how he made his fortune, saying only that he managed and invested the assets of wealthy clients. In 2019, it was revealed that the main bank Epstein used was

Deutsche Bank—the only bank that would lend to Trump after his bankruptcies, the same bank implicated in the Trump Russia scandal.[15]

By the 1990s, Epstein had become a multimillionaire while never revealing the source of his wealth, resting on the prestige of his networks to launder his reputation. The word "prestige" derives from a Latin word meaning "illusion," and Epstein media profiles cloaked themselves in it—his social network of powerful CEOs and NGOs, his affiliations with institutions like Harvard and MIT. The question becomes when "prestige" is no longer an illusion but instead a euphemism for a cover-up. The Epstein case previewed the tactics of the Trump administration: strike a dirty deal, seal the documents, and control the only court left, that of public opinion.

Epstein's first arrest was in 2006, when over forty women came forward with allegations of abuse, many claiming that they were part of a 1990s international underage sex crime ring to service the most rich and powerful men in the world.[16] Underage girls were said to have been lured by Epstein's assistants and forced to perform sexual acts on businessmen, heads of state, and other influential people. Epstein then allegedly kept evidence of the sexual assault as blackmail material.[17] Celebrities who flew on Epstein's jet to the Caribbean island where many of the assaults allegedly took place include Ehud Barak, Prince Andrew, Bill Clinton, and Alan Dershowitz, a close friend of Epstein who also served as his attorney. Dershowitz was accused in 2015 of raping a teenage girl procured by Epstein in the 1990s, and in 2019 he was sued by a victim who claimed he aided in the trafficking.[18] Dershowitz has denied all allegations, saying he had a "perfect, perfect sex life" and insisting that he kept his underwear on during massages at Epstein's mansion.[19]

In 2008, Epstein received a mere eighteen-month sentence for soliciting, molesting, and raping underage girls. The sentence was the result of a strange and disturbing plea deal between Mueller's FBI, which had received testimony from thirty-six of the victims, and Alexander Acosta, who was then the US Attorney for

South Florida and who became Trump's secretary of labor. (In July 2019, following Epstein's arrest, Acosta resigned.) For reasons that remain unclear, the US government agreed to grant Epstein immunity from all federal criminal charges, along with four co-conspirators and any unnamed "potential co-conspirators."[20] As of August 2019, the co-conspirators have not been named.[21]

Epstein's deal with the FBI halted the broader investigation into the international sex trafficking ring. Epstein was soon set free, where he was welcomed by New York elites who seemed either apathetic to or amused by his arrest. Outlets like *The New York Times* praised his fine tastes and Ivy League affiliation, playing down the horror and scope of his crimes. In a 2008 article, Epstein compared himself to "Gulliver shipwrecked among the diminutive denizens of Lilliput" and noted that "Gulliver's playfulness had unintended consequences. That is what happens with wealth. There are unexpected burdens as well as benefits."[22] In response, the *New York Times* reporter gushed about Epstein's private jet, neglecting to mention it was literally a vehicle of rape.

A 2011 *Daily Beast* article describes New York's elites praising Epstein as a man of wealth and taste and even bringing their children to his home for a Break Fast celebration after Yom Kippur, unconcerned that he was convicted of raping other children.[23] Among these elites were future Trump secretary of commerce Wilbur Ross and fellow accused child molester Woody Allen. Almost universally, they mocked and blamed the underage victims, whom they saw as an obstacle to the luxurious life to which they felt Epstein—and they themselves—were entitled. The lone dissenter was a Midwesterner shocked by the cruelty of their culture: "In the Midwest, where I am from, he would be a social pariah," political activist Lorna Brett Howard, the wife of a CEO invited into Epstein's social circle, told *The Daily Beast*. "What I see here is if you have big money or are famous then you get a pass."

One of the things money could buy Epstein was a publicist, and he chose the same publicist as the Trump and Kushner families: Howard Rubenstein. A 2007 *New York* magazine profile reveals how New York white-collar criminals protect their own through a complex PR and media apparatus. This apparatus was pioneered by Roy Cohn and polished by Rubenstein, who had represented other Trump and Epstein colleagues like Rupert Murdoch and Adnan Khashoggi. Epstein was "one of us," the *New York* profile explicitly says—the "us" including New York media itself. Young women were viewed as incidental and disposable—so long as the aggressor was of the right social class and displayed the right cultural cues. The excerpt from this *New York* profile below is typical of Epstein coverage, deviating only in that it admits outright that the story was guided by Rubenstein:

Jeffrey Epstein is under indictment for sex crimes in Palm Beach, Florida, and I'd expected that when he came into the office of PR guru Howard Rubenstein, he would be sober and reserved. Quite the opposite. He was sparkling and ingenuous, apologizing for the half-hour lateness with a charming line—"I never realized how many one-way streets and no-right-turns there are in midtown. I finally got out and walked"—and as we went down the corridor to Rubenstein's office, he asked, "Have you managed to talk to many of my friends?" Epstein had been supplying me the phone numbers of important scientists and financiers and media figures. "Do you understand what an extraordinary group of people they are, what they have accomplished in their fields?"

One of the accusers—a girl of 14—had put his age at 45, not in his fifties, and you could see why. His walk was youthful, and his face was ruddy with health. He had none of the round-shouldered, burdened qualities of middle age. There was nothing in his hands, not a paper, a book, or a phone. Epstein had on his signature outfit: new blue jeans and a powder-blue sweater. "I've only ever seen him in jeans," his friend the publicist Peggy Siegal had reported, saying there was a hint of arrogance in that, Epstein's signal that he doesn't have to wear a uniform like the rest of us.

I told Epstein and Rubenstein the sort of story *New York* wanted to do, and Epstein seemed to find ironic delight in every word. "A secretive genius," I'd said. "Not secretive, private," he corrected in his warm Brooklyn accent. "And if I was a genius I wouldn't be sitting here."[24]

It's hard to read this in 2019 knowing that it took officials over two decades to lock up Epstein—and that he died in prison before his accusers could confront him in court. It's hard to read it like it's hard to see Harvey Weinstein and many other Hollywood abusers living large and walking free. It's hard to read it as someone roughly the same age as Epstein's victims, a 1990s teenager with my own tales to tell, knowing how my words would be devoured and dis-believed if I ever dared speak. It's hardest to read it now that my daughter is the same age as Jane Doe, and I can't tell her that noth-ing has changed since the 1990s, because things have changed: the alleged rapist of a thirteen-year-old is now the president.

The exploitation of women in 1990s tabloid culture reached its apotheosis under Epstein, and no one covered it in real time. When they covered it after the fact, in the 2000s, it was with amusement and disdain for the victims. When they cover it now, in 2019, it is with the knowledge that the complicity of their profession is part of what enabled Epstein, a convicted pedophile sex trafficker, to cover his tracks.

For those still wondering why holding Epstein accountable is in-extricable from holding Donald Trump accountable, I ask again: What was Donald Trump doing in the summer of 1994? Excerpts of "Jane Doe v. Donald J. Trump and Jeffrey Epstein, complaint in the United States District Court of the Southern District of New York," give us one possibility:[25]

7. Plaintiff [Jane Doe] was subject to acts of rape, sexual misconduct, criminal sexual acts, sexual abuse, forcible

touching, assault, battery, intentional and reckless inflic-
tion of emotional distress, duress, false imprisonment, and
threats of death and/or serious bodily injury by the Defen-
dants that took place at several parties during the summer
months of 1994. The parties were held by Defendant Epstein at a New York City residence that was being used by
Defendant Epstein at 9 E. 71st St. in Manhattan. During
this period, Plaintiff was a minor of age 13 and was legally
incapable under New York law of consenting to sexual in-
tercourse and the other sexual contacts detailed herein. NY
Penal L § 130.05(3)(a). [. . .]

9. Plaintiff was enticed by promises of money and a
modeling career to attend a series of parties, with other similarly situated minor females, held at a New York City residence that was being used by Defendant Jeffrey Epstein. At
least four of the parties were attended by Defendant Trump.
Exhs. A and B. On information and belief, by this time in
1994, Defendant Trump had known Defendant Epstein for
seven years (*New York*, 10/28/02, "'I've known Jeff for fifteen years. Terrific guy,' Trump booms from a speakerphone.
'He's a lot of fun to be with. It is even said that he likes
beautiful women as much as I do, and many of them are
on the younger side. No doubt about it—Jeffrey enjoys his
social life.'"), and knew that Plaintiff was then just 13 years
old. Exhs. A and B.

10. Defendant Trump initiated sexual contact with
Plaintiff at four different parties. On the fourth and final
sexual encounter with Defendant Trump, Defendant Trump
tied Plaintiff to a bed, exposed himself to Plaintiff, and then
proceeded to forcibly rape Plaintiff. During the course of
this savage sexual attack, Plaintiff loudly pleaded with Defendant Trump to stop but with no effect. Defendant Trump
responded to Plaintiff's pleas by violently striking Plaintiff
in the face with his open hand and screaming that he would
do whatever he wanted. Exhs. A and B.

11. Immediately following this rape, Defendant Trump threatened Plaintiff that, were she ever to reveal any of the details of the sexual and physical abuse of her by Defendant Trump, Plaintiff and her family would be physically harmed if not killed.

This court document was made available to reporters multiple times during Trump's 2016 campaign. Despite Trump's long-documented history of misogyny, sexual assault, and threats, the press generally avoided the Trump and Epstein allegations, and when they did cover them, they often designated them as irrelevant gossip. One exception was Lisa Bloom, a high-profile attorney who said she was alarmed by the lack of coverage. She wrote in *The Huffington Post*:

In covering a story, a media outlet is not finding guilt. It is simply reporting the news that a lawsuit has been filed against Mr. Trump, and ideally putting the complaint in context. Unproven allegations are just that—unproven, and should be identified that way. (Mr. Trump's lawyer says the charges are "categorically untrue, completely fabricated and politically motivated.") Proof comes later, at trial. But the November election will come well before any trial. And while Mr. Trump is presumed innocent, we are permitted—no, we are obligated—to analyze the case's viability now.[26]

Bloom saw the case as viable, particularly given Epstein's documented crimes and the fact that Jane Doe maintained she had a witness, named in the lawsuit as Tiffany Doe. In fall 2016, Bloom agreed to represent Jane Doe in court. A press conference was scheduled for November 2, 2016, in which Jane Doe was going to tell her story in the same way dozens of other women had told their stories following the release of the *Access Hollywood* video showing Trump bragging of his history of sexual assault. The "grab 'em by the pussy" video gave credence to claims that were once dismissed. But the press conference never happened. According to Bloom, Bloom and Trump's alleged victim were both threatened with violence and Bloom's computer was hacked. Jane Doe, Bloom reported, was terrified into silence, and dropped her lawsuit on November 4, four days before the election.[27]

The Epstein case, the allegations that Trump raped a thirteen-year-old, and the threats toward those who tried to expose them are a shocking story, the sort of high-profile horror that we should expect to dominate cable news shows and inspire books. But much like other aspects of Trump's life that cross from the scandalous to the criminal, the media cowered until it was too late. James Patterson, the bestselling novelist, wrote a quick Epstein biography that received almost no press when it was published in fall 2016. It took #MeToo to get Epstein back into the headlines, and then back into the courts—where both the sex trafficking and the deals with the US government to cover it up are being reexamined. But a large portion of his story remains omitted.

Epstein did not run his operation alone. He had an assistant named Ghislaine Maxwell. Ghislaine is the daughter of Robert Maxwell, a wealthy British publisher who died under mysterious circumstances after falling off a yacht in 1991.[28] His family, and several biographers, claim he was murdered; the police at the time ruled it an accident. Maxwell was also alleged to be an operative for Mossad.[29] His service to the Israeli government began in 1948, when he fought to aid Israel in the War of Independence with a unit from his native Czechoslovakia.[30] His role as an alleged Mossad agent was not revealed until 1986, when a former employee of Israel's Military Intelligence Directorate, Ari Ben-Menashe, identified Maxwell as an agent.[31] This accusation was made after Israeli whistle-blower Mordechai Vanunu attempted to give documents proving the existence of Israel's nuclear weapons to British newspapers, including the *Daily Mirror*, which was owned by Maxwell. Following his offer to the *Daily Mirror*, Vanunu was kidnapped by Mossad and taken back to Israel, where he was convicted of treason and sentenced to eighteen years in prison.

Robert Maxwell denied the allegations that he was a foreign agent, and much in the manner of Trump and Cohn, fought off critical inquiry into his business and political activities with a combination of excessive litigation and media manipulation. Following his sudden death in November 1991, however, his secrets emerged. While posing as a successful tycoon, Maxwell had privately been running his businesses into the ground and had plundered more than 1.6 billion British pounds from his companies' pension funds to save his companies from bankruptcy.[32]

Maxwell was buried in Jerusalem and was given a hero's funeral attended by high-ranking Israeli government officials, who praised Maxwell's contributions to Israel while not specifying what they were.[33] President Chaim Herzog intoned over his corpse: "He scaled the heights. Kings and barons besieged his doorstep. He was a figure of almost mythological stature."[34] Back in Europe, his sons scrambled to keep his empire afloat. They failed, declaring bankruptcy in 1992, and the business documents that were available, including transactions between unidentified parties running into the hundreds of millions, mystified financial analysts.[35] What had Maxwell been doing?

In 2003, journalists Gordon Thomas and Martin Dillon revealed why such enormous sums were moved around and unaccounted for: shortly before the end of his life, Maxwell had begun working with the Russian mafia.[36] They describe a lifetime of inside dealings between Maxwell, the USSR, and Israel, but one of the most revealing passages involves the criminal Robert Mueller once said he would stop at nothing to indict: Semion Mogilevich. According to the journalists, Maxwell had begun partnering with Mogilevich in money-laundering schemes in order to keep his businesses afloat. In return, Maxwell procured for Mogilevich the item that may have changed the world: his Israeli passport.

When the USSR began easing restrictions on travel for Jewish citizens in the perestroika era, including on emigration to Israel, Mogilevich saw an opportunity. He began shaking down fellow Jews by offering to manage their assets and then stealing from them once they had settled abroad. But major lucre required mobility, and in 1988, he found it in Maxwell's passport procurement. Mogilevich abused Israel's "right of return" law to obtain Israeli citizenship and then left Israel to expand his criminal trade around the world—a path that would be replicated by USSR-born mobsters and oligarchs for the next thirty years. (Even in 1988, Maxwell managed to procure Israeli passports for twenty-three Mogilevich associates.)[37] Mogilevich settled in Hungary in early 1991 and began extending his reach into Western Europe. As his international criminal empire flourished, the British intelligence service MI5 began to investigate him, and discovered that one of his main businesses was sex trafficking. Thomas writes that it is difficult to believe Maxwell did not know what Mogilevich was doing. He was either complicit in the operation, or terrified of being murdered himself.[38]

After his death, Ghislaine Maxwell took Robert's place in international high society, becoming a socialite in New York City. Sometime in the early 1990s, she met Jeffrey Epstein and began working for him as a madam, procuring underage girls from around the world and trapping them in sexual slavery. In 2019, a newly unsealed court document cites an Epstein accountant claiming that Robert Maxwell was the true source of Epstein's fortune, but does not elaborate on how or when this happened.[39]

The full story of Mogilevich, the Maxwell family, and how they became connected to fellow sex trafficker Epstein remains a mystery—at least, to the public, due to the refusal of law enforcement officials to discuss it in detail. We know that Robert Maxwell was at the least an acquaintance of Trump in the late 1980s, part of the same corrupt circle of elites.[40] They even bought their respective disastrous yachts from the same arms dealer, Adnan Khashoggi. After Epstein was arrested in July 2019, FBI agents raided his home and found that he had multiple passports, including an Austrian passport that listed his residence as Saudi Arabia.[41] Later that month, reporter Vicky Ward revealed that when she had interviewed Alex Acosta shortly after Trump was elected, he told her, "I was told Epstein 'belonged to intelligence' and to leave it alone."[42] Acosta did not specify to which country's intelligence Epstein belonged.

Unlike Epstein, Ghislaine Maxwell was never convicted for her role in the sex trafficking operation. After striking multiple deals with law enforcement officials, documents discussing her role were sealed, and she is lobbying to keep them that way.[43] She remains the target of lawsuits. One victim, Virginia Roberts, who says she was recruited by Ghislaine in 1998 at the age of fifteen, says she was forced to dress as a prepubescent schoolgirl while rich and powerful men, including Dershowitz and Prince Andrew, raped her.[44] When Maxwell dispatched Roberts to Thailand to study massage, Roberts escaped to Australia.[45] In 2015, she sued both Epstein and Maxwell, and in 2019, she sued Dershowitz. Trump played a role in her case as well. Roberts claims she had been recruited from his Mar-a-Lago club, where Trump had given Maxwell and Epstein unlimited access to teenage and preteen girls, whom they would tell they were recruiting for a modeling or massage agency.[46]

For years, police claimed that they could not locate Ghislaine Maxwell.[47] But after Epstein's alleged suicide, she was reported to have been living in a mansion in Massachusetts, where, among other things, she visited an elementary school in January 2019.[48] (The school realized Maxwell was the accomplice of a child sex trafficker only after the visit.) No effort has yet been made to arrest her, despite her location being made known. The death of Epstein has also prompted associates of Maxwell to come forward, after years of silence, to share insights into her value system. Her friends said she was devoted to Epstein, structuring her appearance to please him by staying rail thin. As one friend put it, "She said, 'I do it the way Nazis did it with the Jews, the Auschwitz diet. I just don't eat.'"[49] Another friend added: "When I asked what she thought of the underage girls, she looked at me and said, 'They're nothing, these girls. They are trash.'"[50]

As I wrote in the introduction, one of the most disorienting things about the Trump era is the feeling like you are living through a rupture in time: the ceaseless revelations about the past; the mix of chaos and inertia that defines the present; and the uncertain future.

The same names and countries appear again and again: the United States, the United Kingdom, the former USSR, Israel, Saudi Arabia. We see the same disturbing patterns: Epstein is not the only pedophile Trump befriended. Other friends and business associates who allegedly ran or participated in underage trafficking rings include his former business partner Tevfik Arif (who was acquitted of the charges despite significant evidence);[51] the modeling agent John Casablancas, for whose company Trump sent teenage Ivanka to work;[52] Mueller probe target George Nader, who has been indicted on, and pled not guilty to, multiple counts of underage sex trafficking and child porn;[53] Dershowitz, a Trump defender who has denied the allegations; and according to Wayne Barrett, Roy Cohn. This list does not include alleged pedophiles like Roy Moore, whom Trump has defended for political purposes, but is limited to the social and business circle he sought out on his own volition. No reporter has asked Trump about his own preteen rape allegation or why he invited so many pedophiles and sex traffickers into his life—not even after Epstein's 2019 arrest. And so we are left with a narrative about rape, espionage, and threats; a narrative of missing pieces. One of those pieces is justice.

In the 1990s, history ended with the specter of the wealthiest men in the world raping teenage girls provided by a mafia-affiliated blackmailer. History ended in a sealed file, history ended in a silent scream, history ended with the last man warning you that if you tell anyone, you'd end too.

As the decade wore on, Trump got some nefarious new neighbors. Trump Tower had effectively functioned as a dorm for the Russian mafia since David Bogatin first used it to launder money in

1984, but the collapse of the Soviet Union had allowed criminals from the former USSR to set up operations worldwide—with New York City a key landing place. New York had a new mayor, Rudy Giuliani, whose prosecution of the Italian mafia as U.S. attorney in the 1980s paved the way for the Russian mafia to dominate New York organized crime in the 1990s, and they found real estate particularly attractive. Pre-Giuliani New York is often mourned as the last era when New York was "real," before it became sanitized by a Disney Store in Times Square or marketed as a playground for wealthy grown-ups through shows like *Sex and the City*. But underneath the sparkling façade was a new rot, one that eventually grew to encompass the United State as a whole.

In 1992, an influential mobster named Vyacheslav Ivankov moved to Brooklyn, having been freed from a gulag after Mogilevich paid off a Russian judge. According to *Red Mafiya*, the seminal 2000 book by journalist Robert I. Friedman—who did the most thorough journalism on the Russian mafia before dying unexpectedly at age fifty-one in 2002—Ivankov was met at JFK airport by a fellow mobster holding a suitcase with $1.5 million inside. He went on to consolidate a crime network and launder money through purchased properties, eluding the FBI, who searched for him for years before realizing he had been living in a luxury apartment in Trump Tower the entire time.[54]

The 1990s were when the term "globalization" came into the popular vernacular, including as a target of protest, most notably in 1999 against the World Trade Organization. Most protesters decried the detrimental effect of globalization on labor both domestically and abroad, as American jobs went to foreign workers who were paid a pittance. They also denounced the rise of income inequality and gentrification, leading to extreme increases in the cost of living in international hubs like New York, San Francisco, and Miami due to the influx of wealthy foreigners driving up rent. Defenders of globalization saw unregulated global markets as a liberating force that went hand in hand with the democratization of former dictatorships that had occurred in the earlier part of the decade.

But what neither side seemed to hold in proper regard was the rise in global organized crime, masked by stately kleptocracies and prestigious corporations employing gangsters in suits and ties.

In a 1995 speech to the United Nations, President Clinton declared international money-laundering a threat to national security.[55] Much like a similar proclamation by President Obama, who declared organized crime a "national emergency" in 2011, his denouncement was hollow in practice. Mogilevich, for example, spent 1995 traipsing around Philadelphia and Miami to monitor his illegal ventures, despite being denied a visa by the State Department after being labeled a major threat at congressional hearings. He gave interviews to American media, telling ABC News in 1999 that he had put a hit out on Friedman, and then claimed he was only joking.[56] Friedman concluded *Red Mafiya* with a warning that the infiltration of this new form of globalized organized crime into businesses and governments in Europe, Israel, and the United States was the greatest threat to world democracy, a menace devouring countries from within. It was a warning unheeded when his book was published in 2000, and largely forgotten after the terrorist attacks of September 11, 2001.

It was a warning that apparently no one in law enforcement thought extended to Donald Trump—despite Trump's long history of corruption, bankruptcies, a tower full of Russian mobsters, and desperate need for money. In 1996, Trump visited Moscow with his longtime associate Howard Lorber, who had made a series of business investments in Russia.[57] The two were allegedly pursuing a Trump real estate venture, although like Trump's many other meetings with Russians over four decades, there was never any building or public arrangement to show for it. When Donald Trump Jr. held his now infamous June 2016 meeting with an assortment of money launderers, campaign staffers, oligarch representatives, and Kremlin representatives in Trump Tower, he made a series of secret phone calls. In February 2019, one of the calls was revealed to have been made to Trump's 1990s buddy Lorber.[58] To this day, Lorber's involvement in Trump's businesses or in the election is not explained. We are simply supposed to accept the end-less reappearance of a cast of characters tied to Russia over multiple decades as an amazing coincidence.

Throughout the late 1990s, Trump rebuilt his business empire in the style of the new criminal elite: blurring the lines between illicit and illegal, polishing the façade with glamour and prestige, and marketing himself as a comeback story of "the new economy." A prime example are his condo sales. In 2018, BuzzFeed revealed that over a fifth of the condos Trump had purchased and sold since the 1980s were financed through secretive, all-cash trans-actions that enabled buyers to avoid legal scrutiny.[59] As BuzzFeed noted, such transactions are not necessarily illegal but they certainly fit the Treasury characteristics for possible money-laundering.

Among them was Trump Tower International, opened in 1996 with 29 percent of its sales raising the possibility of money-laundering; Trump Parc East and 610 Park Avenue Condomini-ums, both opened in 1998 and each with 16 percent of sales raising the same issue; and Trump World Tower, opened in 2000 with 10 percent of sales fitting the same pattern.[60] One of Trump's two publicly available tax returns, which was leaked in 2016 by an unknown source, is from 1995 and shows a $916 million loss—activity incongruent with the alleged boom in business.

As I discuss in greater detail in subsequent chapters, the lack of any consequences for Trump's actions led to a surge in question-able activity over the decade to come. Trump SoHo Hotel, which opened in 2010 in collaboration with mob-connected felon Felix Sater and his business partner Tevfik Arif, had 77 percent of its sales attributed to possible money-laundering.[61] In 2010, Donald Jr. and Ivanka, who oversaw the property, were nearly charged with felony fraud in their Trump SoHo dealings. In a 2017 collaboration between ProPublica, The New Yorker, and WNYC, it was revealed that the case was dropped with District Attorney Cyrus Vance overruling his own prosecutors following a meeting with Trump's attorney, Marc Kasowitz, who had previously donated $25,000 to Vance's re-election campaign and asked Vance to drop the investigation.[62] While

Vance had returned the contribution in advance of the meeting, after Vance dropped the case, Trump's attorney made another large donation and helped raise still more money from others, bringing the total Vance's campaign received to more than $50,000. Vance, who denied any wrongdoing, was tasked in 2019 to oversee the New York–based charges brought forth by offshoots of the Mueller probe.

By the end of the 1990s, Trump felt confident enough to revert to one of his favorite pastimes: running for president. He re-enlisted Roger Stone, the fellow Roy Cohn protégé who had guided his 1988 flirtation with the office and who had been proclaiming Trump would be president since 1985, and set about seeking the nomination of the Reform Party.[63] In a gushing September 1999 *New York Times* article entitled "President? Why Not? Says a Man at the Top," Trump attributed his interest in the nomination to a poll given to readers of the *National Enquirer*. The *Times* article reports: "'Those are the real people,' Mr. Trump declared of the Enquirer readers, earnestly laying his hands across his desk. Roger Stone, his paid consultant, who was sitting across the desk, offering Mr. Trump the occasional pointer during the 45-minute interview, added, 'That is the Trump constituency.'"[64]

The veracity of the poll is questionable, but there is no doubt that the *National Enquirer* itself was the Trump constituency. In February 1999, the *National Enquirer* had been purchased by a new conglomerate which put longtime Trump lackey David Pecker at the helm. Pecker is now known for his "catch and kill" operation to prevent damning stories from reaching the public, a project he conducted with Trump lawyer Michael Cohen. He is also known for his threats toward US opponents of Trump, most notably *Washington Post* owner Jeff Bezos, who maintained that Pecker had targeted him in an extortion scheme in possible collaboration with the Saudi government after the murder of *Washington Post* journalist Jamal Khashoggi.[65]

The *National Enquirer* were very much Trump's people—powerful elites who make threats and tell lies and market it as populism and hidden truths. What's perhaps more disturbing, though, is that there was little difference between the coverage given to Trump's campaign by the *National Enquirer*, a literal Trump tool from 1999 onward, and *The New York Times*. The *Times* made no serious inquiry into finances and asked no hardball questions. "I have been very much an open book. I mean, one thing, people know who I am. While I haven't been public, I am public," Trump told the *Times* interviewer.

In retrospect, "while I haven't been public, I am public" is an apt assessment of a double life lived in plain sight, a life of crimes that gets glossed over because you can see the sheen. The "tycoon or buffoon" strategy is meant to amuse the public, to make Americans believe he either is as successful as he claims to be—after all, *The New York Times* vouches for him!—or is such an obvious phony that he could not be capable of pulling off a massive criminal enterprise without repercussions. He is a public figure, you tell yourself—if he is lying, surely someone will call him out. If he is hurting people, surely someone will stop him.

But they don't. As Trump rose again in the United States, a future political partner was rising abroad, locking himself into the position of power he would occupy for decades. On New Year's Eve in 1999, Vladimir Putin became president of Russia. At the time, he was underestimated as a threat to world democracy and stability. This was in part due to Western perception of Russia as a weakened state, but Putin has also spent decades employing Western public relations specialists to soften his image as a ruthless KGB agent who had skillfully navigated oligarch turf wars.[66] Instead, he sought to be seen as the tough but lawfully elected representative of a fledgling democratic country.

Among those with connections to Putin was Michael Caputo, a longtime GOP operative who worked in Russia for assorted officials and oligarchs throughout the 1990s. (In 2017, Caputo tried to scrub information about these endeavors from the internet.)[67]

After leaving Russia, Caputo returned to the United States to work at a Florida public relations firm with Stone. In 2015, Caputo, like Stone, became one of Trump's campaign advisers. He was yet another longtime Trump contact with decades-long ties to shady Russian businessmen involved in the presidential race.

In February 2000, Trump withdrew from his attempt to become the Reform Party candidate after campaigning as a moderate. The nomination instead went to virulent bigot Pat Buchanan, who ended up being an enthusiastic endorser of Trump's xenophobic 2016 campaign. In 2000, Trump's campaign seemed like a harmless distraction in an era when presidential candidates debated questions like "How do we spend the enormous government surplus in our booming economy?" and the biggest political crisis was Bill Clinton's philandering.

In the media, reality TV continued to thrive, moving from daytime and cable networks into prime time, and forming a new genre in the summer of 2000 with the hit series *Survivor*. *Survivor* became the template for both the construct and ethos of reality TV over the next decade: strangers trapped together in an unfamiliar setting backstab one another in front of the cameras, with one player dismissed in a humiliating weekly ceremony until only the winner remained.

Mark Burnett, the creator of *Survivor*, is one of the most successful television producers of the modern era, but he was never able to realize one of his dream projects. Burnett wanted to create a reality TV show featuring Vladimir Putin that would portray the authoritarian leader to Americans in a flattering light. Burnett's fascination with Putin goes back to at least 2001, when he tried to launch a series called *Destination Mir* and confirmed to *The New York Times* that Putin was involved in the project.[68] For the next decade and a half, he did not stray from this goal. In 2015, *The Hollywood Reporter* wrote:

> Seeing Russia through its controversial president's eyes has Burnett so excited, he already has reached out to Putin, 62,

a noted outdoorsman and former KGB officer. He says he emphasized his show would be devoid of armies and politics; rather, it would focus on "the humans, the nature, the animals of the nation." When it is suggested the Russian leader probably would ignore such a request, Burnett, who recently wrapped filming a *Ben-Hur* remake in Rome, cracks a smile: "How do you know that? I would think I could probably get through to most people."

So, if he did get through, what was the reaction? Responds Burnett coyly, "No comment."[69]

Burnett never got his reality show about Putin off the ground, but he did succeed in increasing the Russian leader's domination over the United States. In 2004, Burnett launched the project that did more to rehabilitate and popularize Donald Trump than anything: *The Apprentice*, the popular reality TV series presenting Trump as a successful and likeable businessman and introducing Donald Jr. and Ivanka to everyday Americans. In 2017, Burnett was hired to produce Trump's inauguration as president, which is being investigated as a mass money-laundering and espionage scheme featuring a variety of Russian mobsters, spies, and oligarchs.[70] (There is no suggestion that Burnett was involved in illicit activity in connection with the inauguration.)

In the end, Burnett got his Putin reality TV series after all. We just mistook it for an election.

4

The Early 2000s: Reality TV Terror

A t twenty-one years old, armed with a liberal arts BA, free-lance clips, and experience creating online content—a novel attribute at the time—I landed a job at America's fifth-largest newspaper, the *New York Daily News*. It was August 2000, and I'd just endured a summer of being so broke I was eating one bowl of rice per day while pretending I was on *Survivor* to feel adventur-ous instead of afraid. I had graduated in May into a fading boom economy that at the time felt daunting but now seems like a bas-tion of riches and ease. I didn't know it then, but I had begun my adult life at the tail end of a dream, one that rapidly transformed into a nightmare of dashed expectations and diminished returns. It was the beginning of a millennium rife with collapse.

I am of the last generation to begin work in a creative profes-sion as a member of the middle class. When I tell young people how I got this job, they respond as if I'm telling them a fairy tale. I was hired after sending my résumé through the mail to strangers. I had no connections, no graduate degree, and no summer internships. I had spent my summers working to save money for college, which meant my résumé included positions like "Record Town cashier" and "Dannon water inventory specialist," a job that consisted of stocking bottled water at supermarkets and did not require the ability to read.

But no one cared back then; the era of elite credentialism was still years ahead. The *Daily News* liked my clips and my skills and especially my willingness to work from 7 P.M. to 3 A.M. The hours were awful, but I didn't mind. I had landed a job that paid $40,000 per year and included health insurance, benefits, and three weeks paid vacation. My apartment, in Astoria, Queens, was a spacious one-bedroom for which I paid $900 per month. I could afford to live alone in New York City as a journalist in my early twenties. In 2000, no one thought that was remarkable, including me. Only in retrospect is it recognizable for what it was: a fluke. A fleeting taste of the American Dream, sweet enough that it still lingers.

By 2010, only one of my former coworkers at the *Daily News* was still working in journalism. I had quit the paper in 2003, but the rest were laid off—casualties of a media recession that began in early 2001 and accelerated with the 2008 financial collapse. The Great Recession that followed led to a massive restructuring in the industry. With the economy tanking, media outlets transformed full-time jobs into contract work and entry-level positions into unpaid internships, and changed worker expectations along the way. Told that advanced degrees would help them keep their jobs, my former coworkers shelled out tens of thousands of dollars for journalism school, where they were taught skills they already knew or that technology would soon render obsolete. In the end, it did not matter—the layoffs came anyway.

By 2010, my old *Daily News* job had been converted into an unpaid internship. My old Astoria apartment rented for over $2,000 per month. The cost of living in New York had skyrocketed, while wages remained stagnant or even decreased as desperate writers took pay cuts to stay in the profession. Outlets that had paid $1,000 per article while I was a college student in the late 1990s had dropped their rates to $200 per article by 2002, and in 2010 were offering zero dollars, otherwise known as "exposure."

Journalism was ahead of the curve in terms of the twenty-first-century opportunity collapse, but the downturn was in every field, though the employment crisis was not widely recognized until the 2010s. (This is what happens when you fire the journalists first.) It made no difference whether a worker had a GED or a Ph.D., whether they toiled in a prestigious field like law or a blue-collar field like retail or a public sector field like teaching. Across all fields, management had realized they could stop paying people a living wage and get away with it.

Younger generations had been trained to work for a future that never arrived. By the time they realized the truth, they were too deep in debt to escape. The past came calling every month in the form of a creditor, dead dreams with soaring interest rates. Everyday necessities—housing, health care, child care—became luxuries, and survival became an aspiration. The 2000s ushered in an era of credentialism that prevented ordinary people from rising through the ranks. Jobs that once required a high school degree now required a BA, jobs that required a BA now required an MA, and the choice was pay to play or get locked out. Sometimes you paid and got locked out anyway, as wealthy elites purchased careers for their untalented offspring. But I discuss Jared and Ivanka in the next chapter.

The three years I worked at the *Daily News*—from 2000 to 2003—were possibly the most transformative in US journalism, and by association, the most transformative in terms of how Americans access and process information. Much of what Americans took for granted was lost within that brief window of time. We lost our faith in the electoral system through the contested 2000 presidential race. We lost our sense of safety from foreign threats through the September 11, 2001, attacks. We lost our sense of prosperity through a recession followed by skyrocketing income inequality. We lost what was left of our shame when we went to war in Iraq based on a lie.

I grieved those losses while working in the industry that tells people what is worth grieving, that defines not only the terms of the debate but the participants. I watched the public shed old illusions only to embrace new ones manufactured in my line of work—fantasies spun out of fear and favor. I watched the media industry scramble to turn chaos into a palatable narrative, one the public could follow, one advertisers could sell.

The country had been upended, and along with it the news industry. When I started at the *Daily News* in 2000, the print newspaper was so popular that they had launched an evening supplement. The website, however, was barely off the ground, and merely an online replication of the print edition. Part of the rationale for this approach was speed: each print article needed to be manually coded in HTML and uploaded into a rigid template, taking five to ten minutes each time. All online articles were published at once in the dead of night, the only time when the website updated.

The laborious nature of running the website made posting breaking news nearly impossible. More significant than the difficulty, though, was a reticence to elevate the paper's online component. The editorial staff of the *New York Daily News* viewed the paper as a holy scripture, one whose screeching, pun-ridden covers—IVANA BETTER DEAL, read the front-page story about Trump's first divorce—lined the hallways like icons in a tabloid church. The internet, where *anyone* could write *anything*, was seen as a threat to the business model and an insult to the industry.

The newspaper had the power to freeze time. When we spent November through December 2000 wondering if the president would be Bush or Gore, our precise point of uncertainty would be captured when the paper closed at 3 A.M. The website would remain unchanged until the next day at 3 A.M., no matter what happened in the intervening hours. I remember going to breakfast with coworkers after an all-nighter on election night and hearing them rejoice that the *Daily News* got the print edition right while the rival *New York Post* had jumped the gun and printed that Bush won—an irony that our nation would have to live with for the next eight years, and not just in terms of preemptive newspaper stories. The print edition was considered gospel, not only to the staff but to the readers.

Reporters had twenty-four hours to figure out and fact-check a story, and in the year 2000, facts were not yet viewed as optional. This is not to say that the *Daily News* was a paragon of journalistic integrity, but that the news still followed the old Mark Twain adage: "Get your facts straight first, and then you can distort them as much as you please." We were not yet in a factual free-for-all: readers had the time to notice if we made mistakes, and we had the time to fix them. I did some reporting for the print side. My first article, in what now seems like ludicrous foreshadowing, was about Robert Hanssen—the FBI agent who was arrested in 2001 after spying for Russia for twenty-two years—writing pornographic stories on the internet, but my primary role was to keep the website operational. My small team was the least important part of the paper, until, one day, we weren't.

I was out of town when the towers fell. I had left New York on September 8, 2001, with my boyfriend to drive to rural Wisconsin to stay at his friend's cabin in the woods. The trip was a birthday treat; I had just turned twenty-three. On September 11, we woke up late and went out to get breakfast. This was the era before smartphones and we hadn't turned on the TV, so we spent the early morning oblivious to the outside world. We were driving on a country road when we turned on the radio and heard Dan Rather saying that the World Trade Center had collapsed. Our first thought was that this was a delayed Y2K joke that had gotten on the air by mistake.

Within minutes we knew the news report was no lapsed parody. We could hear the anguish in Rather's voice as he announced the estimated casualty count to be in the tens of thousands. I remember screaming, "It's real, it's *real*, turn around!" and crying as we raced back to the house, where we spent all day watching the one channel the TV could pick up while calling our friends to see if they were alive. My boyfriend—who later became my husband—worked at the *Daily News* with me; that was where we had met. We knew some of our coworkers would be downtown covering the attacks. We knew the wife of one of our mutual friends worked on the eightieth floor of the South Tower. We couldn't get through to most people because cell phone lines were jammed: millions of Americans were running their own panicked checks.

Twelve hours later we realized we hadn't eaten all day and went to get dinner in a small-town bar, the kind of Wisconsin bar that East Coast reporters now scour to find Trump voters. I remember the unanimity of the grief, and it isn't anything I view with nostalgia. There's no comfort in the ubiquity of the helpless witness, and that's all we were, a packed room of Americans staring at a television with red and swollen eyes. I don't remember returning to the house; I don't remember sleeping, though I suppose I must have at some point. I remember the silence of the plane-free sky, and how we had come to Wisconsin to get away from the stress of the city, to come to a place quiet and still. Now that stillness encompassed the entire country—a purgatory stillness, unwanted and unwarranted.

I remember how badly we wanted to go back to New York. We wanted to get to work, to do something useful, to be home—though the New York we would return to was entirely different than the one we'd left. We hit the highway the next day, driving through Wisconsin and Illinois and Ohio and Pennsylvania, where we must have stopped somewhere to sleep for a few hours before driving on, because I remember it being dawn when we passed under a bridge with a gigantic American flag attached, and saw the smoke rising in the distance.

The next month was something I endured rather than lived. I remember the smell of dust and death when I would get too close to downtown, the exhausted construction workers telling me to turn back, the streets lined with candles and flyers of the "missing" who we knew—but could not say—were the dead. I remember a mother briefly mistaking me for her daughter and both of us sobbing when she was wrong. I remember the silence of the subway, the dazed pain mistaken for stoicism. I remember waking one October night to a booming sound, probably a car backfiring, and my neighbors running out onto the street screaming that the terrorists were back, *it was happening again, it was happening again*. I remember reading op-eds praising the resilience of New Yorkers, and thinking all resilience meant was bearing the big-city burden of living in public, your existence symbolic of something other than the sadness you carried inside.

I remember knowing the rest of my life would be different. We had passed into a darker era when I was barely an adult, and I felt a flicker of resentment quickly quashed by guilt. I was lucky, I told myself: I had been out of town, and no one close to me had died. My friend's wife was late for work in the South Tower and arrived to see the attacks unfold from the ground. Several *Daily News* employees were injured by falling debris, and several people I knew lost friends or family members. My main purpose, as I saw it, was to be useful at work, where we were telling the stories of those who were lost. If that meant sorting through photos of body parts or captioning funeral photos or organizing obituaries for months on end, then I would do it. I would not complain, because every day I was reminded that it could all come undone like it did for the people whose senseless murders I now cataloged. I got engaged to my boyfriend a few months after 9/11. We were grabbing at milestones before they were stolen.

Work also changed—not just my job, but the media industry. In the midst of the terrorist attacks, a decision had to be made— should the *Daily News* update the website? My coworker told me of his anguished, sarcastic remark to the print editors: It would be okay to deviate from the paper and let the world know that the towers had collapsed—maybe, just *maybe*, the public had figured it out, and the website could be used to tell our readers something new. From then on, the website led the paper, gradually improving its technology to mirror the 24/7 news crawl that—once a rarity—

now never left the TV screen. All news was BREAKING all the time, breathless coverage often elucidating nothing. This is one of the longest-lasting artifacts of 9/11.

Time was no longer frozen online. Cable news and the internet now determined the pace, filling a psychic void of trepidation. The public would never again be able to say that nobody warned them something terrible was coming, though the veracity of the terrible thing was often debatable. Every hour heralded a fresh false alarm, a change in the color-coded terror alert system, a foiled but deadly threat. Like every other media outlet, the *Daily News* spent the fall of 2001 on alert for anthrax attacks. At one point spilled Sweet'N Low resulted in a building evacuation and a visit from a hazmat team. New York tabloid media, once known for its jaded toughness, became jittery and hypervigilant. We jumped to update breaking news, we jumped at sudden noises, we jumped to conclusions when the government—the mayor, the police, the president—gave them to us. Conclusions were so enticing—they implied a reason and an end.

The attacks on September 11 hit two of the country's biggest media hubs—New York and Washington, D.C. Proximity to these sites of mass murder left journalists raw, and trauma made them malleable. There was nothing abstract about the devastation, and there was nothing concrete about the cause. Rage and regret were ceaseless and personal, and it was our jobs to streamline our internal and external cacophony into a coherent narrative for public consumption.

That meant creating new heroes and villains. Rudy Giuliani, a washed-up scandal magnet who in August 2001 was making headlines for his illicit affairs and past shady dealings—which include, notably, protecting his longtime friend Trump from being investigated for criminal activity[1]—became recast by the national media as America's Mayor. Reporters who once hated Giuliani were now willing to do anything he said, including vote for Republican billionaire Michael Bloomberg in the mayoral election, and they were reluctant to do things they needed to do, like demand real answers about why Giuliani had not taken greater precautions to protect the World Trade Center from terrorism after it had been attacked in 1993. Too many illusions had been shattered, so we built new ones, illusions that shone like the lights beaming out from the cavernous hole where the towers once stood.

The initial post-9/11 obedience of the media was forged in grief. I blame the media for a lot of things, but I don't blame them for their coverage of the last months of 2001, which was rife with exhaustion and exploited by manipulative authorities. There's an adage that journalism is meant to afflict the comfortable and comfort the afflicted. In late 2001, New Yorkers were the afflicted, and simplistic narrative arcs were a comfort. The complex horror of what occurred could be distilled into black and white, and for a while it felt right to do that—to salute the fallen, to vow revenge, to pretend "with us or against us" was a reasonable belief system. We couldn't get any distance.

When the United States went to war in Afghanistan—the first US war of my adult life—I thought it was probably the right move, unaware that this war would still be going nearly two decades later. My eight-year-old son once asked me, "Has America ever *not* been at war?" and I told him that for about half my life, it was not, but for all of his life, it had been. He asked if America would be at war for the rest of his life. I thought of wars that break out within national borders, and wars that come from computers and aren't called wars, and undeclared wars born of unprecedented treason. I said I didn't know, but that I would try, in my way, to keep him safe. I didn't tell him what he needed to be kept safe from, how deeply the lines between protector and assailant in US government had blurred. I didn't tell him that it was the president, not foreign adversaries, who had called journalists like me "enemies of the people."[2]

I told my son how some of my friends enlisted after 9/11 out of a sense of obligation to country, but that they kept having to fight the same wars over and over, and that this left them hurting inside. My son asked if the government could give them a special reward, like not having to work ever again because they had already tried so hard to protect people, and I held his face to my chest so he wouldn't see me cry.

By 2019, 9/11 had become reduced to slogans and memes of varying severity. Politicians weaponized the tragedy and used it to cast aspersions on their enemies. In April 2019, Congresswoman Ilhan Omar received death threats after Trump tweeted a video falsely implying she approved of the 9/11 attacks. But while the trivialization of 9/11 was a gradual cultural phenomenon, Trump's callousness about 9/11 dates back to the day it happened, when he responded to the death of thousands of New Yorkers by bragging about his buildings. "40 Wall Street actually was the second-tallest building in downtown Manhattan, and it was actually, before the World Trade Center, was the tallest—and then, when they built the World Trade Center, it became known as the second-tallest," he told New York's Channel 9 News hours after the attacks. "And now it's the tallest."[3]

This narcissism is typical of how Trump reacts to American suffering. When the foreclosure crisis and the recession destroyed the American economy, he thought only of how he would profit, saying, "People have been talking about the end of the cycle for 12 years, and I'm excited if it is. I've always made more money in bad markets than in good markets."[4] His predatory mind-set is evident in his obsession with nuclear weapons, which he believes can be used to create profitable catastrophes, and also evident in his interest in causing civilian deaths abroad. When told in 2018 that the CIA had delayed a drone attack until a target left his family, Trump asked, "Why did you wait?"[5] Even as commander in chief, he cannot contain his apathy toward the deaths of others: from US citizens to foreign civilians to US troops whose names he can't remember and whose families he insults.[6]

In 2011, Trump bragged he predicted 9/11 in his 2000 book *The America We Deserve*, a claim that, surprisingly, bears out somewhat.[7] In the book, cowritten with freelance author Dave

Shiflett, Trump wrote of the danger posed by Osama bin Laden and predicted that a mass terrorist attack on American soil was imminent. Though he mentioned the 1993 World Trade Center attacks, he did not specify the buildings as the new target.[8] In 2015, Shiflett said he wrote the book because he needed the money and referred to it sarcastically as his first work of fiction.[9] But he noted that Trump, in 2000, was obsessed with terrorism.[10]

Despite their disturbing nature, Trump's 9/11 comments were not highlighted much by the press during the 2016 campaign. Throughout his run, he added new insults to his litany, including mocking the disability of New York Times reporter Serge Kovaleski, who had corrected Trump's lie that thousands of Muslim Arabs in New Jersey cheered the collapse of the Twin Towers.[11] The muted reaction to Trump's alarming remarks about 9/11 speaks of a reluctance from the press to take him seriously. But there is also a greater theme at play. The tragedy was cheapened in national memory by a cynical frustration with the lack of accountability surrounding both 9/11 and the wars that followed. By 2016, Americans had gotten so used to mass corruption and the commodification of pain that, to some extent, the ability to discern threats had been lost.

The ability to discern threats is related to the ability to discern facts, and preserving that ability was a struggle well before Trump took office. Much has been made of the Trump administration's embrace of "alternative facts," but the confusion dates back to the 2000s: the era of "truthiness" and the rise of reality TV. The Bush years were marked not only by unpunished white-collar and war crimes but blatant confessions of mass manipulation from powerful elites. In 2002, Ron Suskind, a journalist for The New York Times, interviewed a Bush administration official later identified as adviser Karl Rove. Suskind recalls:

> [Rove] said that guys like me were "in what we call the reality-based community," which he defined as people who "believe that solutions emerge from your judicious study

of discernible reality." I nodded and murmured something about enlightenment principles and empiricism. He cut me off. "That's not the way the world really works anymore," he continued. "We're an empire now, and when we act, we create our own reality. And while you're studying that reality—judiciously, as you will—we'll act again, creating other new realities, which you can study too, and that's how things will sort out. We're history's actors . . . and you, all of you, will be left to just study what we do."[12]

Rove made these remarks privately during the 2002 run-up to the Iraq War, when news outlets like the one I worked at ran op-eds claiming war in Iraq to be necessary and protesters to be traitors, worthy of being pelted with freedom fries. There was no question about the Bush administration's agenda that could not be struck down with an outraged "But 9/11!" In retrospect, it is easy to see how the administration exploited not only the fears of the broader American public but the fear of New York and D.C. journalists, who had just spent months covering a mass murder in their backyard. *Of course, we will be attacked again*, the conventional wisdom went, *and of course our authorities must be trusted even if their claims of weapons of mass destruction seem questionable—after all, undermining faith in authority was what the terrorists wanted to do!*

This uncritical embrace of authority for its own sake is similar to the excuses given for the refusal of officials to address the attacks on the 2016 election in depth. (*The Russians want us to distrust the integrity of the US election process*, the pundit explains, *therefore we must never, ever question what the Russians did to the election process!*) The trustworthiness of a process or person was to be dictated from above by "history's actors," not decreed from below by the empirical observations of the masses. What Rove did in that interview—and what Trump does now—was take the ruse one step further, and admit to manipulation openly, not even giving the public the illusion of an honest broker.

When Rove's comments were revealed in 2004, they shocked Americans with their arrogance. When Trump reveled in similar callousness during his campaign, it was decreed plainspoken authenticity by a press so used to seeing the powerful cover up ugly truths with pretty lies that they could not imagine that the ugliness was covering up something even worse.

"Lies are often much more plausible, more appealing to reason, than reality, since the liar has the great advantage of knowing beforehand what the audience wishes or expects to hear," scholar of fascism Hannah Arendt wrote after the release of the Pentagon Papers in 1971.[13] "He has prepared his story for public consumption with a careful eye to making it credible, whereas reality has the disconcerting habit of confronting us with the unexpected, for which we were not prepared."

Trump lives his life like the confirmation of a Hannah Arendt hypothesis—a bad trait in a person and a terrifying one in a president. Arendt, who died in 1975, did not live to see technology evolve to enable new kinds of liars: in particular, the invention of scripted reality as a mass medium. Trump had spent the 1980s and 1990s constructing his own reality through the press, employing methods ranging from telling tabloid tales of himself to reporters, to using vicious lawyers to shut down unflattering coverage, to enlisting the services of well-connected New York PR operatives to fill in whatever blanks remained.

Throughout it all, Trump continued to market himself as a risk-taker. On one hand, this is a euphemistic way to frame a lifetime of bankruptcies. But more to the point, it is untrue. Trump lived his entire adult life in a criminal cocoon, emerging in public to play the greatest version of himself while his backers behind the scenes, as Arendt puts it, "confront the unexpected"—things like laws and lawsuits and loudmouthed women.

This is not boldness: crime ceases to be risky when you know you will get away with it. In the twenty-first century, the corporate loopholes that enable white-collar crime double as nooses around the neck of Western democracy. In the Reagan era, Trump's Republican backers helped devise the dissolution of corporate regulations. In the Bush era, they chipped away at political checks and balances, with the near elimination of accountability as a result. The Republican party provided the structure for an American autocracy enabled by corporate corruption. But it was television producers who gave the future autocrat his most important script.

The impact of *The Apprentice* is possibly the most underappreciated aspect of Trump's presidential rise. For a large percentage of Americans—pretty much anyone born after 1984 and outside the New York area—*The Apprentice*, which debuted in 2004, was their introduction to Donald Trump, one of many rehabbed D-listers to land his own reality show during this decade. While early twenty-first-century reality TV shows like *Survivor* propelled average Americans and little-known hosts to stardom, slightly later series like *The Osbournes* inaugurated a trend of looking into the "real life" of fallen superstars. The most successful reality shows of the 2000s blended the desire for unfettered celebrity access—a desire stoked by gossip magazines like *Us Weekly* that proclaim "Stars—They're Just Like Us!"—with tales of ordinary contestants who battle for a celebrity's approval. This was the format of *American Idol*, *America's Top Model*, and *The Apprentice*—shows that all extended the lifespan of the winner into a "real-life career," albeit one of varying longevity. These ventures lent legitimacy to the industries and, especially, to the host, whose supposed clout jumpstarted the lucky someone's professional endeavors. *The Apprentice* trust-washed Trump's criminal enterprises to an unsuspecting public.

When *The Apprentice* debuted, I was living in Istanbul with my husband. We had quit the *Daily News* in 2003 and decided to teach English abroad, winding up in Turkey, where we lived until 2004. This interlude is another part of my biography that startles people younger than me: "You went to Turkey to get *away* from high-level political corruption, media propaganda, and economic decline?" Common policy worries among my Turkish students included wondering when Turkey would join the EU—it never did—and how soon the Iraq War would end—it stretched on until 2011, destabilizing the entire Middle East. While we lived in Turkey, my husband and I would travel to southern cities like Adana or Mardin as tourists. These border regions now hold camps of Syrian and Iraqi refugees. Recep Tayyip Erdoğan, who in 2003 was a new democratic president greeted with hope, is now a dictator. In 2013, my Turkish friends fell out of touch after Erdoğan's crackdown on free speech made them wary of communicating with political journalists. It has been horrifying to watch the hardship Turkey has endured, and it is surreal to look back and see aspects of its current corruption tangentially linked to an American reality show that debuted while we lived there.

I first heard about *The Apprentice* from my mother, who, nearly two decades after our tasteless christening of Trump Tower, was coming around to the guy. "Sarah, you need to come back home," she told me in winter 2004. "You are missing too much TV. Donald Trump has a show where he pretends to be a businessman and he is *so obnoxious*. He's like, 'You're fired!' I love it; he's terrible. The contestants are all trying to impress him. At first, I was like 'I can't believe this asshole has his own show' but it's perfect. This is exactly at his level, this is what he should have been doing the whole time. They've got him contained!"

For Americans like my mom, who had spent the 1980s and early 1990s gleefully loathing Donald Trump, *The Apprentice* was a hate-watch nostalgia trip: here was everything amusing about The Donald with none of the danger. He was now a scripted NBC product, unable to do harm beyond "firing" game show contestants. For Americans less familiar with Trump's background—which includes most people I've met since moving to the Midwest in 2004—Trump came off as either a ridiculous blowhard (which is to say, an unremarkable reality TV presence) or a charismatic tycoon on a comeback. No one envisioned Trump as the future president of the United States, and few paid attention to what his family was doing behind the scenes—and how he used the show to gloss over his criminal ventures.

On a 2006 *Apprentice* episode, Trump announced the debut of a new property: Trump SoHo. "When it's completed in 2008," Trump declared, "this brilliant $370 million work of art will be an awe-inspiring masterpiece."[14] Ivanka Trump joined the show that year to promote the property, playing the role of Trump's "adviser"—the same amorphous role she now plays in the White House. She pledged to work with that season's winner, Sean Yazbeck, to manage it.[15] But as noted in chapter 2, Trump SoHo appears in significant respects to have been a money-laundering scheme posing as a real estate property. Trump had contrived Trump SoHo with mob-connected felon Felix Sater and his partner Tevfik Arif, both from the development company Bayrock Group. Another partner at Bayrock was Tamir Sapir, whose son Alex later joined Trump's 2013 meetings in Moscow, and who is close with Lev Leviev, an oligarch and Putin confidant.[16] The elder Sapir died in 2014 after a lengthy illness.[17] Managing this crew was a rather ignominious prize offering for a TV game show contestant, and Yazbeck left Trump SoHo after only one year, before the property opened.[18] The exact circumstances of his departure are not known because, as is common for reality television and associates of Donald Trump, everyone on *The Apprentice* had to sign an extensive NDA.[19]

In 2010, the Trump Organization was sued for fraud over Trump SoHo. The lawsuit describes their business practices as "a consistent and concerted pattern of outright lies."[20] In 2012, Donald Jr. and Ivanka were on their way to being charged with felony fraud until the district attorney backed off and received a large campaign contribution from Trump's lawyer.[21] Today Trump claims to have little familiarity with Bayrock and said in 2013 that he "didn't even know what [Sater] looked like,"[22] despite the fact that Sater had worked closely with Trump for years on Trump SoHo and had personally escorted the two oldest Trump children to the Kremlin in 2006, where Ivanka Trump spun around in

Putin's chair.[23] Court documents show Trump is lying, but Sater is a genuine source of confusion for those chronicling the Trump/Russia saga. He is another career criminal who, like Trump, Epstein, and other wealthy New Yorkers, spent decades immersed in a criminal network without repercussions.

Sater was born in Russia in 1966, moved to Israel in 1973, and from there moved with his family to Brighton Beach in New York City, where, according to the FBI, his father, Mikhail Sheferovsky, worked as an underboss for Semion Mogilevich and was later arrested for extortion.[24] A childhood friend of Michael Cohen, Sater was born into the world of organized crime, but he navigated it in a novel way.[25] After a brief career on Wall Street, he was arrested in 1993 for slashing a man's face in a bar fight and served fifteen months in prison. He was arrested again in 1998 in connection to a $40 million penny stock pump-and-dump scheme described by investigative economist James S. Henry as "an innovative joint venture among four New York crime families and the Russian mob aimed at bringing state-of-the-art financial fraud to Wall Street."[26]

This point is crucial to grasp: by the mid-1990s, the influence of the Italian mafia in New York City had severely waned. This decline was first spurred by Giuliani's prosecutions, but was furthered by an influx of criminals from the former USSR due to the loosening of their immigration laws and the abuse of the Israeli "right to return" policy by mobsters who then moved from Israel to the United States. The Russian mafia operated differently than the Italian mafia, focusing less on small-time, local operations. Instead, they infiltrated themselves into Wall Street, corporations, and other avenues of transnational white-collar crime. The loosening of financial regulations in the late Clinton era and throughout the Bush era allowed elite criminal networks to flourish, contributing to the soaring income inequality and corporate corruption that decimated the fortunes of average Americans—a point Mueller himself raised in his 2011 speech about this new incarnation of organized crime.

One of the greatest beneficiaries of 9/11 and the "war on terror" that followed was the Russian mafia and its international associates. US and international law enforcement had been cracking down on the Russian mafia as it grew in the 1990s, but in the aftermath of 9/11, those resources were reallocated. Law enforcement and intelligence agencies shifted their focus to combatting terrorism, and the American public came to see al-Qaeda and other Islamic terrorist organizations as the greatest danger they faced—a grave miscalculation. Since 9/11, 103 people have been killed in the United States by Islamic terrorists, acting either alone or in groups.[27] The death toll from transnational mafia activities including the drug trade, human trafficking, and murder for hire is unclear—due in part to the threat being ignored, and in part to the shadowy nature of their activity—but is larger than the death toll from Islamic terrorism due to the sheer scope of the crimes. Add to that financial crimes resulting in mass economic instability and all its attendant consequences—loss of homes, jobs, health insurance—and you will arrive at an even higher death toll.

Much as Trump and his defenders try to water down the definition of crime by parading their corrupted properties on national television, those fighting for a free and just society must broaden it in response to this new nexus of wealthy, criminal elites. White-collar crime *is* violent crime: it's called blood money for a reason. Over the last forty years, white-collar crime, state crime, and organized crime have merged to the point that criminal networks now control governments, which allows them to redefine what they are doing as legal, exonerate themselves, and persecute those who seek to uphold the rule of law. The mafia manages the military, the crooks control the courts. In other countries, this would be called "an authoritarian coup." In America, mealy-mouthed officials call our transition into a mafia state "deeply troubling" and do little to curb the damage.

Which brings us to the eternal question: why did the FBI and other law enforcement agencies not stop such an obvious threat to national security as Trump running for president? Felix Sater brings a disturbing twist to that tale. Following his arrest in 1998,

Sater turned FBI informant, allegedly providing information on mafia activity until 2001.[28] As part of his cooperation deal, his court records were sealed for ten years by Loretta Lynch, who was then serving as the United States Attorney for the Eastern District of New York, and who later served as attorney general from 2015 to 2017 in the Obama administration. Sater became involved with the Trump Organization through Bayrock after 9/11, when the FBI was preoccupied with Islamic terrorism.

In 2006—the same year Trump SoHo was showcased on *The Apprentice*, the same year Sater took the Trump children to the Kremlin, and the same year Manafort moved into Trump Tower— Michael Cohen became Trump's personal lawyer. In 2015, Sater and Cohen exchanged a series of emails saying they were conspiring to gain Vladimir Putin's support in bringing Trump to power.[29] "Our boy can become president of the USA and we can engineer it," Sater wrote in an email to Cohen. "I will get all of Putins team to buy in on this, I will manage this process."

By 2010, Sater was handing out business cards presenting himself as a senior adviser to Trump, complete with a Trump Organization email address.[30] He had moved into circles of respectability, named the "Man of the Year" in both 2010 and 2014 by the Port Washington, New York, Jewish religious organization Chabad, whose members also included Cohen, and of which Arif, who is not Jewish, is a benefactor. (Mueller investigated this branch of Chabad in 2017 but never revealed his findings.)[31] Sater told the *Los Angeles Times* that he freelanced as an informant to the US government during the 2000s and spent the decade "building Trump Towers by day and hunting Bin Laden by night"[32]—an interesting claim given the rumored connection between al-Qaeda and the Russian mafia operation run by Sater family associate Mogilevich.[33] Former KGB officer Aleksandr Litvinenko, who was murdered by Kremlin agents in 2006, claimed in 2005 that Mogilevich has had a good relationship with Russian president Vladimir Putin since 1994 or 1993 and that Mogilevich is in contact with al-Qaeda and sells them weapons.

Given that Sater had worked as an FBI informant during the crucial years of 1998 to 2001, that the FBI had named Mogilevich their top priority in 2011, and that Sater had worked with the Trump family in a project that appears to have involved significant money-laundering, it is disconcerting at best that the FBI did not raise any concerns when Trump ran for office and won the nomination. Ascending to that level of candidacy not only gave Trump access to classified intelligence, but allowed his campaign team—by that time led by Manafort—access as well. While many of Trump's mafia and illicit Russia ties were already in the public domain, and should have been enough to prompt an investigation as the Kremlin began to show its influence over the Trump campaign, the Sater link makes plausible deniability near impossible. There is no way the FBI could claim that they did not know who Sater was, or that they were unaware he had engaged in illicit dealings with Trump.

But the FBI seemed impassive to this threat—and continued to be so even after Trump won and began firing any federal official likely to investigate him. In his memoir, former FBI official Andrew McCabe—one of several experts on the Russian mafia purged by Trump—wrote that meeting Trump was like meeting a mob boss: "In this moment, I felt the way I'd felt in 1998, in a case involving the Russian mafia, when I sent a man I'll call Big Felix in to meet with a Mafia boss named Dimitri Gufield. The same kind of thing was happening here in the Oval Office."[34] This passage reads like a twisted in-joke about Sater, a man who has been both connected to the mob and informant to the FBI as well as a Trump colleague, and who has spent the Trump presidency hobnobbing with celebrities while blowing off subpoenas, seemingly immune from consequence. Combined with the removal of Mogilevich from the Ten Most Wanted list in 2015 and the FBI's unexplained reexamination of Clinton's emails immediately before the election, this evidence calls into question both Sater's and the FBI's agendas.

Trump tends to flaunt his criminal associations along with his dictatorial ties. He bragged about his friendship with Jeffrey

Epstein and hit the town with scumbag aficionado Roy Cohn. As president, he pardoned notorious criminals like Joe Arpaio and Scooter Libby and cultivated friendships with authoritarian leaders like Kim Jong Un, Erdoğan, and Putin. It is rare for Trump to hide even the sleaziest of contacts, but he has taken pains to conceal his well-documented relationship with Sater. The reasons behind his reticence remain unclear, but may have to do with Sater being a nexus between US law enforcement and foreign oligarchs, and probably a revealing resource into the intricacies of dealings that Trump strives to keep hidden. The unpredictable Sater lives in the unscripted reality in which Trump feels such discomfort.

But that is why the script exists. Trump marketed Trump SoHo as an *Apprentice* prize, covering up a crime scene with the glitz that flourished during the Bush years—an ethos further cultivated by the cutthroat and aspirational ethos of reality TV. F. Scott Fitzgerald once said, "There are no second acts in American lives," but the 2000s were full of them if you had money and lacked shame. The war on terror had made old-school American villains seem quaint and harmless by comparison. In the 2000s, even the Gotti mafia family had its own reality show, while Ivanka made her own reality TV debut on a short-lived 2001 show called *Born Rich*. *The Apprentice* allowed the Trumps to combine glamour and crime into a new family narrative, knowing they could always claim "It's not real; it's just reality TV" if things fell apart.

"Take him literally, but not seriously," faux-sages recommended of Trump after the election.[35] This is the worst advice possible to understand a media-savvy con man skilled at repackaging crimes as ventures and accomplices as advisers and costars. *The Apprentice* is a show built on a lie and the willingness of ordinary Americans to buy into that lie—that Trump is a respected businessman running legitimate enterprises. It is the same lie upon which the Trump presidency is based.

Dictatorship is a branding operation. The ubiquity of the dictator's name and image, the repetition of slogans and symbols, the hollow rituals (like "elections" with preordained winners, like "firings" with preordained losers) all contribute to the building of the spectacular state and its captive audience. This pageantry is something authoritarians and reality TV producers understand in equal measure, and Trump inhabits the worlds of both. His brand of celebrity lent itself to the presidential race and his eventual win, and the dismissal of him as a serious candidate by national security officials was deeply naive. It would be bad enough had Trump merely emerged as a bigoted demagogue, but add long-standing ties to a transnational crime syndicate affiliated with the Kremlin and one ends up with a human road map to an American kleptocracy.

The Apprentice conditioned Americans to accept fraud as entertainment, to expect the reputational rehab of ruined celebrities, and to not consider that behind the fakeness of the show lay something very dark and real. In 2015, after Trump launched his campaign by calling Mexicans rapists and murderers, NBC canceled The Apprentice on moral grounds. Freed from his contract, Trump continued his reality show through cable news, which lacked the fleeting fortitude of NBC. In the end, The Apprentice canceled America.

And so, the grift continued. Between 2007 and 2018, buyers tied to the former Soviet Union made eighty-six cash purchases at Trump properties. In 2018, Congressman Adam Schiff, a member of the House Intelligence Committee, confirmed that the purchases indicated evidence of money-laundering.[36] The Treasury's Financial Crimes Enforcement Network (FinCEN) also noted that the Trump sales fit the prototype: "Criminals can use all-cash purchases to make payments in full for properties and evade scrutiny—on themselves and the origin of their wealth—that is regularly performed by financial institutions in transactions involving mortgages."[37]

Despite this statement, the Treasury did not pursue the legality of Trump's enterprises when he became the nominee. This is perhaps due to the fact that by the 2016 election, the Treasury had been infiltrated by Russia, an event that occurred in 2015 but was not reported on until December 2018 in an explosive exposé in BuzzFeed.[38] When Trump ascended to the White House and showed no anxiety over divestment of his business empire, it was likely not only due to his typical lack of shame, but because his backers had stocked the system with lackeys whose loyalty to Trump and foreign oligarchs overrode their loyalty to America.

To this day, nothing has been done about the infiltration of the Treasury, save the indictment of the whistle-blower, Natalie Mayflower Edwards, who exposed that Treasury officials had been communicating with Russia for years via back-channel Gmail and Hotmail accounts. The magnitude of the Treasury breach has also never been explained by the Obama administration, to which the breach was reported in 2016. According to a senior FinCEN intelligence analyst, illicit coordination with Russia was disguised as an investigation into ISIS. "Russia's subsequent actions suggest that was just a cover," the official said. "What we were seeing with Russia was the fruition of a long-term strategy to try and compromise Treasury by cultivating civil servants. That's why we sounded the alarm and reported it."[39] This internal threat to national security has only grown since 2015. The Treasury is now run by Steven Mnuchin, a lackey of Trump and fellow protégé of Trump's old adviser Carl Icahn. Mnuchin has gone out of his way to ease sanctions on Russian oligarchs—in particular, Manafort's former employer Oleg Deripaska—despite protest from Congress.[40]

Again, basic vetting by state officials—particularly during Trump's "I have nothing to do with Russia" campaign phase— would have highlighted shady connections between the Trumps and Russia that were already in the public domain. Prior to the 2016 election, the guileless nature of the Trump sons made their foreign cash influx easy to trace. In 2008, Donald Trump Jr. announced at a New York real estate conference: "In terms of high-end product influx into the US, Russians make up a pretty disproportionate cross-section of a lot of our assets. Say, in Dubai, and certainly with our project in SoHo, and anywhere in New York. We see a lot of money pouring in from Russia."[41]

Donald Jr.'s comment is the kind of remark Trump defenders like to insist is innocent. After all, there is nothing illegal about doing business in Russia, which in the Bush era was a US partner in the "war on terror." (While claiming to be a partner to the West, Putin was committing his own acts of terrorism abroad, such as poisoning dissidents like the London-based Litvinenko in 2006; much like the United States, the United Kingdom underplayed the Russian threat for decades.) But to rationalize Trump's disproportionate dependence on Russia one has to ignore the broader context every time, viewing each instance as disparate and therefore unimportant.

It is understandable why some find this cop-out appealing: the overall pattern is ominous. Since the dawn of the twenty-first century, the United States has been gutted in every sense: economically, psychologically, and under Trump, militarily, with even the secretary of defense position remaining unfilled for eight months. Post-9/11 America inaugurated an era of panic over fabricated catastrophes and false reassurances about real ones. The Trump era has only exacerbated those tendencies, leaving everyday Americans struggling to process horrific new revelations about which officials rarely provide clear answers. It can therefore be comforting to dismiss disturbing details rather than focus on the big picture. To reconcile with an attack on America as a continuum—instead of the result of an aberrant atrocity like 9/11—is to contend with the prospect of permanent dysfunction.

In the post-9/11 era, proof lost its value along with the people who produced it. The digital revolution that was supposed to liberate journalists—allowing breaking news to flow in real time and provide clarity into ongoing crises—instead led to mass layoffs. Older and experienced reporters were replaced by younger and wealthier content producers who could pay to play in the country's most expensive cities. People who can pay to play are less likely to report on corruption, inequality, or injustice, because they are less likely to recognize it exists. By the end of the decade, the reality of Rove's "reality-based community" had changed. Elites wrote about fellow elites, while the rest of us inhabited an America we rarely saw represented, a ghost world of permanent precarity and dead dreams.

When born-rich Jared Kushner, at age twenty-six, bought *The New York Observer* in 2006, it seemed of a piece with the era. I remember listing it as an example of why I had quit journalism and left New York, where the cost of living had soared under new mayor Michael Bloomberg and where panicked conformity ran rampant in creative fields. Journalism had become an industry designed for the Kushners of the world, not for those who would deign to expose them. The most influential industries—policy, law, academia, entertainment—were restructured to hire and service the wealthy by the end of the 2000s, often using the recession as a pretext to do so.

But the extent of the ramifications for America were not yet clear. A false meritocracy breeds mediocrity. I wrote that in 2013, bemoaning the loss of economic opportunity. I did not realize I was writing about national security as well.

5

The Late 2000s: Heirs to the Crash

n 2008, the world economy collapsed and never recovered. People argued then, and argue now, about who was responsible and what should have been done and when. They argue about why no one heeded the warnings of those who saw it coming and why so many Wall Street predators walked away unpunished. What few argue about, however, is that 2008 was a demarcation point. You remember who you were before the crash. You remember what you expected out of life. And then you try not to think about it.

My thirtieth birthday was the week of the crash. By then, I had left journalism and was studying autocratic regimes in Central Asia, first as an MA student at Indiana University, and then as a Ph.D. student in anthropology at Washington University in St. Louis. My undergraduate work had focused on Russia; Central Asia was a natural extension. At first, I planned to use my expertise to either cover the region as a journalist or, if all else failed, get a government job. There was a popular notion among my generation—a belief shattered with finality under Trump—that no matter how bad the economy got, the US government would always have jobs and seek out people with regional expertise. As it turned out, my expertise on the former Soviet Union would indeed be of interest to the US government, but not in the way I had imagined.

At Indiana University, I learned Uzbek and Russian and worked as a research assistant for an anthropologist, who encouraged me to get a Ph.D. I had never studied anthropology before but I liked it: the in-depth research, the ethnographic writing, the ability to take on subjects that were often ignored in journalism. I also was lured in by the illusion of meritocracy. Academia had a structure that seemed to favor high-achieving lowlifes like me. I loved the liberation of blind peer review: that the reviewers could not learn my identity but were forced to contend with my words. As an MA student, I published scholarly articles with ease. When my professors told me that my success was unusual, and that publishing was a key part of securing gainful employment in academia, I began to do something I had not dared to do since 9/11 and the bottoming out of the media economy. I began to envision a future for myself.

The more I looked at how Ph.D. programs worked, the more they seemed like the answer to not just a professional but personal dilemma. I was never attached to the idea of becoming an academic, but I liked the idea of having kids while on a multiyear fellowship and therefore not having to choose between working or staying home in a time of skyrocketing childcare costs—a "choice" that was killing either the savings or careers of my female friends. I figured I would become a stay-at-home-scholar-of-post-Soviet-authoritarianism mom, structuring my work schedule around my children and avoiding day care, which cost more than my stipend paid. Like most people my age, I did not look for opportunities so much as I navigated obstacles. The biggest obstacle had always been money, and I had finally figured out a work-around.

I got pregnant in my first semester of graduate school, to the dismay of my department. I assured my professors I'd get my work done during nap times, evenings, and weekends. When my adviser expressed doubts over this plan, I reminded him that he was the chair of my dissertation, not my uterus. I followed through, out-publishing the junior faculty of my department, getting mainstream acclaim (for an Uzbekistan expert, anyway), and receiving my Ph.D. in 2012, one year after my second child was born. For six years, my life involved doing things like interviewing Uzbek political dissidents with a toddler in tow or giving interviews to BBC Uzbek from Gymboree. But in comparison with my *Daily News* job of cataloging casualties at 2:00 A.M. while living in fear of terrorism and layoffs, graduate school—even with two babies—seemed easy.

I might have stayed in academia had the economy not collapsed two years into my program. Roughly 50 percent of the jobs in my field were eliminated, and contingent and low-paying prestige positions became the norm. In these jobs, the salary is so low compared to the cost of living that many scholars essentially pay to work. About three-quarters of professors work as adjuncts, most making around $2,000 to $3,000 per course, with many living near or under the poverty line.[1] They stay in these abysmal working conditions because rejecting them risks professional exile. To even briefly leave academia for a more lucrative field while looking for an academic job—assuming an alternative job could be found—is seen as a sign that one is not "serious" about research. In many respects, academia operates like a cult.

In 2011, right after I successfully defended my dissertation, my academic career came to an abrupt end. I realized I could not afford to enter the job market. To apply for jobs, I would have to pay thousands of dollars to attend the academic conferences in expensive cities where job interviews are held. There was no rationale for universities to do this—interviews could have been done through phone or Skype—but it was their way of culling the herd. My husband and I had no money to spare, and I felt like incurring debt was an irresponsible move for a mother of two in a bad economy. I also resented these prohibitive entry costs in a field that was supposed to be based on merit. When I asked my professors what to do, they said most students borrowed money from their parents at this point. I laughed in disbelief, pointing out that I *was* a parent and had lived on my own for over a decade. What kind of infantilizing nonsense was this? They didn't have an answer. A class bias in academia that had been opaque to me was now obvious. In academia, much like in journalism, where you came from determined where you could go. So I said "Fuck this" and stayed in St. Louis.

St. Louis had changed since I had moved there in 2006, and I changed with it. When I came there for my interview at Wash U, the professor who drove me around the area near the university apologized for the lack of luxury and promised it would "improve." He did not know that what I valued most in a city was cheapness and that I feared debt far more than crime. Having grown up in a fairly poor and rough small city, I was fine living in a poor and rough larger city that offered more amenities than I had growing up. When you have children, you start to see your city through their eyes instead of your own.

In St. Louis, I saw parks and free museums and a free zoo and free family events every weekend. I saw a place that was unrefined and looked down upon by outsiders, but whose value revealed itself the more you opened up to it. I became closer to the people I met in my neighborhood, who tended to share my values and frustrations, and moved away from the cloistered world of Wash U. If there's a unifying positive trait to St. Louisans, it's a blunt pragmatism, a radar for bullshit that doesn't quite cross over into cynicism. (I should note that these types of St. Louisans rarely make it into elected office.) And in late 2008, as I was starting to feel at home, I saw St. Louis collapse.

In St. Louis, the brink is a permanent condition. The 2008 recession brought the world of everyone I knew crashing down, with whatever fragile sense of stability they had never to return. Over the next decade, nearly every friend I had in St. Louis lost their job. This group included lawyers, academics, public school teachers, cab drivers, journalists, social workers, service workers, my sister-in-law, her husband, and my husband, whose company was hit by a mass layoff a few years after I finished my Ph.D., when I was working part-time as a journalist. Missouri has the shortest unemployment compensation in the United States, offering only thirteen weeks of pay. (Twenty-six weeks is the national average.) The money did not last long. My husband did not find full-time work for sixteen months, during which time he worked two minimum wage jobs while I balanced freelancing with taking care of the kids. I sometimes refer to my husband's sixteen months without a full-time job as "the time he was unemployed" and then remember he was overemployed. He was working over fifty hours per week but making wages so low that our family of four hovered near the poverty line.

For over a year I would wake up shaking. The economic nightmare I had documented for years as a journalist had finally gotten me, like a monster I had tracked but failed to slay. I developed health problems that I never treated, contemplating the humiliation of a medical GoFundMe but then deciding to wait in case something worse happened—in postrecession Missouri, the odds of something worse happening were always high. We thought about moving, but the new economy had created an unequal economic geography. Expensive cities had better jobs, but the high cost of living made moving anywhere with our meager St. Louis assets impossible. In the cities where we could afford to live—cities similar to St. Louis—there were few full-time positions available.

None of this was reflected in the portrait of the American economy we saw on the news. In Obama's second term, the national unemployment rate was around 5 percent—a number that belied the tenuous and low-paid work that was available. People complain of being treated like a statistic, but I *longed* to be treated like a statistic—to force people in power to acknowledge my family's grim reality instead of counting us as technically employed workers in a false recovery.

In the end, it didn't seem to matter. It made no difference what any of us did or how well we did it. It made no difference what we could offer the world. We only knew what the world could take away.

It takes a long time to go broke in St. Louis; that's part of its charm. My newly struggling friends in rich cities lost their money faster. On the coasts, certain sectors had boomed—technology on the West Coast, finance in New York—but all that did was drive out workers in other professions whose wages stagnated as the cost of living in their gentrifying neighborhoods soared. Many dropped out of fields in which they had trained or worked for years to pursue an occupation that seemed stable, such as health care. Americans weren't going to stop getting sick from being overworked and underpaid any time soon. One of the most influential Central Asia analysts of my generation became a dentist. Another friend who was a well-known pundit on television—a position for which he was paid in "exposure"—works a minimum wage job after years of being exploited by think tanks and media corporations.

There is a vast body of knowledge that has been lost from young people priced out of their professions, specialists whose skills were sharpened but never fully shared. As a group, we drift with the tides of history, trying not to drown. Most of my friends have life stories that are simply a series of reactions to disasters. One friend, after spending thousands of dollars on an academic job search, left St. Louis for the only teaching job she could find, in Puerto Rico. She and her family were then stuck without basic resources in the catastrophic aftermath of Hurricane Maria in 2017. She fled to Florida in 2018 with her husband and children, only to find upon arrival that their new city was temporarily occupied by neo-Nazis. (My friend and her family are Jewish.) She is asking me to write a book called *An End Times Guide for Modern-Day Parents*.

Every ordinary person around my age has a secret self from before the crash, one who dared to dream of more than a life of necessities reclassified as luxuries. There are marriages that never happened, children never born, chances never taken, because the struggle to hang on to what you have is so great that it hurts your heart to hope for more. You can't afford the literal cost, and you can't afford the psychic cost. In the postemployment economy, a generation learned to manage its expectations.

The rage, though—that stays with you.

As opportunity for ordinary people fell, opportunism for the rich and unqualified flourished. The Trump administration is often described as a "kakistocracy," a word that means rule by the least competent.[2] I have never used this word, and prefer the term "kleptocracy," which describes countries where rulers steal their nation's resources to enhance their personal wealth. "Kakistocracy" assumes that the Trump administration's malice is the result of incompetence, and that the dismantling of departments is the incidental result of appointing unqualified people. In the Trump administration, people are hired to dismantle the departments they lead, and the main quality for which they are valued is blind and total fealty.

The Trump administration is, in fact, very competent in achieving its main goal: stripping America down for parts and selling those parts to the highest bidders. That is not kakistocracy but kleptocracy, with elements of burgeoning authoritarianism. Like most kleptocracies, the Trump administration has carried out an enormous number of hirings and firings. Kleptocracies like to move players around to create the illusion of debate and dissent. Changes in personnel give the impression that power is distributed equitably rather than consolidated around a dictator, while also distracting the press from the regime's more substantive flaws. As during his reality television days, Trump shakes up the status of players, and positions are cast more than filled. Firings create court intrigue that reporters will pounce on while ignoring the steady spread of rot.

But there is consistency within the contrived chaos. As in foreign kleptocracies, the glue that holds the Trump administration together is nepotism.

Secretary of Education Betsy DeVos, who opposes public education, is the sister of military mercenary Erik Prince, a key operator in Trump's network of back-channel trades with other kleptocracies. Secretary of Transportation Elaine Chao is the wife of Senate Majority Leader Mitch McConnell, the architect of the GOP coup. In 2019, the appointment of Attorney General William Barr was followed by the appointment of Barr's son-in-law, Tyler McGaughey, as Trump's White House legal counsel and his daughter, Mary Daly, as an employee of the Treasury. These are just a few examples of the nepotism-infested administration Trump has constructed.

The longer autocrats stay in power, the smaller the inner circle becomes, and the more kinship ties tend to dominate. Parties bound by blood or marriage are easier to control. Nepotism allows for an easy accumulation of leverage: if a staffer dares to diverge from the party line, their relative's position—and if necessary, their life—can be threatened. (Witness the deadly kin rivalries in the authoritarian governments of North Korea or Saudi Arabia.) Officials who are not related by family ties in Trump's cabinet are often people who have been working together in corrupt ventures for decades. For example, Secretary of the Treasury Steven Mnuchin and Secretary of Commerce Wilbur Ross were both protégés, like Trump, of Carl Icahn, who stepped down as a White House adviser after a year following a proposed ethics investigation that was, like so many other investigations, mysteriously dropped.

Expand the circle further, and you find political actors who are tied by complicity, including, at this point, the entire GOP, which is contaminated by the influx of dark money in the 2016 election and beyond. For example, in 2017, the GOP made Michael Cohen, Trump's lawyer who would later be sentenced to three years in prison for campaign finance violations, the deputy finance chairman of the Republican National Committee. Corruption breeds loyalty out of fear. The choice is to embrace the crooked gains, hoping that the new regime will consolidate power and rewrite laws to create a sort of preemptive exoneration, or leave politics entirely. The record number of GOP officials—forty-four—who stepped down during Trump's first year in office shows the difficulty Republicans have had with this calculus.[3]

The most egregious beneficiaries of nepotism in the Trump administration are, of course, daughter Ivanka and son-in-law Jared. In the beginning, the elevation of Ivanka and Jared Kushner into the upper echelons of the administration struck many as a violation of basic tenets of American governance. The United States was founded, after all, in rebellion to a monarchy. While there have been numerous political dynasties—Roosevelts, Kennedys, Bushes—there had never been such a blatant insertion of unqualified relatives into such high positions of power. We have never seen adult children operate as official advisers from the moment a president took office. Pundits initially attempted to rationalize their rise with a baseless argument that Ivanka and Jared were a moderating influence. But the two never intervened in Trump's brutal domestic policies, nor did they counter his racist rhetoric. Instead they carried out their own illicit schemes with foreign partners, abusing executive power for personal gain.

The foreign deals Ivanka made that implicate the emoluments laws or that Jared made with Middle Eastern countries who agreed to pay down his debt as he influenced policies that favored them also serve as a perverse method of résumé-padding, especially to a gullible and sometimes compromised American press. That Jared and Ivanka's activity in office has abetted enemies of America (like Russia) or states rife with human rights violations (like Saudi Arabia) has proven irrelevant to media personalities seeking to normalize them: after all, many of these media personalities are themselves the sons and daughters of the rich and powerful. The new American economy runs on purchased merit, and now we bear the consequences on a national security level.

Adult children of authoritarian leaders are useful in multiple ways. First, they tend to be trustworthy confidants in regimes rife with paranoia, as corrupt authoritarian states are. Second, they are excellent vessels for laundering money, creating enough distance that assets stolen from the state are harder to track. Third, they tend to have a warmer public profile, which offsets the brutality of the dictator by distracting the population with pictures of their happy families or glamorous lifestyle. Fourth, a dynastic kleptocracy is the most reliable way to keep assets stolen from the state in the family. It therefore falls upon the authoritarian ruler to legitimize his offspring as successors should he be forced to leave office.

For forty years, Trump hobnobbed with elites from media, business, politics, and entertainment—and then with their offspring, as those professions became dominated by nepotism. In 2016, when Trump's "grab 'em by the pussy" *Access Hollywood* outtakes were released, America was introduced to what I have called "the Billy Bush Principle": for every asshole, there is an equal and opposite asshole. When Trump says something vile, there is an elite laughing alongside him. When Trump makes a corrupt deal, another party makes or enables that deal. They become implicated by the threat of revelation, and power is imbalanced by Trump's complete lack of shame. When Trump's *Access Hollywood* tape was released, Billy Bush (a first cousin of George W. and Jeb Bush) was fired from his job as a TV host for egging Trump on. But Trump, the shameless sexual assaulter, became the president.

The Billy Bush Principle has been an effective deterrent to documentation of Trump team activity. The insularity of the New York and D.C. political and media worlds—combined with the erosion of media and political power in the heartland—means that Trump relies more on self-censorship than state censorship. He has acquired decades of secrets and is willing to weaponize them. One notable example was when he threatened to reveal the sexual relationship between MSNBC cohosts Joe Scarborough and Mika Brzezinski (daughter of Zbigniew Brzezinski, former national security adviser for Jimmy Carter) in 2016 after the two had deviated from their standard sycophancy to raise serious concerns, most notably about Trump's love of nuclear weapons. Called out, they resumed their ass-kissing. Once they divorced their partners and decided to wed, and Trump lost his leverage, they resumed their critiques. In 2017, the two reported that Trump had threatened them with hit pieces in the *National Enquirer* and described the experience as traumatic.[4]

Trump's inner circle has long included dirty operatives like Roger Stone, who is known for withholding incriminating information on political opponents for years and then torpedoing their lives when the interests of the corrupt power brokers he favors are threatened. (Stone helped ensnare Eliot Spitzer in a prostitution scandal, for example, as Spitzer was cracking down on Wall Street;[5] the madam in that scandal, Kristin Davis, was interviewed by the Mueller probe team in 2018 for reasons still unknown.[6]) A lifetime spent scouring the gutter of politics and media gets an operative a lot of dirt, and not a lot of people willing to cross them—in part because they fear for their careers, in part because they fear for their lives, but also because sometimes the dirt extends to relatives who helped them get their powerful positions. A problem of nepotism has become a problem of national security.

The ultimate manifestation of this national security threat is Ivanka and Jared, who have both seemingly violated the law in serious ways during their time in office yet face no consequences. In 2017, it was revealed that Kushner had lied on his security clearance forms more than any person in US history.[7] Ivanka had lied too, but not quite as much as Kushner, who was also reported to have committed the following acts: lobbied for a Qatari blockade after Qatar refused to provide his family a loan to pay off its massive debt; met with the president of a sanctioned Russian bank as part of yet another debt payoff scheme; met illicitly with other Russians connected with plots to subvert the 2016 election; worked with now convicted felon Michael Flynn to devise a secret back channel to the Kremlin; attended the notorious 2016 Trump Tower meeting in which Russian election aid was offered and did not report it to the FBI; helped fire FBI head James Comey in an act constituting obstruction of justice; oversaw the Cambridge Analytica–linked digital influence and data-mining operation that became a key subject of the Mueller probe; helped Saudi prince

Mohammad bin Salman cover up the murder of *Washington Post* journalist Jamal Khashoggi;[8] illicitly proposed giving the Saudis nuclear secrets;[9] conspired with the *National Enquirer* to threaten US media figures and publish propaganda for the Saudi regime;[10] and used personal email and private apps to communicate with foreign leaders.[11] Kushner did all of this while keeping up ties to corrupt oligarchs and disgraced politicians around the world, including his old family friend, now indicted Israeli prime minister Benjamin Netanyahu.

The Jared Kushner Security Crisis exists in a perpetual cycle of déjà news, with documentation of his lawlessness recirculating without repercussions. Every few months, American pundits start to speculate that Kushner constitutes an enormous national security threat, perhaps one greater than Trump, and they begin to discuss his voluminous violations of law and protocol. This cycle lasts about forty-eight hours before its inevitable dismissal and a return to the status quo, where the repercussions of these violations—and what they mean for America—are ignored. In March 2019, I went on MSNBC and proclaimed to *AM Joy* host Joy Reid:

> This is like the twelfth time I've been on your show talking about Jared Kushner and the fact that he lied on his clearance forms, that he's done illicit dealings, that he's giving away state secrets and that he's a massive national security risk and so is Ivanka Trump. The only way we can finally stop having this conversation on national TV is if he's indicted. That is what needs to be done, because this problem is enormous. It's going to persevere. Even if he is gone, he is carrying around this information; other people are carrying around classified information. They do not have loyalty to country. They have debt, they have financial interests, they have personal interests. This problem needs to be handled now. It's ridiculous that we are in this déjà news cycle where I appear on here, as do Malcolm [Nance] and David [Cay Johnston] and others, to have the same conversation again

and again. Just indict Jared Kushner, indict Ivanka Trump, and get this crime family out of the White House!

My commentary was not well received by White House loyalists. But I was speaking from a place of patriotism. I was speaking out for my country, because the elevation of a criminal son-in-law into the world of classified intelligence is not what anyone sought when they cast their ballots—including those who voted for Trump. It is hard to overstate the danger Kushner poses to US national security, and it is hard to explain why this danger was ignored by national security officials during the campaign and continues to be ignored despite warnings and pleas from intelligence experts.

It is easy, however, to explain his rise, for he is as much a product of our times as I and my underemployed friends are. Kushner's rise was made possible by the same institutional rot that left most of my generation scrambling for survival.

Kushner, born in 1981, benefited from the culture of purchased merit and extreme income inequality built by corrupt baby boomers like Trump, and in many ways his life mirrors his father-in-law's. Like Trump, Jared was a bad student who went to an Ivy League college—only in the new Gilded Age, the grift required for Jared's brand-name education had become greater. In *The Price of Admission: How America's Ruling Class Buys Its Way into Elite Colleges—and Who Gets Left Outside the Gates*, journalist Daniel Golden writes that officials at Jared's New Jersey private school were dismayed when Jared was accepted to Harvard. As one former school official put it, "His GPA did not warrant it, his SAT scores did not warrant it," and it meant more deserving students from his high school were rejected.[12] According to Golden, Jared's father, Charles Kushner, donated $2.5 million to Harvard in 1998, the year that Jared applied, to ensure his acceptance.

Like Trump, Jared is the son of a multimillionaire real estate developer linked to criminal enterprises in the New York area. Donald's father, Fred Trump, was investigated in 1954 by a US Senate committee for profiteering, and in 1966 he was investigated for the same by the State of New York.[13] In 2018, *The New York Times* revealed that Fred had spent decades engaged in fraudulent tax schemes, including by selling real estate to Donald for well below its purchase price, and illegally manipulating the financials to benefit from a tax write-off.[14] But unlike Fred Trump, whose team of lawyers helped him avoid federal and state charges, Charles Kushner wound up a convicted felon. He was indicted in 2004 not only for tax evasion and making false statements about campaign contributions, but for a grotesque witness-tampering plot aimed at his brother-in-law, who had been cooperating with a federal investigation of the family businesses.

In 2004, Charles hired a prostitute to seduce his brother-in-law, arranged to record the sexual encounter, and had the resulting tape sent to his own sister to intimidate her and her husband. Instead of being intimidated, they were enraged. The plot—reminiscent of the blackmail tactics Trump, Stone, and others embraced under the tutelage of Roy Cohn—failed, and Charles was sentenced to two years in prison, which he began serving when Jared was twenty-three. In 2019, former New Jersey governor Chris Christie said of the case: "It was one of the most loathsome, disgusting crimes that I prosecuted when I was U.S. Attorney. And I was U.S. Attorney in New Jersey!"[15]

After graduating Harvard in 2003, Kushner, in the manner of modern-day children of millionaires, completed a series of prestigious internships—among them, a stint at the Manhattan DA's office while he was studying law and finance at New York University. His time at the DA's office seeing white-collar criminals face justice does not appear to have had any lasting moral impact on Kushner other than sympathy for the criminals themselves. In a 2014 interview, he complained, "The law is so nuanced. If you're convicting murderers, it's one thing. It's often fairly clear. When you get into things like white-collar crime, there are often a lot of nuances. Seeing my father's situation, I felt what happened was obviously unjust in terms of the way they pursued him. I just never wanted to be on the other side of that and cause pain to the families I was doing that to, whether right or wrong. The moral weight of that was probably a bit more than I could carry."[16]

For Kushner, "moral weight" is opposed to both ethics and law. "Moral weight" is whatever interferes with getting what he wants. And what he wanted in 2005 was to own 666 Fifth Avenue, a forty-one-story tower in Midtown Manhattan that became the most expensive real estate deal in New York City's history—and one of the most disastrous. Kushner bought the property for nearly twice as much on a per-square-foot basis as any previous Manhattan building sale.[17] It is unclear why he found this particular building so desirable, and why he would strike such a terrible deal in 2007, when economic experts were warning of an impending housing crash. Though his motives are unclear, the deal mirrors the kind of fraudulent real estate tax evasion schemes at which Fred Trump had excelled.

Though best known to ordinary New Yorkers for the devil's number of 666 emblazoned on the top, the building also had a storied history among New York's financial elites. It was the favored hangout of corrupt operatives like "Wolf of Wall Street" Jordan Belfort,[18] and the former headquarters of old-time Trump associates like the Lauder family: the powerful corporate dynasty that includes Ronald Lauder, head of the World Jewish Congress and a lifelong friend of Trump.[19] As of 2019, Lauder remains heavily involved with Netanyahu, Putin, and Russian oligarchs like Leviev and Roman Abramovich. Furthermore, according to Trump's book *The Art of the Deal*, it was Ronald Lauder's brother Leonard who held the 1986 dinner party where Trump was introduced to Yuri Dubinin and Vitaly Churkin, the Russian officials who brought Trump to the USSR. After Kushner purchased the property, it continued to be a site of illicit dealings. It was in the Grand Havana Room of 666 Fifth Avenue that convicted felons Paul Manafort and Rick Gates gave Kremlin operative Konstantin Kilimnik US election polling data on August 2, 2016.[20] This transaction, once at the heart of the Mueller investigation, was never fully explored after the probe abruptly ended in March 2019.

Regardless of the rationale for the purchase, there is no denying it was a dud. Following the 2008 crash, Kushner lost $90 million, and the property ended up carrying $1.4 billion in debt, which Kushner was supposed to pay off by February 2019.[21] But Kushner faced no economic or political penalty for this reckless expenditure. Instead, he benefited, and from 2009 to 2016, paid little to no federal taxes.[22] He had achieved the same end that Fred Trump had and his father almost had by "booking heavy losses on reported depreciation of his real estate holdings," according to *The New York Times*.[23] These losses overwhelmed his reported income, resulting in an artificial lowering of his income taxes and a net gain.

In the postrecession era—as young people lost opportunities, middle-aged people lost careers and homes, and elderly people lost their retirement savings—Jared Kushner built a fortune by exploiting a corrupt corporate system rigged to reward deceit. By 2018, his personal wealth had quintupled to nearly $324 million, despite every enterprise he touched—666 Fifth Avenue, the *Observer*, the White House—deteriorating in his hands.[24] This is not including the fortune wife Ivanka had made through various dirty deals, like Trump SoHo, that nearly got her indicted for felony fraud.

Both Jared and Ivanka hold an SF-86 security clearance, which requires a thorough background check in which state officials look for vulnerabilities, like debt, that can be exploited by hostile states, as well as demonstrations of deceit and disloyalty that render an individual a danger to the United States. Kushner's massive debt and tax manipulation schemes should have prevented him from holding any kind of clearance—but not in Trump's dynastic kleptocracy. Kushner's foreign ties were not a deterrent either, even though his lifelong relationship with Netanyahu—a relationship so close that Netanyahu slept in Jared's childhood bedroom when visiting the Kushner family[25]—posed an obvious conflict of interest, one that deepened when he was selected by Trump to be a liaison to the Middle East.

Raised in a strict Orthodox Jewish family, Kushner, like many in Trump's inner fold, now worships at and donates heavily to Chabad, whose religious leadership—including the deceased leader of modern-day Chabad, Rabbi Schneerson—were longtime supporters of Netanyahu and his hard-line, right-wing politics.[26] But Netanyahu is not the only right-wing state leader connected to Chabad. The biggest financial backers of Chabad are Leviev and Abramovich, two of the oligarchs closest to Putin.[27] (In 2018, Abramovich became an Israeli citizen after running into visa troubles in the West.)[28] Putin, who is not Jewish, has also embraced Chabad through his "personal rabbi," Berel Lazar.[29] Branches of the organization, like in Port Washington where Felix Sater became Chabad's "Man of the Year" twice, have served as sites of liaison for some members of the criminal cohort surrounding Trump.[30] These criminal connections of course have nothing to do with the millions of ordinary people who attend Chabad branches for religious or social reasons. The question remains why so many in Trump's circle—especially gentiles like Putin and Tevfik Arif—are so invested in Chabad, and how factions within Chabad influence Kushner's foreign policy. As investigative journalist Craig Unger notes, "Chabad provides some of the richest and unexpectedly direct sets of connections between Putin and Donald Trump."[31]

The Netanyahu connection is less mysterious. The Kushner family are investors in illegal West Bank settlements, meaning that Jared has not only a political conflict of interest by serving as a White House adviser on the Middle East, but a financial one.[32] It is also a humanitarian conflict of interest. As Netanyahu transforms Israel into a more hard-right state, employing extreme violence against Palestinians and lobbing vitriolic rhetoric against liberal Jews in Israel and in the Diaspora, extremist rabbis have flourished—and Kushner favors them. In 2018, Ivanka and Jared were blessed by Rabbi Yitzhak Yosef, who calls black people "monkeys" and believes that non-Jews exist in Israel solely to be the slaves of Jews.[33] This racist rhetoric mirrors that of the Trump administration—including that of Christian evangelicals like Mike Pence or Mike Pompeo who align with Israeli extremists in order to fill their own political ambitions and sate their own religious fanaticism.[34] Contrary to press portrayals, Jared and Ivanka were never outliers in the extremism of the Trump administration.

According to Kushner biographer Vicky Ward, Kushner's devotion to Netanyahu is all-encompassing. Aside from the countries that interest him as targets for kleptocratic shakedown schemes— like Qatar, which ultimately paid off his 666 Fifth Avenue debt through Brookfield, a company backed by the Qatar Investment Authority[35]—Israel is Kushner's major foreign policy concern. Ward writes of a December 2016 attempt by Kushner to rig a UN vote in favor of Israel before taking office (this plan required the aid of the aforementioned Churkin, who had remained in Trump's orbit decades later as Russia's ambassador to the UN):[36] "What was highly unusual was the battle between the transition team and the sitting government. It was as if Kushner viewed Netanyahu as his boss and Obama as his enemy."[37]

Had Kushner not been Trump's son-in-law, he would have never been considered for an advisory role, given his lack of qualifications, history of financial disasters and fraud schemes, and ties to gangsters, oligarchs, and dictators. The same can be said of Donald Trump, and he is the president. Unlike Trump, however, Kushner was not elected. He was appointed by a relative, another blight in a society increasingly based on nepotism. Kushner is like a hellspawn incubated in the "iron triangle" of state corruption, corporate corruption, and organized crime that Mueller warned of in his 2011 speech. But he did not create it: he inherited it.

Kushner entered adulthood in an era in which the conditions of American life had been constructed to benefit young people like him—a small band of nepotistic elites whose pursuit of profit over law or country is condoned by their elders in media and government. Given the ongoing danger his actions pose to US national security, many intelligence experts I've spoken to throughout my reporting assumed Kushner would be indicted by the FBI or special counsel or, at the least, be forced to relinquish his access to classified information. As of 2019, no such accountability has come, and that should not surprise anyone. Kushner does not need to fear the law when his father-in-law can rewrite it. That is how life works in a dynastic kleptocracy. That is how life works now in the United States of America.

Prior to Trump's campaign, Kushner tended to be portrayed as a supporting player in the endless series of puff pieces about the fashionable Ivanka. A 2008 breakup of the couple, who began dating in 2005 and married in 2009, was in part remedied by right-wing media mogul Rupert Murdoch and his then wife, Wendi Deng, who seemed to have great interest in unifying two white-collar crime families in matrimony. The owner of Fox News, the *New York Post*, and other right-wing media properties, Murdoch became a mentor to Kushner after Kushner bought the *Observer*. Meanwhile Deng, a New York socialite, befriended Ivanka, who was over a decade her junior.[38] Following the breakup, Deng invited them separately to the Murdoch family yacht, where they were reunited.[39] Ivanka and Jared soon wed, while Deng went on to divorce Murdoch, allegedly date Putin during Trump's 2016 presidential campaign, and take vacations in Eastern Europe with her old friend Ivanka.[40] Murdoch later insisted that Deng was a Chinese spy, a claim backed up by US intelligence agencies.[41]

These events seem, in retrospect, foreboding and strange. All of the players in this little love story eventually became subjects of the federal probe into election interference, with several suspected of espionage. Corruption in the federal government has become expected to some degree, but a president's social circle being implicated in multiple criminal and espionage plots spanning the course of several decades is not normal. And the refusal of the press and state officials to treat it as abnormal is part of the problem.

Few prior to 2017 believed that Jared and Ivanka would play a major role in government. Many even believed Trump when he denied that the two were being given high-level security clearances.[42]

This belief was in part due to American exceptionalism—surely Trump wouldn't really install his relatives in the White House like a third-world dictator. There was also the mistaken view that Ivanka and Jared represented mere tabloid silliness—surely two *Gossip Girl* guest stars could not destroy US foreign policy through a series of kleptocratic shakedowns. But this complacency was also because influential young people in media and politics had increasingly come to resemble Ivanka and Jared—rich, connected, and unqualified. Their insertion into the White House was consistent with an increasingly nepotistic America.

In November 2016, Jared Kushner's *Observer* newspaper wrote a hit piece on me.[43] It ran thirteen days after the election, a time period where the attention I received for predicting Trump's win and warning of catastrophes to come spurred the worst death threats of my career. These threats of violence were serious enough that I was assigned an undercover bodyguard when I spoke at an international conference three weeks after the election. Some of the people threatening me said they were inspired by the article in Kushner's paper, which proclaimed I was a Soros plant who worked for a website run by Democratic Party operative David Brock, among other falsehoods.

The main tactic of the Trump camp and their backers, I would discover over the next few years, was not to directly threaten you with violence, but to smear you to the point that a fanatic might find murdering you an appealing prospect. This was the strategy they used in "Pizzagate," when a vigilante convinced that Hillary Clinton was running a pedophilic cult out of a D.C. pizza parlor nearly shot up the place. The hit piece on me was standard fare for Kushner. Throughout his tenure as owner of the *Observer* (which he relinquished in 2017), Kushner used the newspaper as a way to target his enemies.[44] The paper was one of two in the United States to endorse Trump in an official capacity: the other was the *National Enquirer*.

My death threats tapered off somewhat once Trump was installed in January 2017. A congressional call for an investigation into Russian interference had arisen and the Trump team had far bigger problems than me. At the height of my 2016 death threats, in December, I gave an interview to *Cosmopolitan* magazine, for a column they called "Get That Life."[45] (I told the interviewer that her readers did not, in fact, want to "get this life," since this life seemed to come with a looming expiration date.) The interviewer asked why I was covering national politics from St. Louis. I answered:

> Trump pretends to speak for the forgotten men and women of the heartland. I am one of those forgotten women. I'm pushed to the sidelines a bit just by virtue of the fact that I live in Missouri. People think, if she were for real, she would live in New York. That's by choice. It allows me some more financial leeway than some of my contemporaries who are bound to the whims of their publishers or worried about their financial situations.
>
> But I don't have freedom in terms of my safety. I'm under a lot of attacks now with Trump being elected. I'm a target because I've been a forthright critic. There have been phishing schemes, threats. I'm worried about my safety and my family's safety. The *New York Observer* wrote a smear piece that singled me out and had inaccuracies; I wasn't contacted for the story. It's unnerving because I'm a journalist from Missouri and the billionaire son-in-law of the president-elect is watching me.[46]

There are people who believe that the current American political crisis began with Trump and will end with Trump if he leaves office. But it is Ivanka and Jared, and their burgeoning kleptocratic dynasty, with whom they should be most concerned. They are the products of an intergenerational crisis of inherited corruption and stolen opportunities. Because their ability to keep their fortunes and dodge prosecution is now intertwined with their ability to hold on to political power, it is unlikely they will relinquish it or leave their enemies alone. Jared and Ivanka and I are all around the same age, and our children are around the same age. They pretend to speak for me and my children—the red state rejects, the "forgotten Americans." They don't like it when we talk back.

Ironically, it's my distance from their insular New York world, my rejection of coastal careerism in favor of an independent life in St. Louis, that has given me the ability to criticize the administration that many journalists with full-time national media jobs lack. (Or, possibly, I'm reckless and stupid.) The Trump administration can't take away my press credentials because I never asked for their permission to speak. They can't get me fired because I hold multiple jobs so that no one entity can screw me over. I'm not interesting enough to blackmail and there's nothing in their rarefied world that I want: not prestige, not wealth, not awards. I'm a twenty-first-century American woman; I don't have enough faith to covet anything but freedom. Over the course of my life, every industry I worked in collapsed, and then my city collapsed, and then my government collapsed.

My career has been a series of reactions to terrible economic and political circumstances caused by the corruption of elites. The same can be said of the careers of Jared Kushner and Ivanka Trump. In the end—in this sick, sad, American story—we all came full circle.

6

2010–2016: Revolution Shakedown

B y 2010, the global recession had caused unemployment rates to soar. As economies tanked and opportunities vanished, protests broke out in North America, the Middle East, Europe, and parts of Asia. While every protest was unique, all reflected the despair citizens felt as rulers responded to economic misery with ruthless indifference. Tunisia's revolution, for example, began in 2010 when a man, Mohamed Bouazizi, set himself on fire to protest government apathy to mass unemployment. The new era of uprisings coincided with the rise of smartphones and social media, meaning that demonstrators not only became more visible, but that their methods of mobilization changed—as did state surveillance and retaliation.

At the time, I could not look away from the protests even if I wanted. Authoritarianism and digital media were the focus of my graduate school research, which had begun with a study of how Uzbeks reacted online to the slaughter of fellow citizens by their government. In May 2005, Uzbekistan's military forces fired on roughly ten thousand people who had gathered in the city of Andijon to protest the unjust imprisonment of Muslim businessmen as well as general regional hardship. On the orders of dictator Islam Karimov, more than seven hundred people were shot to death, and many Uzbek activists and journalists were forced into exile. Western media and international observers were thrown out of the country by Uzbek officials, who were desperate to deny that the massacre had occurred.

But the attempt to silence dissidents through exile backfired. Exiled Uzbeks now had freedom of speech and internet access for the first time. Scattered around the world, they launched blogs and published decades of reporting that had been banned in Uzbekistan, ranging from Soviet-era *samizdat*, underground literature, to banned reports from Andijon. The Uzbek government had claimed the jailed businessmen in Andijon were part of a terrorist group called Akromiya, which in their view had justified their own brutal retaliation. But while doing archival research, I found state documents indicating that Uzbek state propagandists had created Akromiya as a pretext to suppress civilian dissent. The more I read both the official and the eyewitness accounts of Andijon, the more suspicious I became. I published a paper, "Inventing Akromiya,"[1] which was later used by the United Nations to evaluate claims from Uzbek asylum seekers. The paper got me banned from Uzbekistan, curtailing my ability to do research in Central Asia, but I did not care. In 2006, I had to choose between my career and telling the truth. I chose the truth and never regretted it.

The Andijon massacre was one of many protests in the former USSR in the 2000s. These uprisings—which also occurred in Georgia, Kyrgyzstan, and Ukraine—were known as "the color revolutions," a reference to the colors of flowers often used as symbols of nonviolent disobedience. The uprisings yielded mixed results, ranging from democratic reforms followed by backsliding in Ukraine, to the replacement of one autocratic ruler with another in Kyrgyzstan, to the brutal massacre in Uzbekistan. Putin saw the revolutions as a threat: "We see what tragic consequences the wave of so-called color revolutions led to," he proclaimed. "For us this is a lesson and a warning. We should do everything necessary so that nothing similar ever happens in Russia."[2] These changes in governance occurred as the Russian mafia was expanding into Europe and North America, with oligarchs preying on loosened financial laws and then on financial instability. The "we" in Putin's sentence remains undefined, but at that time his network certainly stretched well beyond the borders of his country. A continual global heist requires a stable network of partners.

The Western view of protest has been marred by the fact that we hear most about those that succeed: the toppled dictators, the noble sacrifices, the inmates turned presidents. In reality, many protests fail and the protesters end up unappreciated and even demonized. There are no clear statistics on failed protests for the very reason that failed protests, especially in repressive countries, rarely reach an audience beyond those who participated. But failures have their own impact. In the aftermath of the Andijon massacre, a joke circulated on Uzbek web forums:

Q: Can an Uzbek participate in a demonstration in Uzbekistan?
A: Yes, but only once.

The joke was a dark reminder of what citizens of authoritarian states know all too well, that protest carries great risk and governments kill with impunity. They do not care who knows the extent of their brutality or the audacity of their lies; flaunting power is the point. But state power depends on the dehumanization of the victims to succeed. In the Uzbek case, the victims needed to be erased. For Uzbeks to even joke about Andijon was dangerous, for that meant acknowledging that the massacre was real. To joke, even bitterly, was to reclaim their power as witnesses to an act of state violence. This is a notable lesson about documentation in our current dictator-ridden digital era, when it is easier to be disappeared than ever before.

In the late 2000s, academia resisted examining the increasing importance of the internet to politics. Academia had always been behind the curve when it came to technology—by the 2010s, the first studies of the long-abandoned MySpace were trickling into journals—but the topic was borderline taboo in anthropology. To examine an online community meant to challenge the idea of a field site, which is the foundation of ethnographic methodology. But I saw no clear delineation between virtual and material life—not only among the scattered Uzbek dissidents whom I interviewed via the web for years, but among Americans. For all of my adult life, the digital world *was* the real world. As smartphones and social media took off, the idea that the two were disparate realms became harder to justify.

Despite its pervasiveness, I did not see the internet as an inherently democratizing force. Instead, I worried it exacerbated the worst tendencies of its users, even while giving them new avenues for self-expression. For citizens of authoritarian states dominated by conspiracy theories and lies, the internet proved a terrible tool for building trust. The same features of online discourse that people in free states found liberating—the ability to join and leave a community at will, to write under multiple identities, to preserve and resurrect old arguments—made the internet perilous for participants whose default mode was distrust due to the long-standing oppression they had experienced. You could reinvent yourself on the internet, but you could not start over.

In the early 2010s, most scholars of digital technology and politics emphasized the positive. They envisioned a borderless world in which citizens, buoyed by technology, could expose and thereby rectify structural problems. Their enthusiasm extended to social media corporations, which were often credited for a successful demonstration instead of the actual protesters. In the West, Iran's 2009 uprising was deemed a "Twitter Revolution" and the Arab Spring was called a "Facebook Revolution." Western conceptions of success led to the hardship of protesters on the ground being played down. The potential threat of their corporate supporters was also poorly discerned. Social media corporations that would grow into powerful surveillance monopolies presented themselves in the early 2010s as fellow underdogs in the broader struggle against the system. Vulnerable activists gave them their information.

Meanwhile, the assets of companies like Facebook and Google

were growing exponentially each year. During the first half of the decade, I was invited to a number of lavish events held by what digital media scholar Evgeny Morozov derisively called "cyber-utopians." In 2012, I attended a party Google held in a caravansary in Azerbaijan—another former Soviet republic run by a resource-hoarding dictator—held in part for visitors to the United Nations Internet Governance Forum. Google had arranged for a pro-government blogger to debate an anti-government blogger. They had flexed their corporate muscle to allow the anti-government blogger to get his opinion heard on the ground; a rare event in authoritarian Azerbaijan. The event was well intentioned—and again, it seems remarkable in retrospect that any Silicon Valley company even *sought* to cultivate democracy in the former USSR—but it misunderstood how authoritarian states most effectively use the internet, which is through a process called networked authoritarianism.

Networked authoritarianism, a term coined by social scientist Rebecca MacKinnon, describes an internet that is just open enough so that it can be exploited by bad actors, who use it to bombard users with propaganda, conspiracy theories, and personal attacks.[3] It is the loudest way of silencing the public voice, and is more effective than traditional state censorship, which is what more insular authoritarian regimes like Uzbekistan practice. In Azerbaijan, dissidents were allowed just enough room to speak their mind online, and then were punished by the state for doing so and held up as examples in order to intimidate the public. Two Azerbaijani friends of mine were jailed for two years after releasing a satirical online video where one mocked state lies about agricultural trade by wearing a donkey suit.[4] Another journalist friend was the target of attempted blackmail when a state surveillance agency made a sex tape of her and circulated it, with the goal of humiliating and stoking threats against her.[5] Both were paraded as cautionary tales for aspiring dissidents, and the government used the very internet that was supposed to be the source of liberation to tell them.

In the early 2010s, Russia also practiced networked authoritarianism. "Many have noted the curious absence of censorship on the Russian-speaking internet which largely remains a free-for-all zone, quite unlike traditional media which are kept on a tight leash," wrote journalist Alexey Kovalev in an optimistic 2010 editorial called "Russia's Blogging Revolution."[6] The rationale for the open internet became clear when Russian officials used it to publicize the arrests of popular dissidents like the blogger Alexey Navalny and the punk band Pussy Riot over the next few years. Instead of fearing the open internet, Kremlin officials embraced it, using social media to smear the opposition and to release a firehose of propaganda intended to overwhelm citizens' faculty for critical thinking.[7] The emergence of networks like Facebook, Twitter, and Russia's VKontakte in the 2000s and 2010s made disinformation easier to spread. The arrival of memes allowed eye-catching lies to be delivered via mobile phone, meaning users who lacked home computers could circumvent the internet entirely. Before I left academia for good, networked authoritarianism was my focus—not only because of its danger to citizens of authoritarian states, but because I could see the utility of the model in Western states that were experiencing a similar erosion of institutional trust.

In a 2011 article for *The Atlantic*, I described the Uzbek political internet, focusing on a fake Facebook account that had deceived the Uzbek dissident community—a preview of the type of fake online persona that would be weaponized in the West in 2016. I wrote:

> People involved in Uzbek politics are accustomed to rumor and lies. It's common practice to assume that all information is unreliable and all sources biased, which ensures that all rumors are taken seriously. Rumor is not automatically believed, of course, so much as it is shared, parsed, and discussed—sometimes far beyond what its dubious origins might merit. The result of ubiquitous paranoia is not disbelief. It is credulity.

When all information is assumed fraudulent and all sources suspect, when your worst suspicions about your government are routinely confirmed and denied, when on-line communication—itself nebulous and malleable—is your only means of interaction, what do you do? You follow your principles. . . . But in Uzbekistan, following your principles often gets you nowhere. And there's not much you can do about it.[8]

When I wrote this passage in 2011, I did not know that eight years later, I could substitute "America" for "Uzbekistan" and it would serve as an apt summary of Trump-era politics. I was writing during the last gasps of the internet as a potential force for democracy, before Silicon Valley companies surrendered to the filthy lucre obtained by spying on citizens and data mining personal profiles for the benefit of hostile states. It was a time when people would learn that Google's slogan was "Don't Be Evil" and not burst into ironic laughter. American exceptionalism was always an illusion, and Americans had long been prone to paranoid conspiracies, but even I was surprised by the quickness with which US political culture came to mirror that of surveillance states. I had not anticipated how quickly the cyber-utopianism embraced by internet corporations would turn into nihilist abdication of the public good.

Among the few who saw the threat clearly was computer scientist Jaron Lanier, who, in 2010, warned the public of a new danger: WikiLeaks. At the time, free speech advocates were hailing WikiLeaks, and its founder, Julian Assange, as defenders of government transparency. Their lionization of the leaker organization was largely due to frustration with the criminal impunity of the Bush administration. In February 2010, soldier Chelsea Manning exposed war crimes by sending classified documents to WikiLeaks, which WikiLeaks then published online. The emphasis on civilian victims led human rights advocates to believe that WikiLeaks would prove a formidable opponent for autocratic regimes. But after WikiLeaks dropped hacked documents from the US State Department in November, Lanier predicted the opposite—that WikiLeaks would ultimately ally with dictators and that social media networks would abet them:

> The WikiLeaks method punishes a nation—or any human undertaking—that falls short of absolute, total transparency, which is all human undertakings, but perversely rewards an absolute lack of transparency. Thus an iron-shut government doesn't have leaks to the site, but a mostly-open government does.
>
> If the political world becomes a mirror of the Internet as we know it today, then the world will be restructured around opaque, digitally delineated power centers surrounded by a sea of chaotic, underachieving openness. WikiLeaks is one prototype of a digital power center, but others include hedge funds and social networking sites.
>
> This is the world we are headed to, it seems, since people are unable to resist becoming organized according to the digital architectures that connect us. The only way out is to change the architecture.[9]

Social media sites didn't change the architecture. Instead, over the course of the 2010s, the architecture changed us. The calculus of post–Cold War politics—that democracy spreads through engagement, that technology enhances freedom—was reversed. Hostile states used digital technology not only to attack their own citizens but to attempt to transform foreign democracies into dictatorships. We saw this with Russian influence operations in elections in the United States, France, and in the Brexit referendum, among others.[10] The social media corporations that had once bragged of the internet's liberating power now helped the hijackers of democracy. Networks like Facebook abetted, whether intentionally or not, the "iron triangles" of organized crime, state corruption, and corporate criminality, and they were aided by complicit Western actors content to let their own countries die while turning a profit.

In late January 2011, I gave birth to my son. There were complications. I had to have a C-section, and my son was born with fluid in his lungs, requiring him to stay in the newborn intensive care unit. During this time, St. Louis was bracing for an ice storm so severe that most of the hospital staff was ordered to evacuate, and once my insurance ran out, I was ordered to leave too—even though that meant I would be separated from my baby and unable to see him or nurse him for days. I refused, saying I'd sleep on the waiting room floor if the insurance company kicked me out of my bed. The staff felt sorry for us and decided to let my son—who seemed to have no major problems and who turned out to be fine—leave a day early. My husband and newborn and I raced the storm home, arriving right before the roads became impassable.

There are a few things I remember about our arrival: the gratitude that we were finally home safe as a family, the way my three-year-old daughter looked back and forth between me and her new brother and said, "Oh, it got out," before returning to playing with her blocks, and the television, which was showing some kind of revolution. I had not checked the news in two weeks.

"What'd I miss?" I asked, as the screen filled with chanting protesters.

"Oh yeah, I forgot to tell you," my husband said. "Egypt had a revolution while you were in the hospital and Mubarak is on his way out."

I remember thinking that I was witnessing something beautiful. I felt inspired that my son had been born into a world that was changing for the better at last—a world where decades-long dictatorships were crumbling in the face of a new generation of resilient protesters. If it could happen in Egypt, maybe it would happen in Uzbekistan, and maybe my exiled friends could finally go home and live in peace. Maybe we were witnessing the start of a worldwide movement for freedom akin to the revolutions that had toppled communist dictators in the late 1980s and early 1990s.

In retrospect, I was extremely high on postsurgery Percocet as I thought this, but it wasn't just the drugs or the sentimentality of new motherhood talking. In 2011, the world seemed to hang in the balance between good and evil, with rapid technological change bringing new visibility to the weaknesses of autocratic regimes. We did not know that evil had already launched its own plans, transnational criminal ambitions that were far beyond the scope of a sole state fighting its citizens. Mueller's "iron triangles" speech was also in January 2011. Obama declared organized crime a national emergency a few months later. Our day-to-day lives carried on, though, and no one paid much attention to either development.

The rest of the year brought live-streamed revolution. The protests erupting throughout the Middle East and later in Russia were encouraged by sympathizers watching online from abroad. Americans began to rise up against corporate corruption: Occupy Wall Street emerged in the summer of 2011, accompanied by similar protests against austerity and income inequality worldwide. By the end of 2012, a mass movement for a fifteen-dollar-an-hour minimum wage had taken off in the United States, and in May 2013, St. Louis became the third US city to hold a large grassroots protest in favor of a living wage and a workers' union. I had been to protests in St. Louis many times before, but this one was racially integrated and not stamped out by the police, a relative rarity. I had long felt that I was born in a bad era, forever in the wrong place at the wrong time—but now I felt we had a chance for change.

In the early 2010s, activists around the world often organized together with the expectation of good faith. There was a sense in the early 2010s that awareness in and of itself mattered, that the new mediums making people more aware of citizens' suffering would therefore make them more empathetic and more likely to stand up for the afflicted. This was most evident in Syria, where activists in 2011 and 2012 sent out daily documentation of Assad's brutality, with the hope that if his war crimes were witnessed, rather than masked by state propaganda, they would be stopped. Instead, Syria became the most well-documented war in history, a shame and a failure of the international community.[11] Protesters were screaming into a moral void.

The complicity and greed of the global elite seemed the biggest barrier to change. What it both masked and enabled was worse: the rebirth of global fascism. The fringes had not yet become the center—or moved into the White House—but the movement was there. The weaponization of social media by authoritarian states and corporate intelligence agencies like Cambridge Analytica had begun; they were mapping the terrain as we obliviously inhabited it.[12] Protesters were not yet cauterized by the vicious cynicism that dominates political culture today. A nightmarish act of violence was still viewed by most as a nightmarish act of violence; not a meme, not a joke. Now we live in an era when mass shooters livestream their massacres while online forums cheer the body count like it's a video game.[13] This is the architecture of the internet that Lanier warned about, an algorithmic facilitation of cruelty and pain.

Something had broken in how we treated each other. It wasn't about civility or respectability, but about empathy, kindness, and respect. By the end of 2014, I was exhausted from a year of documenting nonstop and often inexplicable atrocities: the Syrian war, the rise of ISIS, Ebola, Russia invading and annexing Crimea, the disappearance of Malaysia Airlines Flight 370, the shooting down of a passenger airliner in Ukraine by Russia, the kidnapping of girls by Boko Haram in Nigeria, and the Israeli massacres of Palestinian civilians in Gaza. Mass harassment and threats had exploded online, fueled by misogynist movements like Gamergate and the rise of neo-Nazis—often halting productive discussions and driving participants off social media.[14] Despite pleas from the victims, social media companies did almost nothing to stop it.[15]

The troll epidemic and spread of toxic online culture is not merely a source of anguish for many users, but an ignored national security threat. Throughout 2014, female and nonwhite online activists—and in particular, black women on Twitter—noticed a shift in social media discourse that left them suspicious. In summer 2014, writers Shafiqah Hudson and l'Nasah Crockett launched the hashtag #YourSlipIsShowing to expose accounts impersonating black users and making obnoxious political claims.[16] Many of these accounts were later revealed to be Russian troll accounts seeking to map the US political landscape and prepare to influence the 2016 election.[17] Other trolls were right-wing users in the United States linked to the Russian effort: Steve Bannon (then the editor of Breitbart) and Cambridge Analytica were experimenting with social media to see how social groups could be manipulated online for political gain. According to Cambridge Analytica whistle-blower Christopher Wylie, Bannon asked employees to "test messaging around Russian President Vladimir Putin and Russian expansion."[18] However, few in power paid attention—in part because social media companies almost never took seriously the most common targets, women of color. Had Twitter taken harassment seriously and investigated the source, this facet of the Russian effort to influence the 2016 election could have been detected early. It took Congress years to identify an intelligence operation that black women pointed out in real time. The systemic racism enabling this willful ignorance put democracy in jeopardy.

Above all else, what dominates my memory of 2014 is Ferguson. The Ferguson uprising that summer marked the divide between the tentative hope of the early 2010s demonstrations and the chaotic brutality of the rest. Like other tragedies of 2014, the Ferguson protests against police brutality were a spectacle of online voyeurism, exemplified and exploited in hashtags, and a mainstay of cable news.

But I live in St. Louis. Ferguson is not a hashtag for me, it is a town five miles from my house. Ferguson is where I sent my kids to camp and shopped at strip malls. Ferguson is where most of

the workers I interviewed for my articles on the St. Louis minimum wage strikes lived. In April 2014, I published a long history
of St. Louis's impoverished black suburbs, including Ferguson,
and their residents' struggle for civil and economic rights.[19] I saw
Ferguson, and the surrounding area of North County St. Louis,
as likely to rise up against long-standing injustices. The story of
Ferguson was always there, but like most stories about St. Louis,
people did not want to hear it—including many white people in
the St. Louis region.

In Ferguson, the world saw St. Louis's heartache laid bare, and
decided it was something to devour and then dismiss. Ferguson
was a flash point, and it hurts to live through a flash point. A flash
point glimmers, it burns, sometimes so brightly it eclipses the pain
of day-to-day life. And then it is gone, and you are left alone with
that pain, amplified by the apathy with which it was so abruptly
received.

On August 9, a St. Louis friend texted me a photo of a middle-
aged black man in a tank top and jeans holding a sign, handwrit-
ten on a torn piece of cardboard, proclaiming: FERGUSON POLICE
JUST EXECUTED MY UNARMED SON!!! The photo had been posted
to an Instagram account and circulated throughout St. Louis social
media. The man holding the sign in the photo was Louis Head, the
grieving stepfather of eighteen-year-old Michael Brown. Because
violence is so common in St. Louis, my initial fear upon hearing
of the killing was that it would not be covered, making justice for
the victim's family less likely. I was worried people wouldn't care
what had happened, and in many ways, I was right. If Ferguson
taught me anything, it was that noticing and caring are two very
different things.

People often say the story of Ferguson began with a body in
the road. But Ferguson attracted attention not because of a body
but because of a person, Michael Brown, and those who loved
him—an anguished community who took to the streets and refused to leave. They were joined by a steady stream of sympathizers, and soon Ferguson dominated national headlines. Within

a week, the country learned the identity of the shooter—Officer Darren Wilson—and that Brown had been unarmed. Between August and November 2014, activists demonstrated daily, calling for Wilson to be indicted for the killing of Brown. A grand jury was convened to debate Wilson's fate, and protesters vowed to stay in the streets until justice was served. The vigil had become a protest, which became a movement.

Understanding Ferguson is not only a product of principle but of proximity. The narrative changes depending on where you live, what media you consume, who you talk to, and who you believe. In St. Louis, we still live in the Ferguson aftermath. There is no real beginning, because Brown's death is part of a continuum of criminal impunity by the police toward St. Louis's black residents. There is no real end, because there are always new victims to mourn. In St. Louis, there is no justice, only sequels.

Outside of St. Louis, Ferguson is shorthand for violence and dysfunction. When I go to foreign countries that do not know what St. Louis is, I sometimes joke, darkly, that I'm from a "suburb of Ferguson." People respond like they are meeting a witness of a war zone, because that is what they saw on TV and on the internet. What they missed is that Ferguson was the longest sustained civil rights protest since the 1960s. The protest was fought on principle because in St. Louis County, law had long ago divorced itself from justice, and when lawmakers abandon justice, principle is all that remains. The criminal impunity many Americans are only discovering now—through the Trump administration—had always structured the system for black residents of St. Louis County, who had learned to expect a rigged and brutal system but refused to accept it.

In the beginning, there was hope that police would restrain themselves because of the volume of witnesses. But there was no incentive for them to do so: no punishment locally, and no repercussions nationally. Militarized police aggression happened nearly every night, transforming an already traumatic situation into a showcase of abuse. The police routinely used tear gas and rubber bullets. They arrested local officials, clergy, and journalists for things like stepping off the sidewalk. They did not care who witnessed their behavior, even though they knew the world was watching. Livestream videographers filmed the chaos minute by minute for an audience of millions. #Ferguson, the hashtag, was born, and the Twitter followings of those covering the chaos rose into the tens of thousands. But the documentation did not stop the brutality. Instead, clips were used by opponents of the protesters to try to create an impression of constant "riots" that in reality did not occur. The vandalism and arson shown on cable news in an endless loop were limited to a few nights and took place on only a few streets.

National media had pounced on St. Louis, parachuting in when a camera-ready crisis was rumored to be impending, leaving when the protests were peaceful and tame. Some TV crews did not bother to hide their glee at the prospect of what I heard one deem a real-life Hunger Games, among other flippant and cruel comments. The original protests, which were focused on the particularities of the abusive St. Louis system, became buried by out-of-town journalists who found out-of-town activists and portrayed them as local leaders. The intent was not necessarily malicious, but the lack of familiarity with the region led to disorienting and insulting coverage. Tabloid hype began to overshadow the tragedy. Spectators arrived from so many points of origins that the St. Louis Arch felt like a magnet pulling in fringe groups from around the country: Anonymous and the Oath Keepers and the Nation of Islam and the Ku Klux Klan and the Revolutionary Communist Party and celebrities who claimed they were there out of deep concern and not to get on television. Almost none of the celebrities ever returned.

In fall 2014, the world saw chaos and violence, but St. Louis saw grief. Ask a stranger in those days how they were doing and their eyes, already red from late nights glued to the TV or internet, would well up with tears. Some grieved stability, others grieved community, others simply grieved the loss of a teenage boy, unique and complex as any other, to a system that designated him a menace on sight. But it was hard to find someone who was not grieving something, even if it was a peace born of ignorance. It was a loss that was hard to convey to people living outside of the region. I covered the Ferguson protests as a journalist, but I lived it as a St. Louisan. Those are two different things. It is one thing to watch a region implode on TV. It is another to live within the slow-motion implosion. When I would share what I witnessed, people kept urging me to call my representative, and I would explain: "But they gassed my representative too."[20]

A few days before Thanksgiving, Bob McCulloch—a prosecutor with a history of being biased in favor of police—sauntered into an evening press conference and declared that no charges would be brought against Wilson.[21] Nothing would be done to punish the killer of a teenage boy whose corpse was left in the blazing sun for four and a half hours. That November night, St. Louis the region erupted with predictable fury. Buildings were burned, activists were gassed, residents barricaded themselves inside their homes and wept. Everything about it felt sick—the mix of inevitability and uncertainty, the feeling of being watched but not seen. During the three months McCulloch had been making his case for Wilson's innocence, two more St. Louis black men, Kajieme Powell and VonDerrit Myers, were killed by police. A movement born in grief kept gaining martyrs.

In 2016, a locally well-known Ferguson protester, Darren Seals, wrote in a Facebook post: "Black death is a business. Millions and millions flowing through the hands of these organizations in the name of Mike Brown yet we don't see any of it coming into our community or being used to help our youth. I've been calling out this shit for months. People see this as an opportunity to not only build a name but make bank at the expense of the lives of people like me."[22] Seals complained about how out-of-town NGOs and online celebrities associated with Black Lives Matter had gained attention off the Ferguson brand, used that attention to raise money, and then left with the resources meant to help St. Louis—a slight

St. Louis regional activists, who had suffered severe psychological and economic hardship as a result of the protests, never forgot, as it devastated their community even further. Soon after his post, Seals was shot to death in his car, which was then set on fire. His murderer was never found. But his killing set off another Ferguson media frenzy, and the media Seals derided for their apathy toward the plight of black men created clickbait from his death.

When I look back at Ferguson now, I look back not only at Brown, who I did not know, but at dead friends and acquaintances like Seals. I look back at protesters who died due to the common reasons people die young in St. Louis: murder, denial of health care, self-medication through drugs—and whose conditions were made worse by the trauma they experienced during months of protest, and the lack of care they received in the aftermath. In July 2019, a famed Ferguson protest leader, Bruce Franks, who had been elected to Missouri's legislature in 2016 in an underdog win, announced he was resigning from politics and leaving the region to try to heal. "If I don't make this move, St. Louis is going to kill me," he said.[23] The trauma endured during Ferguson was worsened by the exploitative way violence against black and brown protesters was portrayed and consumed by mass media. At times the voracious consumption reminded me of postcards from a century ago showing white crowds cheerfully watching lynchings.

The Ferguson protests turned some local activists into online stars—the worst kind of celebrity, the kind that gives you notoriety but no protection. One of my friends, Bassem Masri, was a Palestinian-American livestreamer who achieved brief national fame for his passionate speeches denouncing police brutality and racism. Bassem was a sweet and generous person, a friend who checked in on my family when we fell on hard economic times. In November 2018, Bassem died of a heart attack at age thirty-one, and he too became the subject of online news stories full of conspiracy theories and vitriol. When one of my friends from the Ferguson movement dies, I am forced to process their death in two ways: through my own grief, and through the media coverage of distant reporters seeking to again capitalize off the Ferguson brand, pretending to care about the local activists they disregarded in daily life. There are not words for the double conscious agony of this experience.

The most reliable export of St. Louis is pain; its most reliable import is predators. All I have asked since 2014 is to stop treating people like prey, and it's not a request made out of sanctimony but a plea for survival. It's a request that goes out to everyone; it's a request that underlays everything I write. Michael Brown lost his life because Darren Wilson denied him his basic humanity. The casualties that followed included activists who refused to accept that dehumanization as the final say. To protest dehumanization, in the digital media era, is to risk your own life. It's to make yourself a target in a medium that distorts and devours you until you are no longer recognized as real.

At the one-year anniversary of the Ferguson events, reporters began relaying the lies of a new commentator: presidential candidate Donald Trump. Speaking at an Iowa news conference, he proclaimed, "You know a lot of the gangs that you see in Baltimore and in St. Louis and Ferguson and Chicago, do you know they're illegal immigrants? They're here illegally," Trump said. "And they're rough dudes. Rough people."[24]

Trump's comments were not tethered to reality in any way. Undocumented immigrants make up less than 1 percent of the population of Missouri and the foreign-born population of Ferguson is 1.1 percent. Given that the Ferguson protests were filmed around the clock for months on end, one would think someone would have noticed the presence of roving immigrant gangs. But Trump's comments were covered nonetheless, simply because he said them.

Trump had spent his life spreading dangerous racist myths and his comments on Ferguson only continued this lifelong libel streak. In 1989, he notoriously took out a newspaper ad in multiple newspapers, including the *New York Daily News,* calling for the execution of five black and Latino boys, the Central Park Five, who were falsely accused of rape and battery.[25] Accompanying his racist rhetoric about the Central Park Five and deceitful commentary on Ferguson, was his fervent multiyear "birther" campaign against President Obama. Starting around 2010, Trump began claiming Obama was not born in America and was therefore an illegitimate president. This theory gained traction at the behest of Trump and his lawyer, Michael Cohen, who ordered the lies to be printed in the *National Enquirer*.[26] It was then amplified by a network of Republicans and racists. New right-wing websites trafficked in racist propaganda, which was then echoed by the Tea Party at rallies and online. The website Breitbart, established in Israel in 2007 by the American libertarian Andrew Breitbart,[27] became more bigoted and conspiracy-oriented after Breitbart died suddenly in 2012 and was replaced with future Trump campaign manager Steve Bannon.

But the peddling of the birther myth was not limited to right-wing extremist sites. As I mentioned in chapter 2, in the early days of the internet most news sites were a replication of print. While flawed in many ways, this system still employed fact-checking as a standard practice. During the 2000s, print media and online media coexisted uneasily, with the latter often being dismissed as inherently unreliable. By the 2010s, the media industry had been so gutted by the recession that it relied on online clickbait for profit, creating an echo chamber of lies. Decontextualized tweets began to appear in articles in lieu of interviews with people whose statements—and even existence—were verified. An article would then be written about that article, and then another article about that article. Discernment was rejected for speed. All information was news, and all news was now fit to print. If a statement was uttered on television by someone famous, it was worth an article, even if the statement was untrue. Trump understood this system and capitalized on it, spreading the birther myth across cable news and onto the internet, and from his Twitter account to cable news: his own ouroboros of bullshit.

The internet strategy of Trump's team is reminiscent of "the

Big Lie," a theory of control employed by the Third Reich. Adolf Hitler—whose speeches Trump long kept by his bedside[28]—praised the strength of this mechanism and used it to turn a country against itself. He describes it as such: "In the big lie there is always a certain force of credibility, because the broad masses of a nation are always more easily corrupted in the deeper strata of their emotional nature than consciously or voluntarily. Thus in the primitive simplicity of their minds they more readily fall victim to the big lie than the small lie, since they themselves often tell small lies in little matters but would be ashamed to resort to large-scale falsehoods. It would never come into their heads to fabricate colossal untruths, and they would not believe that others could have the impudence to distort the truth so infamously."[29]

The big lie, today, finds its strength in numbers—in bots created by propaganda ministries, validated by retweets and trending topics, and repeated through aggregated content. The big lie is not only big in its audacity, but in its pervasiveness. The big lie goes unquestioned not only because of the authority behind it, but because assumptions about media integrity endured just long enough for people like Trump to use them to their advantage. Would so many outlets really reprint claims so obviously false, knowing that repetition, even in the process of rebuttal, was what made the lies linger? The answer was yes, and Republicans and racists reaped the benefits.

Birtherism was never about where Barack Obama came from. It was about where he was allowed to go. Power, for Trump, a wealthy real estate scion, was rooted in birthright, and birthright was inseparable from race. In the last few chapters, I laid out networks of nepotism and power: almost everyone in them is not only wealthy, but white. As the son of a Kenyan, bearing the middle name Hussein, Obama shattered the image of what an American president could be. To many Americans, this change was exhilarating. To wealthy white men of limited merit, who had long benefited from racial and ethnic exclusion, it was a threat—and a rich source of propaganda. As the false recovery from the 2008 crash wore on, Trump insisted to white people that illegitimate outsiders, including Obama, had taken what should have been theirs. In ways both overt and subtle, Trump promoted whiteness as assurance of immunity from hard times.

The overt racism stoked by Trump and his cohort was reflected in major policy changes. Racism never fixes itself. Throughout US history, bigotry has had to be constrained through law, often through measures that were unpopular with white people at the time. Whiteness was always social and economic currency in America, and the myth of a "postracial" society after Obama's win was as illusory as the myth of a post-2008 economic recovery. These twin myths enabled a crisis that liberal power brokers did not seem to recognize, even though it is the classic path to demagoguery. They did not see the danger of a rise in bigotry coinciding with an explosion of economic pain—or how savvy political operatives could play the two off each other if the law did not constrain their malicious intent.

During Obama's tenure, the inability of lawmakers to see US society for what it was shattered the rights of vulnerable Americans. Two major Supreme Court rulings—the 2010 *Citizens United* ruling and the 2013 partial repeal of the Voting Rights Act (VRA)—shifted power away from the people and into the hands of elites with extremist views and shady foreign ties. The long-term domestic agenda of the radical right, aimed at disempowering ordinary people and especially people of color, made gains while other threats—like transnational organized crime—exacerbated them. People like Paul Manafort were ideal stewards of this new machinery, and the lack of attention given to them when it mattered is, in the worst sense, a validation of their skill.

The *Citizens United* ruling allowed dark money to dominate elections, removing accountability and transparency from the process and allowing not only corporations but foreign money to shape the political process. Kremlin-affiliated oligarchs poured money into the National Rifle Association, which then dispersed it to their preferred Republican candidates under the guise of American donorship. This meant that many Republicans—and some Democrats—took money that had likely been collected and laundered by the Russian mafia, as well as by other international criminal operations; an act that renders them either witting or unwitting actors in a criminal plot, and possibly even targets of blackmail by those who carved out the cash.

Meanwhile, the partial repeal of the VRA—which the Supreme Court passed with a statement saying that protections against racism were no longer necessary, one month before George Zimmerman was acquitted for murdering Trayvon Martin—allowed states to pass new repressive voter ID laws that disenfranchised black and Latino voters. In Wisconsin, over two hundred thousand voters were blocked from the polls. Clinton lost the state by only twenty-three thousand votes.[30] There are many ways to rig an election. This one was carried out in plain sight, under the auspices of lawmakers who proclaimed America to be well and good. The bedrock of autocracy is laid with the abdication of vigilance.

In December 2012, Congress passed the Magnitsky Act, named for Russian tax accountant Sergei Magnitsky, who died in a Russian federal prison after exposing large-scale theft from the Russian state, sanctioned and carried out by Russian officials. Magnitsky had been tortured and deprived of medical care before his sudden death at age thirty-seven. The Magnitsky Act was intended to bar Russian officials believed to be associated with his death from entering the United States or using its banking system. In 2012, the bill passed overwhelmingly through a bipartisan resolution, which Magnitsky's American advocate, Bill Browder, attributed to the fact that there "wasn't a pro-Russian-torture-and-murder lobby to oppose it."[31]

Times have changed.

The Magnitsky Act was one of the few serious attempts by Congress to curb Russian organized crime and influence-peddling during the Obama administration. During his 2012 presidential debate with Mitt Romney, Obama laughed off the Russian threat, telling Romney: "The 1980s called—they want their foreign policy back."[32] But even after the dangers of Putin's Russia were clear, the administration did little to combat them. Obama's second term was particularly egregious in its dereliction of duty. In 2013, Russia gave shelter to Edward Snowden, an NSA employee who had fled there with an enormous cache of stolen classified documents. In 2014, Russia invaded Crimea and then held an illegal referendum that allowed the Kremlin to annex Ukraine territory. In 2015, Russia committed war crimes in Syria and began its illicit influence operations in Western elections—not only in the United States, but in the United Kingdom prior to the Brexit referendum. Before and while this was happening, the Obama administration continued to cut funding for research on the former Soviet Union and did not behave as if its actions posed a serious threat to the United States.

At the time, this negligence seemed of a piece with Obama's lack of interest in the former USSR as well as his obligation to confront a cavalcade of other disasters: in particular, Syria, ISIS, and domestic crises like the recession and a sharp rise in gun violence. But when does complacency turn into complicity? The Obama administration was far from unique in its lenience toward corrupt Russian actors. James Comey had removed Russian mob boss Semion Mogilevich from the FBI Ten Most Wanted list in late 2015, right when Trump's lackeys Felix Sater and Michael Cohen were conspiring to bring him into power with Putin's assistance. Meanwhile, members of the GOP were actively pursuing financial and personal relationships with Russian oligarchs, mafiosos, and spies. Some of these relationships were revealed during Mueller's investigation, and showed ties going back years and even decades. Again, where was law enforcement when it mattered?

Throughout Obama's second term, Trump solidified his already strong relationship with the Kremlin and related parties. In November 2013, Trump hosted the Miss Universe pageant in Moscow in concert with the Agalarov family, Azerbaijani-Russian billionaires who are also associates of the Kremlin.[33] "Do you think Putin will be going to the Miss Universe pageant in November in Moscow?" Trump tweeted that June. "If so, will he become my new best friend?"[34]

Three years later, in June 2016, the lawyer of the Agalarovs, Rob Goldstone, attended Donald Trump Jr.'s infamous Trump Tower meeting with other Kremlin allies and Trump campaign members. At this meeting, they discussed easing the sanctions that had been enforced by the Magnitsky Act presumably in exchange for Russia helping to ensure a Trump victory.[35]

The sheer volume of Trump officials who have done and are still doing questionable business with Russian oligarchs is startling. In 2013, Exxon chief and future secretary of state Rex Tillerson received the Order of Friendship medal from Putin.[36] In 2018, Trump legal lackey Rudy Giuliani was asked to register as a foreign agent by the Senate due to his work for entities affiliated with Ukraine's Kremlin-affiliated Party of Regions, the same party for which Manafort worked.[37] Attorney General Bill Barr worked for the law firm representing Alfa-Bank, which was a target of the Mueller probe, and received money from Vector group, a holding company with deep financial ties to the Russian state.[38] Treasury Secretary Steven Mnuchin was a target of Senate inquiry due to his financial ties to oligarchs Len Blavatnik and Oleg Deripaska, the latter for whom he relieved sanctions when he took over at Treasury in defiance of congressional rulings.[39]

Then there are the campaign managers. One can start, of course, with Paul Manafort, whose entire career was dedicated to the pursuit of blood money, including his years in the 2010s spent working as an operative in Ukraine alongside GOP consultant (and now convicted felon) Rick Gates in order to benefit a pro-Kremlin candidate, while doing the bidding of Russian oligarch Deripaska on the side. Manafort was not the only campaign manager from the 2016 election to engage in this activity. Multiple political operatives from both sides of the aisle have worked for

Kremlin allies, oligarchs, and mobsters, including Bernie Sanders's chief strategist Tad Devine, liberal lobbyist Tony Podesta (the brother of Hillary Clinton's 2016 campaign chairman John Podesta), and Lanny Davis, a family friend of and former consultant for the Clintons. In 2018, Davis, an attorney, was simultaneously representing oligarch Dmitry Firtash, who has been indicted on racketeering and worked with Mogilevich, and Michael Cohen, who is linked to Mogilevich through his family's business connections.[40]

Then there is the FBI. During the Bush and Obama eras, two former heads of the FBI, William Sessions and Louis Freeh, began working as attorneys for the Russian mafia they used to fight. In 1997, Sessions traveled to Moscow and came back warning the world that the Russian mafia, headed by Semion Mogilevich, posed a severe threat to global stability—but a decade later, Mogilevich became his client. Louis Freeh, who succeeded Sessions, took on Russian clients including Prevezon, a real estate firm accused by the US government of laundering more than $200 million in a Russian tax fraud scheme, after his tenure in the FBI ended. Prevezon is the same company whose scandal culminated in the death of Sergei Magnitsky.[41]

Most of this activity is technically legal, but exceptionally strange. The Magnitsky Act was supposed to punish oligarchs and curb their influence. It offered clear moral and legal guidelines, and its importance as a foundational document was enhanced when Russia illicitly influenced our election and helped install a Kremlin puppet as president. Why did so many officials who had sworn to protect the United States, including two FBI heads, go on to work with the Russian mafia? Why would this be an attractive prospect after they themselves had alerted the world to the mafia's danger? There are plenty of routes to personal profit. Why choose the one that is in direct ethical conflict with current US policy and may endanger your country?

As American officials capitulated, Russian oligarchs shored

up influence through other means. They spent the postrecession era investing in US banks, corporations, real estate, social media companies, and nongovernmental organizations, to the point that the head of the Hudson Institute's Kleptocracy Initiative, an American organization dedicated to exposing the threats of kleptocratic regimes to civic life, quit in protest when it was found that the Kleptocracy Initiative was secretly bankrolled by Ukrainian-born oligarch Len Blavatnik.[42]

The Trump administration is a transnational crime syndicate masquerading as a government. The foundation of this edifice was formed not when Trump took office, but decades before, through prolonged engagement with criminal or criminal-adjacent actors linked to hostile regimes, in particular, the Kremlin and its oligarch network.

For a few years after my Ph.D., I served on occasion as an expert witness in court for asylum seekers from authoritarian states in Central Asia, some of whom had escaped the Andijon massacre. I did not get paid for this work. I did it because people needed help, and I was one of few people who could give it. One family paid me with a home-cooked Uzbek meal—one that was delicious and went on for several hours, as home-cooked Uzbek meals tend to do.

Another man couldn't afford to give me anything. But after he became a US citizen, he wrote me a letter of gratitude that I used to look at when I was feeling bad. It reminded me that I had done something indisputably good: I had helped save a man's life. After Trump was elected, that man wrote me again, because he was terrified he was going to be placed on the Muslim registry. I hadn't saved anyone. I had fucked it all up, I had helped him go from one hell to another, a hell that now endangered me, too. The nightmares I had been fending off had come home in the form of the Trump administration: a white supremacist kleptocracy linked to a transnational crime syndicate, using digital media to manipulate reality and destroy privacy, led by a sociopathic nuke-fetishist, backed by apocalyptic fanatics preying on the weakest and most vulnerable as feckless and complicit officials fail to protect them.

You can be prepared for something but that does not make the pain of it any less: the pain you feel for others, or the pain you feel inside, the pain you push away daily because if you gave in to it you would never get out. You lie to your children all day because you have to tell the truth in public, and because your heart can't bear breaking theirs.

The truth you tell is what the world does not want to hear. People are afraid, and fear makes them furious. You become the object of their wrath because the real threat feels unstoppable. When they're angry, they send you graphic threats and tell you that will be your fate if you keep talking about investigations or indictment or impeachment. When they feel good, they offer you their delusions born of fear and nostalgia and groupthink, a category they like to call "hope." When they are desperate, they rhapsodize about secret saviors and their impenetrable agendas to fix it all, insisting that things cannot be this bad, that there must be sealed indictments and steady hands. They sing you a liturgy of "trust the plan" and you want to cover your ears and scream but you know in a few months, when the plan falls apart and the saviors are revealed as empty vessels, they are going to need someone to listen to them about that too.

You know what's coming but you don't know how to stop it. There's no logic to this orchestration, there's just raw power, and you, with your stripped-down city and low-down life, seem to have the exact wrong amount: enough to make the wrong people angry, not enough to make the right people act. When you write, you imagine the censorship of your material as you go, wondering how many times the word "allegedly" will get slapped on these cold hard facts. You realize this is how your writer friends in autocratic states tell you they write their works too, and you try to

shake the mind-set off, but it's impossible. Despite your sanctimo-
nious struggle, it still got you, it's inside you: you've arrived.

You wonder if—should things go the way they tend to go for
people like you at times like these—if the new deep fake technology will alter you in your digital afterlife, so that you never said
the things you said and never did the things you did. You wonder
whether your children will see it and if they will be able to tell
truth from fantasy when you are not around to teach them anymore. You cannot believe people still talk about the legacy of leaders like it constitutes leverage—like the future is going to be real,
like the continuum hasn't been disrupted, like the ability to erase
the past were not easier than ever before.

You wish you lived in a time when people were more haunted
by the past than by the future.

The television tells you not to stress so much, *there's a plan*,
take it easy, *there's a plan*, of course officials would never just let
this happen, of course they hadn't been letting it happen for your
entire life. You look to your leaders, since they must have some
value: after all, everyone is so into being followers these days.
Most leaders have gone ominously silent on the obvious threat,
but you find some unexpected advice on dealing with stress from
Donald Trump. The quote is from Trump's 2004 CNN interview
with Larry King, who you remember as a celebrity interviewer
from your childhood but who was paid $225,000 in 2011 to do
a puff piece interview with a Kremlin-friendly oligarch and whose
show now airs on Russian state media, because seemingly everyone on earth now has a side hustle with the Kremlin.[43] But since
calming down and obeying the leader are the orders of the day—
the orders, repeated like the drumbeat of a racing heart—you decide to see what he has to offer:

> Caller: I'd like to know how you handle your stress.
> Trump: I try and tell myself it doesn't matter. Nothing
> matters. If you tell yourself it doesn't matter—like you do
> shows, you do this, you do that, and then you have earth-

quakes in India where 400,000 people get killed. Honestly, it doesn't matter.[44]

You try to tell yourself that this interview doesn't matter either. But of course, it does. It all matters. And you're locked alone again in realization, staring into the tunnel at the end of the light.

7

2016–2019: "A Threat More Extensive Than Is Widely Known"

On Halloween 2016, I took my kids trick-or-treating in my neighborhood, came back, and found my Twitter timeline looking like a John le Carré novel.

What I had been suggesting for months had been confirmed: Trump was a Kremlin asset. To say that Trump is an asset is not to say he directly follows Kremlin orders, but that the Kremlin had exploited or compromised him in order to carry out their goals. This had seemed probable for years given his relationship with Russian oligarchs and his unwavering reverence for Putin. In fact, his admiration of Putin was his most consistent foreign policy stance. His relationship is only further exacerbated by the many Trump campaign staffers with ties to the Kremlin or subsidiaries like WikiLeaks, and by summer 2016 it seemed obvious that the Kremlin saw the Trump campaign as a useful vehicle for its anti-American objectives—*at the least*—and that Trump had no objection to being used.

The best argument that Trump was *not* a Kremlin asset was the belief that, if a Kremlin asset were running for president, surely someone would step in and stop it. Every day of inaction by state officials therefore validated the Trump camp's insistence that the

Russia story was a hoax, or at the least, not a serious threat to US security and sovereignty. Every time Trump's lies were normalized, every insistence that Clinton was destined to win, every day someone proclaimed that even if he won, checks and balances would constrain his agenda, served to soothe the consciences of reluctant Trump voters and cynical nonvoters alike.

As evidence mounted, however, accepting Trump's assertion that he had "nothing to do with Russia"[1] became an act of willful denial. Trump asked Putin to get him Clinton's emails at a July 27 press conference; the RNC platform was altered by Paul Manafort in August to appease his Kremlin-friendly oligarch benefactors by reducing aid to Ukraine.[2] That same month, Senate Minority Leader Harry Reid warned that the threat from Russia "is more extensive than is widely known and may include the intent to falsify official election results"—a damning assertion that received little attention.[3] In October, Hillary Clinton proclaimed from the debate stage that Trump was a puppet of Putin—an evidence-based claim that was framed by much of the media as a subjective smear. The Obama administration largely remained silent, but finally admitted on October 7 that "the Russian Government directed the recent compromises of e-mails from U.S. persons and institutions, including from U.S. political organizations."[4] But that admission—an admission of a foreign attack—was drowned out by the release of the *Access Hollywood* video the same day.

On October 28, James Comey reignited suspicion against Clinton by declaring that an FBI investigation of her emails had been reopened. The FBI targeting of Clinton, who turned out to be innocent, and simultaneous silence on Trump prompted a second letter from Reid, who stated: "In my communications with you and other top officials in the national security community, it has become clear that you possess explosive information about close ties and coordination between Donald Trump, his top advisors, and the Russian government . . . The public has a right to know this information."[5] Reid accused Comey of violating the Hatch Act, a federal law that prohibits partisan activity by federal employees.[6]

On November 7, Comey backtracked on Clinton, stating that there was no longer a new investigation, but refused to comment on the FBI's inquiry into Trump. During that ten-day period, roughly eight million Americans voted early, with Comey's insinuation of Clinton's guilt the final word they heard on the issue.

But the truth, or at least a rough cut of it, was working its way out. On October 31, 2016, journalist David Corn at *Mother Jones* published the first summary of what would become known as the Steele dossier.[7]

Corn reported that an intelligence source, who in January 2017 was revealed by BuzzFeed to be veteran British intelligence officer Christopher Steele, had, during the course of an investigation for a private intelligence firm, discovered that Trump had been working with the Kremlin since at least 2011. Corn said Steele maintained that "Trump and his inner circle have accepted a regular flow of intelligence from the Kremlin, including on his Democratic and other political rivals."[8] Steele told Corn that he was shaken by what he had found, and that he had gone to the FBI with evidence, only to see those members of the FBI turn around and give the information to members of Trump's inner circle. Later, the founder of the private intelligence firm who hired Steele to compile the dossier, Fusion GPS, stated that the publication of the dossier had led to the sudden death of one dossier source, implying that Steele's life might also be at risk.[9]

Steele was horrified when *The New York Times* ran a story on November 1—the day after Corn's bombshell—titled INVESTIGATING TRUMP, FBI SEES NO CLEAR LINK TO RUSSIA. The article, which was frequently cited over the next year to validate Trump's claim that his illicit ties to Russia were an elaborate hoax, contradicted what both Steele and other interviewees had said. The editor of *The New York Times*, Dean Baquet, had ordered the article to be rewritten so that it reflected an alternate and inaccurate narrative—one contradicted by his writers' own interviews with FBI officials.[10] One of the authors of the article, Eric Lichtblau, later quit the *Times* in part because of the way Baquet had handled that article. The *New York Times* public editor, Liz Spayd, wrote about how the newspaper had chosen to ignore or play down Trump's Russia ties and illicit attempts to influence the election in a November column.[11] She was harshly criticized by upper management,[12] and in May 2017 *The New York Times* fired Spayd and then eliminated the public editor position entirely.[13]

Corn's exposé shook loose the hesitation many journalists felt about revealing what they had heard about Trump's decades of illicit activity, a hesitancy based not only on fear of retaliation, but fear of sounding hysterical. After all, the story sounded far-fetched. Obviously, the host of *Celebrity Apprentice* could not be a foreign asset, even though all evidence indicated that he was? Disparate political observers began revealing the details they had heard about the Steele dossier, which I had first encountered through the 2016 rumor mill, as well. The main rumor was that the Russian government had obtained recordings of Trump engaged in illegal or compromising sexual activity abroad.

As I scrolled through Twitter, I noticed that an independent journalist, Andrea Chalupa, had tweeted: "In intel circles, the story goes FSB filmed Trump in an orgy while in Russia. Yes, this all ends in a Trump sex tape." I added my own tweet to hers— "OK, I guess since it's out there now, I've heard this multiple times as well . . . with some very nasty details. No confirmation though." The next day, the two of us ended up side by side in a *New York* magazine piece detailing the numerous Trump sexual kompromat theories.[14] We refer to this article now as our "wedding photo." It was the perverse beginning of an enduring friendship.

Andrea and I began to text each other about what we had heard. What she told me went beyond even my worst suspicions. Her sister, Alexandra Chalupa, had been working as a part-time researcher for the Democratic National Committee when she heard that Manafort had joined the Trump campaign. The Chalupa sisters, Ukrainian-Americans from California, were alarmed since they had tracked Manafort's dangerous intervention into Ukraine's politics in 2014, as well as his long history as an operative working for blood money.

In spring of 2016, Alexandra informed the Democratic Party of her suspicion that Manafort was going to intervene in the race on behalf of Russia. She also alerted the FBI. She told them that her email had been hacked and that she was afraid Russia had penetrated the DNC and would use their private emails to blackmail or humiliate them. Her claim was soon validated by the summer 2016 release of over twenty thousand stolen emails by WikiLeaks, and was further validated by the Mueller Report and the multiple indictments Manafort faced in 2017. Manafort's criminal history was so expansive he was initially set to potentially face over three hundred years in prison[15]—until the judge in his case, T. S. Ellis, was threatened to the point that he had to be protected by US Marshals.[16] Ellis said that the jury was also receiving threats. He refused to make their names public, saying he feared for their safety.[17] Despite the threats, Manafort's trial led to a conviction, which Manafort then attempted to circumvent through a plea deal with Mueller—a deal that he broke. At Manafort's sentencing months later, Ellis shocked the country by proclaiming Manafort—now well known by Americans as a crime machine—a man who had led an "otherwise blameless life." He reduced his sentence to below the recommended guidelines, prompting a series of ethics inquiries that were later dismissed.[18] No one followed up on the threats to Ellis—a frightening pattern that played out with many who attempted to hold the Trump team accountable.

Alexandra Chalupa was one of the first Americans to face threats for investigating illicit activity between the Trump campaign and Kremlin operatives. Throughout 2016, she endured break-ins into her home and car, menacing voicemails, stalkers who followed her while she was out with her children, and other acts of intimidation intended to silence her.[19] In fall 2017, when the Manafort indictment had made it impossible for Trump's team to deny their relationship with Russia, they tried to flip the script and say the *real* danger was Alexandra Chalupa asking Ukrainians about Manafort during her independent research—an inquiry she had made out of concern for the national security of the United States. Among those who have targeted her include Rudy Giuliani, the Kremlin, Sean Hannity and other Fox News hosts, and Matthew Whitaker (later interim attorney general), whom Manafort told to target Chalupa well into 2017, when Manafort himself was under FBI investigation.[20] Alexandra Chalupa contends today that Manafort was targeting her even from prison, a plausible claim given he was indicted for additional criminal activity behind bars, which he was able to commit after inexplicably being given internet access.

Along with her sister Alexandra, Andrea Chalupa became the subject of hit pieces meant to inspire people to discredit their findings and incite people to commit violence against them through inflammatory allegations. As Andrea's friend and later her partner on a podcast we cohost, *Gaslit Nation*, as well as an outspoken public figure myself, I was similarly targeted. Death threats are now part of my life. Over the years, the threats have varied in their intensity, and I have had to have a private security team at several speaking events. As a writer, I lack the ability to afford that level of security at home. But as someone who has studied authoritarian states my whole life, I know how this tends to end. I try to take the attitude my fellow St. Louisan writer Elijah Lovejoy held over a century ago and speak out while I have the chance.

One of the most horrific realizations when your government is hijacked from the inside is that there is no official to whom you can turn—because it is rare to find an official who cannot be turned by a corrupt operator. Living for legacy, living for security, living for money—it makes no difference, they are not living for you. There had been a coup, and we were on our own.

By November 2016, the FBI had begun to exhibit bizarre behavior, including tweeting out files praising Fred Trump as a philanthropist from its little-used Twitter vault account, while simultaneously releasing negative files about the Clintons. Combined with Comey's actions, this contributed to one of Trump's most successful methods of attack: ceaseless insinuations of wrongdoing that provide little new information about their target but create confusion and suspicion.

On November 1, a former State Department official, Steve Pieczenik, announced in a video that the Trump campaign had pulled off a coup with FBI assistance and that Obama was standing down.[21] Most people ignored this because Pieczenik is regarded as a kook, but this dismissal displays a gross miscalculation of how authoritarian states operate in the digital age. In authoritarian states, conspiracy narratives function both as a method of intimidation and as a way to rally followers. To dismiss those who propagate such narratives as "only conspiracists" is to ignore that *Trump* is a conspiracist who is surrounded by other conspiracists— and that the narratives of seasoned intelligence officials like Steele and alleged lunatics like Pieczenik were lining up in horrific ways.

There is no "normal" narrative anymore. The paranoia of American politics is nothing new, but in the twenty-first century, it was newly exploitable. "In a populistic culture like ours, which seems to lack a responsible elite with political and moral autonomy, and in which it is possible to exploit the wildest currents of public sentiment for private purposes, it is at least conceivable that a highly organized, vocal, active, and well-financed minority could create a political climate in which the rational pursuit of our well-being and safety would become impossible," wrote Richard Hofstadter in his 1964 book *The Paranoid Style in American Politics*.[22] That minority buried itself in institutions for decades, infiltrating, debasing, and over time merging with the organizations they sought to destroy. They hid in plain sight, pulling the fringes to the center, and thereby ensured that the center could not hold—and that exposure of this corruption would be dismissed as conspiracy-mongering. What Americans rejected in 2016 was not trust but discernment. A criminal can bury the truth in a conspiracy because no one will believe it except those accustomed to parsing absurdities, who are then mocked as insane.

By midnight on November 8, my worst fears came true. Trump had won the election, and the GOP had won the Senate by margins that went wildly against polling expectations, including in my state of Missouri. I thought it was plausible that Trump had legitimately won Missouri, but the results of the governor and Senate races were unexpected. I was not surprised when the loser of the Senate race, Jason Kander, started an election integrity advocacy group after his loss, though Kander never linked this effort to his own defeat. I was also not surprised when, over the course of the next few years, officials gradually revealed that Russian hackers had targeted election systems in 2016 in all fifty states.[23] The most damning evidence of this was brought forward by NSA whistleblower Reality Winner, a twenty-five-year-old Air Force veteran who anonymously sent proof of the attacks to the website *The Intercept*. *The Intercept* then published the leaked information in a way that made Winner easy for officials to identify and then arrest.[24] *The Intercept* is home to Glenn Greenwald, the journalist famous for aiding Kremlin abettor Julian Assange and Edward Snowden, who gained asylum in Russia after fleeing the United States with classified documents.

In 2018, Winner was jailed under the Espionage Act and was given the longest sentence in US history for her particular offense, totaling sixty-three months.[25] She is banned from speaking to the press. No government official has bothered to interview Winner about her explosive findings, not even Robert Mueller.[26] There remains to this day a publicly available NSA document showing that US voting infrastructure was attacked. It floats around cyberspace like an unheeded warning, attracting no hearings beyond the one that sent Winner to prison. Winner was soon joined by other federal whistle-blowers: Natalie Mayflower Edwards, indicted for exposing that Russia had infiltrated the Treasury in 2015; and Tricia Newbold, a White House employee suspended for exposing that security clearances had been knowingly given to staffers who violated national security protocol.[27] Among those staffers were Jared and Ivanka. The Trump administration whistle-blowers have all been women whose findings are marginalized by officials and the press. This is not surprising. To take the evidence seriously means to challenge the fundamental legitimacy of Trump's election, and all of the decisions—appointments, laws, arrests—that came after. Trump has spent his life silencing inconvenient women, and as president he does the same.

At 3 A.M. on November 9, after Trump had been announced as president-elect, I called Andrea Chalupa. We had never spoken on the phone, but I did not know who else to turn to. She was among the few people unsurprised and determined to face this grim new reality head on. We spent hours reviewing the results and examining the possibilities of what had happened. By the morning, we had come to the conclusion that Trump, working with an international criminal syndicate connected to the Kremlin, had illegally influenced the 2016 election, possibly altered vote results, and would build a kleptocracy while curtailing civil rights, starting with immigrants and anyone who is not white. This turned out to be what happened, but at the time our serious concerns were dismissed as hysteria. The level of denial in the media, especially among New York and D.C. establishment reporters, was staggering. I spent weeks privately begging high-profile reporters with more connections and resources than me to follow the Trump team money trail. I urged them to start with Manafort, only to be told by them that Manafort was not a problem. Manafort had been on the Sunday shows, they assured me, and networks don't put criminals on the Sunday shows.

Despite these obstacles, Andrea and I kept going. Autocracy moves fast, and once an autocrat gets in, it is very hard to get them out. We figured we had two and a half months to educate the country about what to expect when your country is expecting a dictator. We were joined in our efforts by many other journalists, scholars, activists, and concerned citizens. We launched a movement demanding a vote audit in the three states with the closest victory margins—Michigan, Pennsylvania, and Wisconsin. On November 4, Manafort had abruptly reemerged on Twitter to declare that "battleground states" were "moving to Trump en masse."[28] The Mueller report later revealed that Michigan, Pennsylvania, Wisconsin, and Minnesota were the states Manafort had designated as "battleground states" during his illicit meetings with alleged Kremlin operative Konstantin Kilimnik.[29] But the vote audit movement failed. Not only was there no audit, but the call to action was hijacked by Putin gala guest and Green Party presidential candidate Jill Stein, who used some of the money panicked citizens had donated to pay her own legal fees.[30]

I barely slept from Election Day until the inauguration. I reached out to everyone I saw expressing the same concerns I did in an attempt to build a coalition. I did multiple interviews nearly every day, trying to warn the public. I wrote a series of articles explaining how American authoritarianism would happen. This is the same work I had done throughout 2016, writing mostly for Canadian and Dutch outlets because they were more willing to print stark criticisms of Trump than American outlets. They were also more willing to abide my most controversial Trump thesis, which was that he would win. Meanwhile, my book *The View from Flyover Country*, a collection of essays discussing the collapse of institutional stability and social trust in the United States, suddenly became a bestseller. People asked me if I was happy about that and I told them if they thought I could possibly be happy right now, then they had missed the point of the book.

Over the course of 2016, I never played down what I saw coming except on a few occasions when I thought voicing my worst fears would do more harm than good, and those instances haunt me still. An acquaintance in St. Louis told me with nervous excitement that his mother, from Pakistan, had become a US citizen, and was voting for the first time. He asked me to assure them that Trump would not win, because his mother was terrified of being persecuted as a Muslim immigrant who wears a hijab. I told him I thought Clinton had a good shot, which was the best I could offer without lying outright, and he texted me a picture of his mother in line for the voting booth that I still keep on my phone. I am the last person who needs to be reminded of the human toll of this administration, but I cannot bring myself to delete this photo, a reminder of what we once had, and how in a single day so much more than an election was lost.

From Election Day onward, I took every public speaking invitation I was offered, most unpaid, in order to try to reach people more powerful than me and convince them that our country was in grave danger. This effort included debating Matthew Boyle, a staff writer at Breitbart, at an international conference on media in Denmark in late November 2017. I had been asked to speak at this conference before the election, with the organizers assuming that Clinton would win and we would be discussing Trump's next media moves. But with Trump the president-elect, Brexit architect Nigel Farage a featured conference speaker, and a series of threats indicating that I was not safe abroad, I was assigned a round-the-clock undercover bodyguard. This was kept secret throughout the conference and I have never discussed it in public. My bodyguard watched silently from the sidelines as I answered a question about Breitbart hiring members of ethnic minorities to write bigoted articles about other ethnic minorities:

> I do think it matters what your editorial makeup is, and I think that if our media wasn't dominated by white men you might see different coverage and different concerns being emphasized. But I think the most important thing is: What is the result of this coverage? It doesn't matter who is working there if you're putting out anti-Semitic content, anti-Muslim content, anti-black content, conspiracy theories—things that lead to actual hate crimes, things that lead to physical assaults, things that lead to kids in schools getting bullied

right now as a result of this rhetoric. That rhetoric matters. Whether you say that you're just kidding, whether you say someone of this ethnicity or race works there—that doesn't matter. What matters is who gets hurt. And the obligation of a journalist is to serve the public. The obligation of a politician is to serve the public. And the public is not getting served. The public is being served conspiracy theories and hate rhetoric, and it's leading to actual repercussions that are terrible for our democracy, and have hurt people badly, and I don't think that journalists are doing a good job standing up for the most vulnerable citizens which is absolutely what their priority should be.[31]

The audience, comprised of journalists from around the world, applauded hesitantly, most looking stunned, a few looking angry, and fewer still looking pleased. I do not think most of the white journalists understood why I spoke with such urgency, but maybe they do now. I hope so.

In January, I was invited to a conference of journalists and tech corporation employees in Palo Alto to discuss the problem of "fake news," a hot topic after the election. This event was one of many post-Trump misadventures in which I was invited somewhere fancy as a token "red state journalist who had predicted Trump would win," leading people who had apparently never read anything I had written to assume I also approved of that outcome. When I opened my mouth to speak, they seemed as startled by my warnings about Trump as they were that I had all my teeth. I learned over the next year that many in coastal media seemed to assume I led a *Deliverance*-style life surrounded by a squad of MAGA acolytes. At one point, NPR requested an interview with me about rural life, which I declined, explaining that I lived in St. Louis. They said that's why they asked me, and I then had to explain to them that St. Louis was a metro area of three million people. Finally, I had to clarify, once and for all, that yes, I lived in Missouri, and no, I did not live on a farm. A variation of this theme has followed me for years, often recited by the same people who accuse the residents of my state of living in a bubble.

Almost no one I met at the Palo Alto conference seemed to grasp the severity of the Trump crisis, which was disappointing given the oversized role social media companies had played in fueling it. But there were encouraging developments happening elsewhere. That week, the Steele dossier was published on BuzzFeed. I remember sitting in my California hotel room, relief rushing through me. I was grateful that it had dropped before the inauguration, thinking that its publication *had* to bring repercussions or at least a straightforward inquiry. It is a bad moment in American life when you are praying that the president-elect allegedly hiring hookers to piss on a bed may be what forces state officials to stop a transnational crime syndicate. But there were no meaningful consequences. The salacious details stuck; the serious problems lived on. No one could see the forest for the treason.

The night before Trump's inauguration, I was invited to speak about media and democracy at a panel held by the Chicago Council on Global Affairs. I went to Chicago planning to emphasize the work of Wayne Barrett, the New York journalist who had done more to shed light on Trump's illegalities than any other reporter. Five minutes after I got onstage, I received a text telling me Barrett had died. (Given that this book is full of suspicious deaths, I will state that by all accounts, Barrett died of cancer.) I was saddened to hear of his passing, because he had done the work every journalist should do: speak truth to power and follow the money. In Chicago, I encouraged the audience to examine Barrett's public archives chronicling Trump's criminality, reciting what would become a mantra so frequent people have joked it will be emblazoned on my tombstone—"It's in the public domain, it's been there the whole time!"—and flew back to St. Louis the next day.

I had scheduled my flight so that I would be sure to miss the inauguration. But my plane landed a half hour early, meaning I arrived just as Trump's speech was starting. I was at the opposite end of the terminal from the exit. This meant that in order to get out of the airport I had to walk down a long hallway lined with two dozen gates, and in each gate was a television blaring the same sick spectacle, with Trump's voice booming over the otherwise silent terminal. As I walked down the corridor, I glanced at the faces of waiting travelers watching the speech. I tried to guess where they were from and how they were feeling, wanting to gauge the public mood as Trump bleated out his hostilities.

But after a dozen gates the hypnotic sway was too much for me. It reminded me of the Trump rally I had attended at the Peabody Opera House eight months earlier, the one where I had watched a crowd become a mob. Now that same dynamic, that familiar fascist script, was playing out on the Capitol steps. I ran down the corridor past the dystopian duplicate screens, out the airport doors into the freezing air, into a cab driven by an immigrant who also wanted the damn thing off, past the landmarks from the airport drive that mark the familiarity of home, the parade of Dollar Tree and Dollar General and Family Dollar, the strip mall with China King and the husk of an empty Firestone, the rotting remains of a century-old theater from St. Louis's bygone boom days, and then onto my street, inside my house, where I felt like I should cry, but by then I didn't have it in me.

Trump was part of a wider movement of white supremacists and international kleptocrats seeking to dismantle Western democracy. I was one of the few American journalists to warn of this crisis in advance, and this unwanted distinction resulted in my being in great demand to speak on the issue abroad. In January, I was flown to the United Kingdom for a conference on press freedom and disinformation, where some Brits told me horror stories of Brexit while others assured me that they would figure it out, they would keep calm and carry on, this idiotic crisis surely would not undo a millennium of British sovereignty. I was not so sure. Brexit was a direct precursor of the US election, featuring not only the same largely unexpected result, but the same players behind the scenes.

In early 2017, a tenacious UK journalist, Carole Cadwalladr, had started to investigate the role of social media in the Brexit referendum, especially the company Cambridge Analytica and the interlocking parties who benefited from it—Nigel Farage, Steve Bannon, Jared Kushner. Eventually, she got a whistle-blower from Cambridge Analytica to come forward about the extent of their data-mining and election-influencing operation, and both the whistle-blower and Cadwalladr received scorn and threats.[32] She was not alone. A few other UK journalists were examining Russia's influence over UK institutions that had been infiltrated by Russian mafia associates over decades, much in the same way our institutions in the United States had been. As in the US, laws were loosened; as in the US, the line between white-collar corruption and organized crime had blurred.

US and UK citizens who protested this criminal impunity read each other's works from across the pond, while also watching the developments in our respective governments. Each side hoped the other would enforce accountability and thus prompt our own side to do so as well. A blatant crime would occur—Trump confessing to obstruction of justice on television in May 2017; the Kremlin poisoning a woman to death on UK soil in Salisbury in March 2018[33]—that would make the danger so immediate and obvious that we would tell ourselves, "OK, now they *have* to act." But no officials did—not with the courage and speed required, and not on behalf of the people they were supposed to serve.

From the United Kingdom I headed to the Netherlands, where I had been invited to give a public talk about authoritarianism in Amsterdam. When I arrived, Dutch citizens were watching the rise of their own Trump-like figure, the bigoted demagogue Geert Wilders, who was running for office. I envied the Dutch parliamentary system, which mitigated the damage Wilders could do even with his coalition. The Dutch audience asked whether a Trump phenomenon could happen there, and I said, "Yes, it can happen anywhere." This is the same answer I give everywhere I go, because the surest route to a kleptocratic takeover is to deny it's happening, and the surest way to solve it is to sever it before it blooms.

I gave the same answer again in Montreal a few weeks later, when I was on a panel about whether Canada would turn into a giant mess like its southern neighbor or its overseas cousin. I remember sitting in the audience reading about the new phenomena of "American exiles"—mostly black immigrants terrified of Trump's persecutory policies—who had crossed the American-Canadian border into Manitoba.[34] Canada was now the new America, taking in our huddled masses yearning to breathe free while the Trump administration condemned the Statue of Liberty.[35] But the illusion of Canadian respite did not last. As I write this in mid-2019, white supremacist movements are moving into mainstream Canadian politics while the country wrestles with financial corruption similar to that which weakened the US and UK economies before our respective collapses.

When people ask me if they should leave the United States, my answer is always, "And where, exactly, is it safe to go?"

In May 2017, I flew to Estonia to give a conference talk on a panel to a host of foreign dignitaries, including the presidents of Estonia and Finland. I had flown to Tallinn right after Trump had fired FBI director James Comey, which at that time was the most flagrant act of obstruction Trump had committed. Much of the audience was still processing what had happened, especially when Trump capped off the Comey firing by celebrating it with Russian state officials Sergei Lavrov and Sergei Kislyak in the Oval Office and giving them classified information about US intelligence operations in Israel—a brazen act of disloyalty for which he faced no consequences.[36]

I have great respect and sympathy for Estonia, which both suffered under and fended off Russian domination and which has some of the smartest cybersecurity measures of any state. I was placed on a panel with one conservative who disliked Trump, and two conservatives who glorified him, one of whom, Stephen Biegun, ended up becoming Trump's special representative to North Korea in 2018. The two Trump boosters offered supplicative platitudes like "we should feel empathy for Trump, because he is just not prepared to be president." A picture of me giving them an incredulous side-eye went viral after that comment.

An audience member asked the panel about what the election of Trump meant for American values. I couldn't help the answer that came out from me:

> There is a gulf between the president and the public. I love my country. But I am horrified that this man, this autocrat, who is struggling against a democratic framework of checks and balances that may or may not hold, has become my president. I want to point out that his victory was both narrow and flawed. Only about 25 percent of the country voted for him. The election was marred by Russian interference, baseline voter suppression, and flaws in our electoral system that go back to the founding of the United States. We have never been a perfect democracy. We have never been an equal country. But generally, at least through my lifetime, we have tried to progress toward that kind of change.
>
> I live in the center of the United States. I live in St. Louis, Missouri. I live in a majority black city in a bright red state that voted for Donald Trump. What I saw when he came into St. Louis and campaigned was that he was preying on people's pain, and he was preying on people's prejudice. He was taking the economic devastation that is real in the heart of America—he was right about that—and exploiting it for the most awful and xenophobic instincts that you could bring out in Americans. He is hurting the most vulnerable and disadvantaged people in our country, and as he stays in office, that's going to get worse. I don't think that this

is distinct to his foreign policy. There is a linked quality in how he views other human beings. He views them as disposable. He views them as people who don't deserve rights, or dignity, or respect. That kind of attitude will extend into other countries; we have already seen it in his treatment of Angela Merkel. We need to be wary. We are dealing with someone with autocratic leanings, who is not rational, who is destructive, who will break those American values.

I am proud of the American public for pushing back. I am proud of the representatives who are struggling to keep our constitution and respect our checks and balances. But I do not think that those are the aims of this president.[37]

After my remarks, the president of Estonia, Kersti Kaljulaid, countered me, saying she had been personally assured by Paul Ryan, Mike Pence, and other officials that the relationship between Estonia and the United States was strong and the US would remain a reliable partner. I responded the only way I could: with brutal honesty. It is a terrible feeling to tell the president of a foreign country not to trust my own government for the sake of their national security. This is different than telling a foreign country that your own country is flawed—all countries are flawed. Self-criticism of your own government is healthy. It is a crucial aspect of being in a democracy. Given that so many people in repressive states are forbidden from such critiques, criticizing the government should be considered both an obligation and a privilege. But this was new terrain. I had to tell a foreign leader that my own government might hurt Estonia, our ally, in order to please Russia, a hostile state that had brutalized her own country.

I told Kaljulaid I hoped that she was right and I was wrong, but that the Trump administration was untrustworthy and duplicitous, and that she and other Estonian officials should "watch your back and hope for the best." As it turned out, the Trump administration had indeed lied to her. A few months later Trump stunned the world by meeting secretly for an hour with Putin at the G20 summit and then suggesting that he and Putin become partners in cybersecurity. In early 2018, Trump threatened to withdraw US troops from the Baltics, a threat he has made repeatedly since.

The year went on with nonstop writing and nonstop travel. I went to Germany to give a series of talks to university students in Giessen. For the first time, I was receiving warnings rather than giving them. Germans knew the signs of dictatorship and warned me that the American media was blowing it in their inability to discern propaganda and strengthen institutions against autocratic abuse. I went to Hungary for a multiday conference on authoritarianism and global change and watched Hungarian officials whose dreams of democracy came true in the 1990s hold back tears as they detailed the brutal policies of their authoritarian leader, Viktor Orbán. Hungary was a key example of how fast a country can fall from fragile democracy into a burgeoning autocracy; Poland and Turkey are two other recent cautionary tales. All three are countries I have visited several times and to which I have an emotional attachment—my ancestors are from Poland, and I had lived in Turkey for a year—and seeing the loss of freedom firsthand broke my heart.

I went to Hungary for the first time in 1998, as a college student, and stayed in a five-dollar-a-night hostel with a group of Serbians who were fleeing political turmoil. In 2003, on my way to Belgrade to visit a Serbian friend with whom I'd stayed in touch, I stopped in Budapest for a day, and was shocked by the transformation. The struggling but fascinating city of five years ago was dynamic and much more expensive, and Hungary was set to join the EU. In fall 2017, I was back in Budapest again, but this time it felt heavy to walk around visiting the same landmarks I had first laid eyes on in my twenties. There were the centuries-old synagogues that stood as symbols of both Jewish resilience and a horrific reminder of the Holocaust's toll. There was the Liberty Statue that had removed its Russian inscription in 1989 to serve as a genuine emblem of Hungarian freedom and independence. Now anti-Semitism was on the rise; universities and media outlets were closing under state pressure; and the spirit of promise was gone, struck down by over a decade of economic decline and the rise of dictatorship. I went back to my hotel room and watched Trump threaten to nuke North Korea again.

The year went on like that, frenetically, with more and more crimes of the Trump administration revealed each month. I warned that if criminals were not countered now, we would be stuck hashing out their crimes the next year, and that the backlog combined with agency purges and court packing would make the pursuit of justice nearly impossible. This all came to pass, and the Mueller probe, which served to placate the public and instill a passive reverence among lawmakers, made the situation worse. As institutions crumbled, I kept speaking out, in New York and New Haven and Austin and Oakland and Toronto and more places than I could count in Missouri and Illinois.

I discussed immigration and Islamophobia at the invitation of the Muslim Students' Association at St. Louis University. I sat on a panel with former Black Panthers at an Afrofuturism conference at Harris-Stowe, a historically black college in St. Louis, and agreed that state-sanctioned autocracy had already happened to black Americans and that the notion that America is "exceptional" is not only an illusion but an insult. I gave a talk to a mixed audience of conservatives and liberals in the Missouri Ozarks who were receptive to my warnings—after all, they were Missourians, they knew corruption had no bounds. I wanted to talk to everyone I could and hear everyone's story—in part because we are all in this together, in part because I hoped someone would know a way out. I felt like I had been elected to a position for which I never ran.

In June 2017, I spoke under the Gateway Arch in St. Louis at the "March for Truth," a national demonstration demanding a justice system with integrity, an independent investigation of Trump's relationship with Russia, and transparency about the 2016 election.

I closed with this statement:

We need not only investigators that we can trust to do their jobs honorably, but a justice system that can be trusted to act on the findings of the investigation, and if crimes are confirmed, to hold criminals accountable.

The administration likes to portray citizens, especially out here in the Midwest where we live, as passive, as compliant, as uninterested in justice and law. What they are really hoping for is that we will be complacent, that we not defend the honor of our country or the sanctity of our laws, that we'll just stand by silently and let them get away with it.

But we are St. Louis! We have witnessed injustice so many times, and we do not always win, but Lord knows we let everyone know when justice has not been served. We correct the lies. We come for the liars, and the grifters, and the traitors. We come hard, and we will not quit.

Never let anyone tell you that you do not deserve the truth or that truth itself has no value. When they say that, what they're really saying is that you, as a citizen, have no value, that you have no voice. You deserve so much better than this. You have value, and you have a voice, so use it.[38]

Two years later, as the Mueller probe wound down with a whimper, it is hard to remember this earlier era of mass protests. There were so many—the women's marches, the march for science, the march against migrant abuse, the march against gun violence. Some of the marches were the largest in our nation's history.

Americans like to romanticize protest. As a scholar of the Andijon massacre in Uzbekistan and a firsthand witness to the brutality of Ferguson, I tend to do the opposite and emphasize that demonstrations rarely achieve an instantaneous result and are often dangerous. But the way in which the mass protests of 2017 and 2018 have been dismissed is disturbing, particularly since most participants and organizers were women. Women also comprised the grassroots efforts behind the 2018 Democratic wins, organizing while dealing with the endless agonizing revelations of the

#MeToo movement. In the years after Trump's election, more women ran for and won office than ever before. This flurry of female activism should surprise no one, given that the policies of the Trump administration, whether economic or social, disproportionately hurt women. In Trump's America, women run for their lives.

On July 29, 2016, two days after he had asked Russia to get him Hillary Clinton's emails, Trump gave a speech that strikes me as his most revealing. "Look, we have the greatest business people in the world and we don't use them," he told the crowd at a rally in Denver, Colorado. "We use political hacks. Some of these business people are not nice people. Who cares? You care? I don't think so. Some of these business people are vicious, horrible, miserable human beings. Who cares? Who cares?" he muttered.

Then Trump began to scream.

"Some of these people, they don't sleep at night! They twist, and turn, and sweat!" he cried, twisting his hand furiously, "and their mattress is soaking wet! Because they're thinking all night about victory the next day against some poor person that doesn't have a chance."

His eyes flashing with panic, Trump kept going.

"And these people—unfortunately, I know them all," he laughed bitterly. "These people would love to represent us against China, against Japan, against all of these countries . . . These people. They feel crazy! They feel angry! They cannot believe the deals that are made. We will do things we have never done before."[39]

When I heard the speech, I did not know if it was an autobiography, a confession of collaboration, or both. Trump loves to be caught and not be punished. Throughout the 2016 campaign, he recited the poem "The Snake," a story of treachery that mocks the victims: "You knew damn well I was a snake before you let me in." It is not enough for Trump to commit a crime. He needs to let you know that he got away with it. Others in his camp, like Roger

Stone, share the same predilection. The thrill is in the flaunting, the in-jokes, the admissions so blunt that, perversely, few take them seriously. That's also where the tell is, if you are working for law enforcement, but these days, federal law enforcement works for Trump.

In June 2017, the Mueller probe was announced as a replacement for the investigation into the 2016 election that had been led by James Comey, who Trump admitted he had shut down because Comey had been nosing into his business with Russia. From the start, the media was bullish on Mueller taking down Trump. This was in part due to the Trump family confessing major campaign crimes in the public domain twice in a two-month period—Trump telling Lester Holt about obstruction of justice in May 2017, and Donald Trump Jr. tweeting out emails in July 2017 about an incriminating June 2016 Trump Tower meeting attended by Manafort, Kushner, and Kremlin operatives. How hard could this be if the evidence was right in front of us, so obvious that ordinary people could hear straight from the perps that they had committed the crimes?

This confidence was compounded by the valorization of Mueller as a consummate G-man, a neutral arbiter whose fealty was to the law and not to the leader. Mueller's reticence to speak to the press led many to assume he was the strong and silent type instead of what he was revealed to be at end of his probe—a weak-willed bureaucrat who either failed to understand the stakes or found them tolerable. Though I wanted the Mueller probe to succeed, I was wary of its odds from the start.

Autocratic consolidation is a matter of power, not protocol, and if you cannot tell the difference between the two, you have no business leading an investigation. You cannot go by the book while the book is burning. As an institutionalist, Mueller seemed only as strong as our institutions, and our institutions had been pushed to the brink of collapse. A forceful and transparent probe could have constrained criminality and saved American lives. The timid and plodding investigation Mueller carried out instead, abetted by the cowardice of a Congress that refused to act upon his findings, obfuscated the American past and fostered its fallen future.

Mueller had long been an enabler, intentional or not, of the corruption he was tasked to investigate. He headed the FBI from 2001 until 2013, doing little to stop the criminal behavior carried out by operatives from his own political party. When Paul Manafort was indicted by Mueller in October 2017, for example, it was for crimes he had committed in the early 2000s. Why did Mueller not arrest Manafort earlier? If Mueller was so aware of the danger of this transnational crime syndicate that he gave a speech warning it would destroy democracy in 2011, why did he do so little to stop it—and why did he not speak out when Trump began receiving classified information during his campaign? At best, Mueller was guilty of negligence—but in 2017, negligence seemed a forgivable sin given the stakes and the competition. Negligence was a step up from money-laundering or treason or rape. The country was willing to overlook negligence and naivete in return for someone willing to root out the rot.

By the end of 2017, "Mueller will save us" had become an internet mantra, chanted by legal experts and armies of trolls alike. "Mueller will save us" had replaced "Comey will save us," and was later supplanted by "Pelosi will save us" and "the 2020 election will save us," all while the damage of the Trump administration grew more irreparable. Rumors swirled throughout 2017 and 2018 about imminent indictments and secret plans, and Mueller disciples found a funhouse mirror in the "QAnon" cult surrounding Trump. The QAnon phenomenon—in which Trump acolytes believe an anonymous high-level official named "Q" leaves them coded tips about secret prosecutions as well as other enticing developments, like the underground revolution they claim is being led by a still-alive JFK Jr.—is a disturbing example of savior syndrome.

Savior syndrome is a mind-set that flourishes during the unstable period of autocratic consolidation, when frightened citizens seek to find meaning in the inexplicable actions of their failed leaders. To those under the sway of savior syndrome, once trusted officials are not incompetent or corrupt: they are merely "playing 3-D chess." It doesn't matter if officials are, in reality, resorting to the weakest moves ("When you don't know what to do, push a pawn" could have been the motto of the Mueller probe), their motives must be presented as pure, their tactics impeccable and impenetrable. The abdication of the admired is too much for those seeking saviors to process, no matter their political predilection. And so, for two years, one group of political junkies lit Mueller-themed prayer candles while another parsed Trump tweets for coded clues. Both sides told the skeptics to shut up and "trust the plan." Neither side got what they wanted.

The delusion was disheartening to watch. I felt sorry for those QAnon acolytes who were nonviolent and would occasionally hit on something real, like the Epstein case, and be dismissed as conspiracists by onlookers while Trumpian manipulators drew them deeper into the QAnon cult. But I was also frustrated with the side proclaiming allegiance to logic and law: the legal scholars and political pundits who baselessly assured the public of Mueller's forthcoming success as Mueller continued to blow the case.

Those who noted Mueller's missteps were pummeled with insults from those clinging to the vestiges of institutionalism. Those who had studied or lived through autocratic consolidation screamed about these missteps like spectators on the sidelines of our own demise. To point out the failures of the Mueller probe—many of which were caused by the Trump administration's purges and threats; but some of which were caused by the Mueller team's poor judgment—was to become a heretic. But it's better to be a heretic than a liar. A heretic these days is a temporary occupation: the sin lies in telling the truth too early. Much like Trump's crimes, Mueller's failures were hiding in plain sight. Establishment analysts were afraid to discuss them because of what these failures signified—that the system was broken and the good guys had lost. Or worse, that the good guys were never that great in the first place.

But regardless of the probe's failures, one should still read the Mueller report, as it does document a multitude of crimes including at least ten instances of obstruction of justice. That the Mueller report could discuss Trump campaign criminality for over four hundred pages and only scratch the surface of what they've done is a denunciation of far more than Mueller. The problem lies less with his report than with the lack of consequences for the criminals he probed. Mueller's main sin is omission. He failed to interview key players, including Trump, and refused to indict the most dangerous parties, like Jared Kushner. Despite these flaws, his report nonetheless gave a clear signal to Congress to launch an impeachment inquiry, but the House Democrats have thus far failed to do so successfully, cutting off another avenue to accountability.

Impeachment hearings should have begun after the report's release, and the report inspired many elected officials to deem them necessary. But it's critical to remember that Congress could have started in 2017, when the first articles of impeachment were filed by Representatives Brad Sherman and Al Green. The Mueller report was never necessary for impeachment, because Trump had committed impeachable offenses outside the purview of the probe—like emoluments violations, abuse of migrants, and abuse of the pardon power—every week for over two years. Impeaching the person responsible for these ongoing atrocities was deemed by Nancy Pelosi in March 2019 to be "not worth it." The House, presented with a menu of incriminating offenses, took the pursuit of justice off the table.

Over the last two years, when people have asked me for advice on dealing with the Trump regime, I told them to learn to think like the enemy (but not act like them) and have infinite backup plans. Given that the enemy telegraphs its intentions, the first part of this strategy should be easy to achieve, yet officials often do not practice it. The failures of the judiciary, the strongest bulwark against authoritarianism, led to terrible political calculations. When officials saw the Mueller probe flailing, they should have sought other avenues to protect the American people. Instead,

Mueller and his boss Bill Barr—notorious for being the Iran Contra cleanup guy[40]—were given the benefit of the doubt even after the probe was shown to be in trouble.

In October 2017, Mueller indicted Manafort for conspiracy against the United States, but followed that up in November with a loose bail deal that allowed Manafort to roam around without GPS tracking. My immediate thought was that Manafort would flee the country—wouldn't you, if you were a career criminal with vast foreign ties and assets?—but it took Manafort plotting more crimes for Mueller to create a stricter arrangement based on adherence to law and not personal trust. Following his arrest, Manafort went on to pen propaganda and tamper with witnesses.[41] While whistle-blowers like Reality Winner have been banned from speaking to the media, Manafort was given phone and internet access, which he used to ghostwrite articles for Ukrainian websites and chat with Trump mouthpiece Sean Hannity.[42]

Throughout 2018, Mueller continued to fall for Manafort's tricks. In August 2018, Manafort was convicted in federal court of tax and bank fraud. Days later, Mueller's team announced that Manafort had agreed to cooperate with the special counsel. My heart sank. This career criminal's sudden cooperation had arrived right after he had been convicted by a judge and jury—both of which had been threatened with violence but convicted him anyway. Meanwhile, another criminal implicated in the Mueller probe, Trump foreign policy adviser George Papadopoulos, had received a sentence of only two weeks—even after it was revealed he hadn't cooperated with the Mueller probe at all, and had in fact impeded it. It seemed obvious that Manafort would do the exact same thing. Manafort's choice was simple: take a chance on the judiciary system, which had not yet been consolidated by Trump, or strike a fake plea bargain and run out the clock.

I warned of Manafort's plans for months on end, in articles and on national TV, hoping Mueller's team knew what they were doing and that they had a backup plan for when Manafort screwed them over. In November 2018, it was revealed that Manafort had not cooperated and had impeded the probe. He ended up with two small sentences not commensurate with the monumental nature of his crimes. He may well get out within a few years and go back to targeting my colleague's sister, among other citizens.

Those who treat this as a game seem to not grasp—or care—that ordinary Americans have been caught in the crossfire and that Manafort poses a public safety threat. At the time of Manafort's sentencing, I was in disbelief that Mueller's team could not see this outcome coming, and it has made me wonder whether, in fact, they did, and found it acceptable. I remember looking at a photo of Mueller heading to church in spring 2019, shortly after Barr had issued a misleading summary of his probe, and wondering what kind of god this man could believe in to allow his country-men such preventable pain. We were living in Mueller's America. One nation, under God, collateral damage.

There were other egregious errors. Manafort crony Rick Gates was also given loose travel restrictions and even had the destina-tion of his future travel plans announced.[43] This seemed asinine, given that Gates was both a flight risk and a potential assassina-tion target. Eventually, the Mueller team realized this and gave him travel restrictions and tracking.[44] The "Mueller is playing 3-D chess" analogies began to take off at this point among those des-perate for a rationale for why Mueller's team were making rookie errors. Some pundits liked to claim that Mueller was doing a classic mafia roll-up, where he would go easy, nab the low-level players first, and then arrest the key instigators all at once.[45] That illusion was shattered when Mueller ensured that Michael Flynn walked free in fall 2018, at least so far.

Flynn was a central figure in the Mueller probe. A foreign agent for both Russia and Turkey who aspired to illicitly deal nuclear material and kidnap a Turkish cleric living in the United States, Flynn was the first national security adviser for Trump before re-signing less than a month into his term after his Russian campaign ties were revealed. In December 2017, he struck his own deal with Mueller and pled guilty to lying to the FBI. In December 2018, Flynn was supposed to be sentenced, and it was expected he would get the maximum penalty. In an unusual rebuke, the judge, Emmet Sullivan, said to Flynn, "Arguably, you sold your country out," adding, "I'm not hiding my disgust, my disdain for this criminal offense."[46] Sullivan was the rare official ready to make a Trump associate pay for his crimes—until Mueller stepped in and recommended that Flynn serve no time at all.[47] There remains no logical explanation for this move. Mueller chose to coddle a plausible traitor. Flynn remains a national security threat who roams the country meeting with right-wing extremists.[48]

There are many questions here: Why did Mueller give cushy plea deals to Flynn and Gates when the information from those deals did not lead to indictments of the most dangerous perpetrators? Why were other key players, like Roger Stone, allowed to threaten people—including a judge—without consequence after their own indictments? Why was there no mention of Semion Mogilevich and his crime syndicate in the Mueller report, especially when they had been a key target during Mueller's tenure in the FBI? Why was the broader context of the case—*the mafia*—omitted by the Mueller team? Why did the probe abruptly end on March 5, one day after the House Judiciary Committee sent out a list of eighty-one people they sought to interview about Trump administration corruption—the first sign that the House would flex its prosecutorial muscle?[49] Did Mueller end the probe voluntarily, or did Barr shut it down?

We do not know the answers to these questions because Mueller refuses to answer them. Perhaps by the time you read this, the truth will have come out, but I cannot imagine who has the fortitude to force it. When Mueller testified to Congress in July 2019, it was under subpoena and after months of delay. Under oath, the Godot of prosecutors became the Bartleby of witnesses: Mueller spoke with extreme reluctance, deflecting or declining to answer questions 155 times. He refused to answer basic inquiries about key players in his own probe, like whether he had wanted to interview Donald Trump Jr. He never discussed the Russian mafia, and none of the members of Congress would raise the topic. It is unlikely that Mueller will ever give a straightforward account to the American people, because that would involve Mueller laying himself bare, explaining why he failed to stop a plot against America both during his tenure as FBI director and as special counsel. We would get closer to learning whether the answer lies in negligence or malice, but even that would not compensate for the harm his botched probe has already caused.

For as the Mueller probe plodded along, Trump purged agencies and packed courts, including the Supreme Court appointment of Brett Kavanaugh, who has implied that he will never allow Trump to be indicted.[50] The only time Mueller broke his silence during the probe was to condemn a BuzzFeed article claiming that Trump had directed Michael Cohen to lie to Congress, a report that generated widespread talk of impeachment.[51] Mueller spoke out more strongly about that BuzzFeed article—which turned out to be accurate—than he did when Barr released a deceitful memo misrepresenting his two years of investigative work. The two BuzzFeed reporters who broke the Cohen story were the same who broke the story of Russian infiltration of the US Treasury less than a month before. An effort to discredit them seemed to be at play, but the Treasury story was never disproven, and Cohen later confirmed the central thesis of their report on him.

"They may try to manipulate those at the highest levels of government," Mueller proclaimed in 2011. "Indeed, these so-called 'iron triangles' of organized criminals, corrupt government officials, and business leaders pose a significant national security threat." By 2019, Mueller had become a point in his own triangle.

People keep looking for the smoking gun that will end Trump's corrupt reign. But it has been there the whole time. The gun is in his hand, and it's still smoking.

It's smoking because he is shooting our country to death. It's smoking because no one will take away the gun. It's smoking because the very people tasked with protecting you reload it for him again and again. They will keep firing until all constraints are removed and there is no one left to gaze at the carnage and ask why nothing is being done.

Epilogue

End Times Road Trip

I n fall 2016, I said to a friend, "I don't know who has it worse—the people who understand what is going to happen, or the people who don't."

Her answer was simple: "Neither of them: it's the kids."

For the past four years, I have been taking my children on road trips around America, in the event of its demise. This compulsion began in September 2016, when I became certain that American authoritarianism loomed. National landmarks that I had long taken for granted seemed newly vulnerable to destruction or desecration. It was important to me that my kids see America with their own eyes, and not through mine. I want my children to have their own memories of the United States, so that if they're confronted with a false version years from now, they can say, "No, I saw it. We had that. This was real. That America was real."

I began driving my children to historical sites in Missouri and Illinois whenever I could. I wanted them to see the sites of our states alongside other Americans who, whatever our political differences may be, wanted their kids to see them too. I took my children to the Dred Scott courthouse in St. Louis where the rights of slaves were debated; to the estate of Ulysses S. Grant and his slave quarters; to the Trail of Tears State Park in southern Missouri commemorating the deaths of Native Americans; to the rural Missouri homestead of Daniel Boone, the frontiersman and slave owner; to the tomb of Abraham Lincoln in Springfield, Illinois. My youngest did not understand; my oldest knew enough to recognize the incongruity between virtue and cruelty. How could political leaders betray what were supposed to be national values? How could brutal practices be embraced by ordinary Americans?

Or, as she put it, "Why did no one stop people from doing bad things?"

The answer you're supposed to give to children—one I heard myself as a child—is "That's just the way things were." You're supposed to say, "Lots of good people owned slaves," or, "It was legal then." You're supposed to pretend that historic injustices have either been resolved or that they were never that bad, that they didn't linger and structure the politics of the present. You're supposed to normalize cruelty, and in doing so exonerate those who practiced it.

But as I tried to answer her question, my mind flashed forward to what my children might be asking thirty years from now, when their own children are trying to figure out what happened to America. How did a president commit impeachable offenses on a weekly basis—refusing to divest from his businesses, abusing private citizens and migrants, obstructing justice—without facing consequences? How did mafia associates infiltrate US institutions right under the nose of federal officials? How did white supremacist groups rise from the shadows into the spotlight, countenanced by the president and his advisers? How could a politician show more respect to foreign dictators than to US veterans and civil rights leaders, yet still be treated as legitimate by his party?

There is no "That's just the way things were" to answer the question of what happened to the United States of America. It's "That's the way things became," as a transnational crime syndicate took the place of government. There is a difference between institutions weakening, as they did throughout the wars and recessions of the twenty-first century, and the institutions that protect freedom and national security being hijacked or gutted by hostile, anti-American actors. US history is beset with partisan divides and corruption, but we have never been ruled by a man whose only loyalty beyond himself is to an authoritarian foreign power.

I don't know what my children will remember of the America I have shown them. I am trying to teach them while I can, so they will know the difference between a deeply flawed democracy and a country that ceases to be a democracy at all. They know that practices like slavery that were accepted as "normal" in US history are today considered an abomination, and that rationalizing cruelty was what allowed them to last for so long. I told them to never consider cruel policies as normal, no matter what politicians and pundits tell them.

I am trying to show them our country was always vulnerable, always flawed, but that people fought back. We've survived as long as we have due to self-criticism and sacrifice, a willingness to examine our faults and try to fix them. In the past, we survived because good Americans answered the question "Why does nobody stop people from doing bad things?" with laws and actions that prevented people from doing them. If we survive the current era, it will not be due to a savior from above, but to the refusal of ordinary people to accept elite criminal impunity as normal.

When my family and I get the chance to travel outside Missouri, like many Midwestern families, we drive. There is nothing I love more than being on the open road; if I had the choice, this is all I would do. In the Midwest, distance is measured in time, not miles. Three hours to a destination and back is a nice day trip; a fifteen-hour haul is "doable." This mind-set is alien to those in crowded coastal regions, whose highways are glutted with traffic and unpleasant to drive. I don't blame people there for choosing to fly over us, but they are missing out. When your trip begins in Missouri, you can see America from every direction.

My children have never left the United States—leaving is an

unfathomable luxury that will hopefully not become a sudden necessity—but they have seen, in ways big and small, the determination and tragedies of our diverse population. They have been to Native American reservations in Oklahoma and South Dakota, and heard Cherokee and Lakota spoken by members of tribes. They have seen the house where Martin Luther King Jr. lived in Montgomery, Alabama, and the bomb crater on its porch, and heard the tapes of him refusing to abandon his cause. They have seen the sites of the Salem witch trials in Massachusetts, and learned how paranoid misogyny and mob mentality culminated in death and shame. They have seen centuries-old churches in Santa Fe and were fascinated, in New Mexico, to hear more people speaking Spanish than English—and were amazed to discover the Spanish-speakers were there before the English speakers. They have been to the oldest mosque in America, in Cedar Rapids, Iowa, where they were given Ramadan candy by a welcoming imam.

They have been to countless cities and small towns in the South and Southwest and Midwest and Great Plains. Their favorite state to visit is Texas, because so many of the restaurants and storefronts are covered in Texas-themed objects and Texas-shaped items, just in case you forget for one second that you're in the amazing state of Texas. Their cousins live in suburban Dallas, their grandparents live in rural Wisconsin, their other grandparents live in a city in central Connecticut, and we drive hours on end to see them, watching the landscapes and cultures transform along the way, punctuated with a steadfast tawdriness that makes every place feel like home: the truck stop megaplazas, the "world's largest object" tourist traps, the ubiquity of giant American flags, which in our violent era usually fly at half-staff.

We have met a lot of interesting people and heard a lot of strange things. My kids don't find any person out of the ordinary in America because they know there is no archetypal American. When I explain that there is an ongoing debate in the media about which Americans are "real Americans," they are confused. When I explain that this facile debate has spilled over into government, with Trump challenging the American-ness of different ethnic groups, they are horrified.

My kids have been dragged to more presidential museums and libraries than they wanted to see: Harry Truman, Abraham Lincoln, George W. Bush, Lyndon B. Johnson, and poor Gerald Ford, who was so boring that I had to tell the kids he was an undercover wizard and encouraged them to scour his museum for "magic clues." (I realized years later while reading a first-grade writing assignment that I had not corrected this myth.) They roll their eyes but absorb the information, as well as the disparity between then and now. I don't need to spell out the rupture between every past US president and Trump. It is evident in every museum and national monument we visit, even though so many of the problems we face today—systemic racism, economic decline, foreign aggression—are the same as before.

In 2018, we visited the Dwight Eisenhower museum and tomb in Abilene, Kansas. Engraved on its wall is a quote from his 1953 speech "The Chance for Peace." It says: "Every gun that is made, every warship launched, every rocket fired signifies, in the final sense, a theft from those who hunger and are not fed, those who are cold and are not clothed. This world in arms is not spending money alone. It is spending the sweat of its laborers, the genius of its scientists, the hopes of its children. . . . This is not a way of life at all, in any true sense. Under the cloud of threatening war, it is humanity hanging from a cross of iron."

I don't get sentimental about presidents. As a rule, I oppose making heroes out of public servants. But the vast gulf between the present and the era of Eisenhower's speech hurts, not because our problems are so different but because our leaders have so profoundly failed us. We live in Eisenhower's nightmare realized. "This is not a way of life at all" could be the motto of our time. My son was impressed by the giant statue of Eisenhower that stands in front of the museum. He was surprised, and touched, that surrounding it was a plea for peace from a man who was a general.

Since Trump was elected, all of our vacations have been at

national parks, sites of awe that I share with my children and sorrow that I keep to myself. In January 2017, Trump declared war on the national parks, resulting in a number of "rogue national park" Twitter accounts from which park employees tweeted out information about now forbidden topics like climate change.[1] This was one of Trump's first aggressive moves against an administrative body, and it struck me as profoundly dangerous. National parks are among the few things nearly all Americans think are a good idea, so the attack was an early sign that the public had little leverage over policy. The attack on the parks also signaled a broader attack on the environment and on cultural preservation, which became blatant when Trump called for a mass reduction of Bears Ears and Grand Staircase-Escalante National Monuments, two wonders that are also sacred Native American sites.

In March 2017, my family drove west to New Mexico. My children saw the mountains and desert for the first time, and I tried not to cry when they talked about wanting to return and see the same landscapes on their own when they are grown. One morning we woke up early to go sledding on the dunes at White Sands National Monument. We were the only people there. I remember sitting on top of the white crystal sand, with no sound but my children laughing as they sped down the hillsides, thinking that I would never have a happier moment than this, because my gratitude that I could still show my children a place this beautiful was so profound. I felt the same overwhelming emotion, gratitude interlaced with grief, when we took the kids to Colorado and Utah a year later, where they saw the Rocky Mountains and Arches and Canyonlands and Mesa Verde; and the year after that, when we saw Yellowstone and Glacier and Grand Teton and Theodore Roosevelt National Parks. We still had the freedom to travel, and there is so much to see.

Every day since 2016 has felt like a clock ticking down—for every one of us and for America as a country. Climate change has exacerbated the pressure, as fires burn and waters rise. As I write this, Missouri is flooded, and no one is intervening except citizens, who construct sandbags from scratch, trying to keep the rivers at bay before they swallow whole what's left of our landscape. I spend evenings watching otherworldly sunsets caused by forest fires in Alberta reflect on the floodwaters covering the St. Louis streets.

There is a fragility to life now that nearly breaks me, one I could handle as a child and as an adult but not as a mother. Children force you to envision the future, and doing that today is an act of mental violence. But children also force you to fight for the future—to insist that there will be one, to bend the arc of the moral universe toward justice through sheer force of will, because it sure as hell doesn't bend that way on its own.

I have tried to prepare my children for the future by showing them America firsthand, the horrors and the resilience, the diversity of regions and people. Part of me feels most at home on the road, part of me has always wanted to run away without leaving, and America has always offered respite for the restless. But another part of me is inoculating my children against future propaganda: fake memories marketed as memes, fake archives duplicated by algorithm, false assurances uttered by everyone.

I want them to remember this country, and that I loved it despite its flaws, that it was part of me, and in turn part of them. It is our heritage and our responsibility. I want them to know that I fought for it in the only way I knew how: by telling the truth. But I don't want them to parrot my views or anyone else's. I want them to learn and think for themselves. I want them to see their homeland firsthand and draw their own conclusions. To paraphrase George Orwell, those who control the past control the future. I want my children to see the American past before it is gone.

I don't expect to see peace in my time. I expect a continued erosion of freedom coupled with horrific shifts in our environmental climate and our national law. I expect surveillance culture will exacerbate fear to the point that submission is no longer recognizable as such; it will just be called life. I expect elite criminal impunity to prosper so long as officials refuse to enforce accountability. I expect recessions and censorship and violence.

But there is a difference between expecting an American autocracy and accepting it, and I refuse to accept it. Every loss we endure is a reminder of the gifts we still hold, and of our obligation to fight for a better future for the next generation. I will never settle. I want to settle the score.

Acknowledgments

I wrote this book between January and August 2019, which means I wrote a dark American history as the country faded to black. This was not easy, and I was only able to do it thanks to the support and encouragement of many people—too many to list in this space.

First, I'd like to thank my wonderful readers. You made my first book, *The View from Flyover Country*, a grassroots hit and created the demand for more. I've enjoyed reading your emails, tweets, and letters, and meeting some of you while on tour. I am very fortunate to have such an engaged and thoughtful audience. I believe that an informed public is a powerful public, and I hope you take that message to heart while reading *Hiding in Plain Sight*.

My profound gratitude to my agent, Robert Lecker, who always had my back and whose advice throughout this process was indispensable. Robert is both principled and pragmatic, and one of the best professional decisions I ever made was signing with his agency in 2016.

Thank you to everyone at Flatiron Books, especially my editor, Bryn Clark, who offered useful suggestions at every stage of the process, came up with a great title, and stayed both flexible and tenacious as the news cycle necessitated constant updates to the material. *Hiding in Plain Sight* can get very depressing, and Bryn had to read every line over and over, so major credit to Bryn for putting up with that. Thanks also to the copy editors and production designers for bringing this book to fruition, and to my Flatiron publicist, the always helpful and organized Amelia Possanza, who brought my work to a larger audience.

Thank you to all the friends and fellow writers with whom I discussed this subject matter over the years. Foremost among them is Andrea Chalupa, who is not only my partner on our podcast *Gaslit Nation* but a terrific friend and a brilliant thinker. I could not have gotten through the last few years without Andrea. Congratulations on baby Alice! Others whose insights and support I particularly appreciate include Malcolm Nance, Leah McElrath, Melissa McEwan, Olga Lautman, and Josh Manning. Thank you to all the *Gaslit Nation* guests who came on the show and shared your wisdom with me and Andrea, and thank you to the shows who had me on in turn. Thanks also to the many editors who have supported my work these last few years, especially Amberly McAteer at *The Globe and Mail*.

Deep appreciation for the activists inspired by my writing, especially Indivisible St. Louis and Annie Marshall. It has been encouraging to see people continue to fight for our rights nationwide, but particularly here in Missouri, where life was already hard and no hell was all that shocking. Thank you also to the Ferguson activists and others in the St. Louis region who keep demanding justice no matter the odds.

Most of all, thank you to my family for making every day worthwhile, even in these dark times. Thanks to my parents, Barbara and Larry—and special thanks to my mom for taking her cameos in this book in stride. Thanks also to Lizzie, Mike, Jack, and Kate; Sally and Phil; Liz and Dave; and babysitters extraordinaire Karl and Julia.

To my favorite people, Emily and Alex: I love you so much. You made writing this difficult book easier just by being yourselves. Every time I'm with you, the horrible complexity of the situation

I've found myself in fades away and I know what matters in life. I am so happy to be your mom.

Finally, to my husband, Pete: thank you for everything. Thank you for standing by me during a very tumultuous time, for hearing out my ideas, for reading the initial drafts of this book and offering comments, for being a wonderful father, for buying me Guns N' Roses tickets as a reward for finishing the book, and for your incredible patience. We may not have gotten the future we envisioned twenty years ago, but, for once, I've got no complaints.

Notes

Introduction

1. Laura Adams, *The Spectacular State: Culture and National Identity in Uzbekistan* (Durham, NC: Duke University Press, 2000).
2. Sarah Kendzior, "Reclaiming Ma'naviyat," in *Ethnographies of the State in Central Asia: Performing Politics*, ed. Madeleine Reeves (Bloomington: Indiana University Press, 2014).
3. Human Rights Watch, "Creating Enemies of the State: Religious Persecution in Uzbekistan," March 2004, https://www.hrw.org/reports/2004/uzbekistan0304/2.htm#_Toc65397893.
4. Sarah Kendzior, "Kim Kardashistan: A Violent Dictator's Daughter on a Quest for Pop Stardom," *The Atlantic*, August 8, 2012, https://www.theatlantic.com/international/archive/2012/08/kim-kardashistan-a-violent-dictators-daughter-on-a-quest-for-pop-stardom/260885/.
5. Betsy Woodruff and Tim Mak, "Top Trump Aide Led the 'Torturers' Lobby,'" *Daily Beast*, April 13, 2016, https://www.thedailybeast.com/top-trump-aide-led-the-torturers-lobby.
6. Rob Wile, "Is Vladimir Putin Secretly the Richest Man in the World?," *CNN Money*, January 22, 2017, http://money.com/money/4641093/vladimir-putin-net-worth/.
7. "Donald Trump's 2014 Political Predictions," Fox News, February 10, 2014, https://video.foxnews.com/v/3179604851001/donald-trumps-2014-political-predictions/?#sp=show-clips.
8. "Дональд Трамп: Хватит придираться к России!" ["Donald Trump: Stop Picking on Russia!"], *RT*, February 11, 2014, https://russian.rt.com/article/22064.
9. Sarah Kendzior, "Donald Trump's bromance with Vladimir Putin underscores an unsettling truth about the two leaders," *Quartz*, August 19,

2016, https://qz.com/761656/donald-trumps-bromance-with-vladimir
-putin-underscores-an-unsettling-truth-about-the-two-leaders/.

10. The Moscow Project, "Bailed Out By Russia," 2019, https://themoscow
project.org/collusion-chapter/chapter-1/; The Moscow Project, "Banks
Refused to Lend to Trump, Citing 'The Donald Risk,'" 2019, https://
themoscowproject.org/collusion/banks-refuse-lend-trump-citing
-donald-risk/.

11. Ed Caeser, "Deutsche Bank's $10-Billion Scandal," *New Yorker,*
August 22, 2016, https://www.newyorker.com/magazine/2016/08/29
/deutsche-banks-10-billion-scandal; Allan Smith, "Trump's Long and
Winding History with Deutsche Bank Could Now Be at the Center of
Robert Mueller's Investigation," *Business Insider,* December 8, 2017,
https://www.businessinsider.com/trump-deutsche-bank-mueller-2017-12.

12. David E. Sanger, "Harry Reid Cites Evidence of Russian Tampering in
U.S. Vote, and Seeks F.B.I. Inquiry," *New York Times,* August 29, 2016,
https://www.nytimes.com/2016/08/30/us/politics/harry-reid-russia
-tampering-election-fbi.html.

13. Sarah Kendzior, "How State Politicians Are Quietly Working to Steal
the 2016 Election," *Quartz,* May 20, 2016, https://qz.com/687408/how
-local-politicians-are-quietly-working-to-steal-the-us-presidential
-election/.

14. Sarah Kendzior, "Welcome to Donald Trump's America," *Foreign Policy,* August 3, 2016, https://foreignpolicy.com/2016/08/03/welcome-to
-donald-trumps-america/.

15. Sarah Kendzior, "Be Afraid: Trump May Have Bought the Fourth Estate,"
Globe and Mail, September 9, 2016, https://www.theglobeandmail
.com/opinion/be-afraid-trump-may-have-bought-the-fourth-estate
/article31789981/.

16. Naomi Klein, *The Shock Doctrine: The Rise of Disaster Capitalism*
(Toronto: Alfred A. Knopf Canada, 2007).

17. Sarah Kendzior, "We Are Heading Into Dark Times—This Is How to
Be Your Own Light," *De Correspondent,* November 18, 2016, https://
thecorrespondent.com/5696/were-heading-into-dark-times-this-is-how
-to-be-your-own-light-in-the-age-of-trump/1611114266432-e23ea1a6.

18. Anna Politkovskaya, *A Small Corner of Hell: Dispatches from Chechnya* (Chicago: University of Chicago Press, 2003), 216.

1. The Bellwether of American Decline

1. Omair Ahmad, "A Cassandra in Trumpland: Sarah Kendzior's Pithy Comment on Privilege," *The Wire,* December 9, 2016, https://thewire.in/84913
/sarah-kendzior-cassandra-in-trumpland-privilege/?fromNewsdog=1.

2. https://www.sos.mo.gov/archives/history/slogan.asp.

3. Rachel Lippmann, "Missouri Lawmakers Look to Undo Voter-Approved Initiatives," St. Louis Public Radio, April 22, 2019, https:// news.stlpublicradio.org/post/missouri-lawmakers-look-undo-voter -approved-initiatives.

4. T. S. Eliot, *The Hollow Men* (Redlands, CA: IC Press, 1988).

5. Jim Gallagher, "A Survivor Describes the Great Quake of 1811," *St. Louis Post-Dispatch*, August 1, 2015, https://www.stltoday.com/news /local/a-survivor-describes-the-great-quake-of/article_83ac1f82-7cd2 -5d20-b570-74efc8355aee.html.

6. Helen Wilbers, "New Madrid Threat Leaves Generals Quaking," *Fulton Sun*, November 18, 2018, http://www.fultonsun.com/news/local /story/2018/nov/18/new-madrid-threat-leaves-generals-quaking /752890/.

7. Phillip Longman, "Why the Economic Fates of America's Cities Diverged," *The Atlantic*, November 28, 2015, https://www.theatlantic .com/business/archive/2015/11/cities-economic-fates-diverge/417372/.

8. Elaine X. Grant, "TWA—Death of a Legend," *St. Louis* magazine, June 28, 2006, https://www.stlmag.com/TWA-Death-Of-A-Legend/.

9. Reuters, "Icahn: Mnuchin and Ross 'Would Be Great Choices' for Trump," November 15, 2016, https://www.businessinsider.com/r-update-1 -icahn-mnuchin-and-ross-would-be-great-choices-for-trump-2016-11.

10. Alan Greenblatt, "Rex Sinquefield: The Tyrannosaurus Rex of State Politics," Governing.com, June 2015, https://www.governing.com /topics/politics/gov-rex-sinquefield-missouri.html.

11. Dan Schnurbusch, "The Wild Mid-West: Missouri Ethics and Campaign Finance Under a Narrowed Corruption Regime," *Missouri Law Review* 80, no. 4 (2015), https://scholarship.law.missouri.edu/cgi/viewcontent .cgi?referer=&httpsredir=1&article=4175&context=mlr.

12. David A. Lieb, "Missouri Campaign Limits Repealed," *Missourian*, July 22, 2008, https://www.columbiamissourian.com/news/state_news /missouri-campaign-contribution-limits-repealed/article_0778898c -9e58-5e00-a6e9-dbcfcdeabd2c.html.

13. Open Secrets, "Political Nonprofits (Dark Money)," Last updated August 14, 2019, https://www.opensecrets.org/outsidespending/nonprof _summ.php.

14. Bruce Wilson, "Roy Blunt (R-MO) Tells Racism-Tinged Monkey Joke at DC Conference," *Huffington Post*, November 21, 2009, https://www .huffpost.com/entry/roy-blunt-r-mo-tells-raci_b_292260.

15. Monica Davey and Jeff Zeleny, "Obama Returns to Missouri, Site of Slim 2008 Loss," *New York Times*, July 6, 2010, https://www.nytimes .com/2010/07/07/us/politics/07missouri.html.

16. Jeff Nesbit, "The Secret Origins of the Tea Party," *Time*, 2016, https:// time.com/secret-origins-of-the-tea-party/.

17. Andrew Fowler, "NAACP Calls Out Tea Party for Racism," *St. Louis American*, July 15, 2010, http://www.stlamerican.com/news/local_news /naacp-calls-out-tea-party-for-racism/article_ba2aa555-432f-5424 -bea4-d231be68709b.html.

18. https://ballotpedia.org/Missouri_elections,_2016#cite_note-4.

19. Greenblatt, "Rex Sinquefield."

20. Nicholas Lemann, "Claire McCaskill's Toughest Fight," *New Yorker*, October 22, 2018, https://www.newyorker.com/magazine/2018/10/29 /claire-mccaskills-toughest-fight; Andy Kroll, "Dark Money's Top Target: Claire McCaskill," *Mother Jones*, September/October 2012, https:// www.motherjones.com/politics/2012/08/claire-mccaskill-missouri-karl -rove/.

21. Chris Gentilviso, "Todd Akin on Abortion: 'Legitimate Rape' Victims Have 'Ways to Try to Shut That Whole Thing Down,'" *Huffington Post*, August 19, 2012, https://www.huffpost.com/entry/todd-akin-abortion -legitimate-rape_n_1807381.

22. John Eligon, "McCaskill Ad Features Victims of Sexual Assault," *New York Times*, October 10, 2012, https://thecaucus.blogs.nytimes.com /2012/10/10/mccaskill-ads-feature-victims-of-sexual-assault/.

23. "America's Choice 2012: Election Center," Missouri Senate race results, CNN.com, December 10, 2012, http://edition.cnn.com/election /2012/results/state/MO/senate/.

24. Hannah Arendt, *The Life of the Mind* (New York: Harcourt, Inc., 1971), 180.

25. Jenna McLaughlin and Pema Levy, "What We Know About the Mysterious Suicide of Missouri Gubernatorial Candidate Tom Schweich," *Mother Jones*, February 27, 2015, https://www.motherjones.com/politics /2015/02/tom-schweich-missouri-suicide/.

26. Alex Stuckey, "Spence Jackson's Note: 'I Can't Take Being Unemployed Again," *St. Louis Post-Dispatch*, March 31, 2015, https://www.stltoday .com/news/local/crime-and-courts/spence-jackson-s-note-i-can-t-take -being-unemployed/article_e623c1eb-343a-568d-9bae-a18d350175f3 .html.

27. Erin Richey, "Missouri Gets D-Grade in 2015 state integrity investigation," Center for Public Integrity, November 9, 2015, https://publicintegrity.org /state-politics/state-integrity-investigation/missouri-gets-d-grade-in-2015 -state-integrity-investigation/.

28. Ibid.

29. Associated Press, "Court Says Pro-Greitens' Group Must Comply with Subpoena," Fox4kc.com, May 29, 2018, https://fox4kc.com/2018/05 /29/court-says-pro-greitens-group-must-comply-with-subpoena/.

30. Jason Hancock, "House Says Greitens' Nonprofit Must Comply with Judge's Order and Turn Over Records," *Kansas City Star*, May 31,

2018, https://www.kansascity.com/news/politics-government/article212 279384.html.

31. Jo Mannies, "Greitens' Political Nonprofits Take Center Stage in Missouri; Common for Governors Around US," St. Louis Public Radio, April 4, 2017, https://news.stlpublicradio.org/post/greitens-political -nonprofits-take-center-stage-missouri-common-governors-around -us#stream/0.

32. Kurt Erickson, "Greitens Campaign Operation Is Sharing Space with Dark Money Group," St. Louis Post-Dispatch, January 20, 2018, https:// www.stltoday.com/news/local/govt-and-politics/greitens-campaign -operation-is-sharing-space-with-dark-money-group/article_61fe730c -80a4-5221-82df-bff1be22794a.html.

33. The National Interest, "Proposed Missouri Law Would Require Residents 18 to 35 to Own an AR-15 (There's a Catch)," Yahoo News, May 5, 2019, https://news.yahoo.com/proposed-missouri-law-require-residents -110000807.html.

34. "New Analysis Finds Gun Violence Takes a $1.9 Billion Toll on Missouri," Giffords Law Center, January 2019, https://giffords.org /wp-content/uploads/2019/01/Economic-Cost-of-Gun-Violence-in -Missouri-1.pdf.

35. "Drug Overdose Mortality by State," CDC, https://www.cdc.gov/nchs /pressroom/sosmap/drug_poisoning_mortality/drug_poisoning.htm.

36. Joe Millitzer, "Stenger Resigns After Federal 'Pay-to-Play' Indictment," Fox 2 News, April 29, 2019, https://fox2now.com/2019/04/29/st-louis -county-executive-steve-stenger-indicted-in-pay-to-play-scheme/.

37. "Post-Dispatch Coverage of the West Lake and Bridgeton Landfills," St. Louis Post-Dispatch, January 7, 2019, https://www.stltoday .com/news/archives/post-dispatch-coverage-of-the-west-lake-and -bridgeton-landfills/collection_f524db66-ffa9-54df-a131-b759a94ec 3dd.html.

38. "NAACP Missouri Chapter Issues Travel Warning for People of Color," NPR, August 6, 2017, https://www.npr.org/2017/08/06/541929796/naacp -missouri-chapter-issues-travel-warning-for-people-of-color.

39. "The US State Where Women 'Could Be Fired' for Using Contraception," BBC News, January 31, 2019, https://www.bbc.co.uk/bbcthree /article/dad7562f-05b5-428c-8568-b5648674dcda.

40. Jo Mannies, "Missouri to Give Trump Commission Limited Voter Details, as Illinois Waits for White House Request," St. Louis Public Radio, January 30, 2017, https://news.stlpublicradio.org/post/missouri -give-trump-commission-limited-voter-details-illinois-waits-white -house-request#stream/0.

41. Jason Hancock and Bryan Lowry, "Missouri Gov. Eric Greitens Resigns, Ending Political Career Once Aimed at Presidency," Kansas

City Star, May 29, 2018, https://www.kansascity.com/news/politics
-government/article212114314.html.

42. Chisun Lee, "Dark Money and the Downfall of Eric Greitens," *American Prospect*, June 6, 2018, https://prospect.org/article/dark-money
-and-downfall-eric-greitens.

43. Hancock, "House Says Greitens' Nonprofit Must Comply with Judge's Order."

44. Danny Wicentowski, "'This Place Is Hell': An Undercover Trip Inside St. Louis' Workhouse," *Riverfront Times*, August 7, 2017, https://www.riverfronttimes.com/newsblog/2017/08/07/this-place-is-hell-an
-undercover-trip-inside-st-louis-workhouse.

45. Samuel King, "'Dark Money' Groups Spent Millions to Influence Missouri Voters, Report Finds," St. Louis Public Radio, April 18, 2019, https://news.stlpublicradio.org/post/dark-money-groups-spent
-millions-influence-missouri-voters-report-finds#stream/0.

46. Christopher Hooks and Mike Spies, "Documents Show NRA and Republican Candidates Coordinated Ads in Key Senate Races," *Mother Jones*, January 11, 2019, https://www.motherjones.com/politics/2019
/01/nra-republicans-campaign-ads-senate-josh-hawley/.

47. Steve Vockrodt, Lindsay Wise, and Jason Hancock, "Missouri Secretary of State Begins Investigation into Josh Hawley," *Kansas City Star*, December 6, 2018, https://www.kansascity.com/news/politics-government
/article222741630.html.

48. Mike Spies, "NRA Accused of 'Elaborate Scheme' to Evade Campaign Finance Law," *Mother Jones*, October 23, 2018, https://www
.motherjones.com/politics/2018/10/nra-josh-hawley-campaign-finance
-starboard-strategic/; Hooks and Spies, "Documents Show NRA and Republican Candidates Coordinated Ads."

49. Mark Follman, "Why the National Rifle Association Is Under Fire Like Never Before," *Mother Jones*, March 27, 2019, https://www
.motherjones.com/politics/2019/03/nra-russia-butina-torshin-trump
-investigations/.

50. Sue Blesi, "843-Acre Property Is Don Robinson's Legacy," River Hills Traveler, https://www.riverhillstraveler.com/843-acre-property-is-don
-robinsons-legacy-to-outdoor-lovers/.

2. The 1980s: Roy Cohn's Orwellian America

1. Lois Romano, "Donald Trump, Holding All the Cards: The Tower! The Team! The Money! The Future!" *Washington Post*, November 15, 1984, https://www.washingtonpost.com/archive/lifestyle/1984/11/15/donald
-trump-holding-all-the-cards-the-tower-the-team-the-money-the-future
/8be79254-7793-4812-a153-f2b88e81fa54/?utm_term=.c610b02e7d79.

2. Susan Mulcahy, "Confessions of a Trump Tabloid Scribe," *Politico Magazine*, May/June 2016, https://www.politico.com/magazine/story /2016/04/2016-donald-trump-tabloids-new-york-post-daily-news -media-213842.

3. Marcus Baram, "Donald Trump Was Once Sued by Justice Department for Not Renting to Blacks," *Huffington Post*, April 29, 2011, https:// www.huffpost.com/entry/donald-trump-blacks-lawsuit_n_855553.

4. Alex Henderson, "Here's Why Trump's Ideal Lawyer, Roy Cohn, Was Such a Vile Figure in US Politics—and Why His Name Lives in Infamy," AlterNet, April 20, 2019, https://www.thenewcivilrightsmovement .com/2019/04/heres-why-trumps-ideal-lawyer-roy-cohn-was-such-a -vile-figure-in-us-politics-and-why-his-name-lives-in-infamy/.

5. Baram, "Donald Trump Was Once Sued by Justice Department."

6. Judy Klemesrud, "Donald Trump, Real Estate Promoter, Builds Image as He Buys Buildings," *New York Times*, November 1, 1976, https:// www.documentcloud.org/documents/2186610-donald-trump-real -estate-promoter-builds-image.html.

7. Marie Brenner, "How Donald Trump and Roy Cohn's Ruthless Symbiosis Changed America," *Vanity Fair*, June 28, 2017, https://www .vanityfair.com/news/2017/06/donald-trump-roy-cohn-relationship.

8. Ron Elving, "President Trump Called for Roy Cohn, but Roy Cohn Was Gone," NPR, January 7, 2018, https://www.npr.org/2018/01/07 /576209428/president-trump-called-for-roy-cohn-but-roy-cohn-was -gone.

9. Juan Gonzalez and Amy Goodman, "Trump's 'Greatest Mentor' Was Red-Baiting Aide to Joseph McCarthy," *Democracy Now!*, July 5, 2016, https://truthout.org/video/trump-s-greatest-mentor-was-red-baiting-aide -to-joseph-mccarthy/.

10. Alex Shephard and Theodore Ross, "'There's No Check on Trump Except Reality': A Q&A with Wayne Barrett," *New Republic*, December 1, 2016, https://newrepublic.com/article/139094/theres-no-check -trump-except-reality-qa-wayne-barrett.

11. Brenner, "Donald Trump and Roy Cohn's Ruthless Symbiosis."

12. Ibid.

13. Peter Manso, "My Bizarre Dinner Party with Donald Trump, Roy Cohn and Estee Lauder," *Politico Magazine*, May 27, 2016, https:// www.politico.com/magazine/story/2016/05/donald-trump-2016 -dinner-party-213923; GLBTQ, "Cohn, Roy (1927–1986)," http:// www.glbtqarchive.com/ssh/cohn_r_S.pdf.

14. Craig Unger, "Trump's Russian Laundromat," *New Republic*, July 13, 2017, https://newrepublic.com/article/143586/trumps-russian-laun dromat-trump-tower-luxury-high-rises-dirty-money-international -crime-syndicate.

15. Ibid.
16. Michael Winerip, "High Profile Prosecutor," *New York Times*, June 9, 1985 https://www.nytimes.com/1985/06/09/magazine/high-profile-prose cutor.html.
17. The photo is viewable on Getty Images at https://media.gettyimages .com/photos/football-portrait-of-lawyer-roy-cohn-at-home-posing -with-stuffed-toy-picture-id621089776.
18. Robert Mueller, "The Evolving Organized Crime Threat," Federal Bureau of Investigation, Citizens Crime Commission of New York City, January 27, 2011, https://archives.fbi.gov/archives/news/speeches/the -evolving-organized-crime-threat.
19. Jon Tuleya, "Reputed Philly Mobster Bumped from FBI's 'Ten Most Wanted' List," *Philly Voice*, December 17, 2015, https://www.phillyvoice .com/reputed-philly-mobster-bumped-fbis-ten-most-wanted-list/.
20. Ibid.
21. Federal Bureau of Investigation, "Top Ten Fugitives: Global Con Artist and Ruthless Criminal," October 21, 2009, https://archives.fbi.gov /archives/news/stories/2009/october/mogilevich_102109.
22. Callum Borchers, "The Amazing Story of Donald Trump's Old Spokesman, John Barron—Who Was Actually Donald Trump Himself," *Washington Post*, May 13, 2016, https://www.washingtonpost.com /news/the-fix/wp/2016/03/21/the-amazing-story-of-donald-trumps-old -spokesman-john-barron-who-was-actually-donald-trump-himself/ ?utm_term=.a2d07ab7231c.
23. Glenn Thrush, "To Charm Trump, Paul Manafort Sold Himself as an Affordable Outsider," *New York Times*, April 8, 2017, https://www .nytimes.com/2017/04/08/us/to-charm-trump-paul-manafort-sold -himself-as-an-affordable-outsider.html.
24. Michael Kruse, "'He Brutalized For You,'" *Politico Magazine,* April 8, 2016, https://www.politico.com/magazine/story/2016/04/donald-trump -roy-cohn-mentor-joseph-mccarthy-213799?o=0.
25. Becky Little, "Roy Cohn: From Ruthless 'Red Scare' Prosecutor to Donald Trump's Mentor," History Channel, 2019, https://www.history .com/news/roy-cohn-mccarthyism-rosenberg-trial-donald-trump.
26. Harold Meyerson, "The State of Work in the Age of Anxiety," *American Prospect*, https://prospect.org/article/40-year-slump.
27. Dwight Eisenhower, "Address 'The Chance for Peace' Delivered Before the American Society of Newspaper Editors," online by Gerhard Peters and John T. Woolley, American Presidency Project, https:// www.presidency.ucsb.edu/documents/address-the-chance-for-peace -delivered-before-the-american-society-newspaper-editors.
28. *Axios*, "Chart: How Pay Level Relates to Worker Productivity," May 7, 2019, https://www.axios.com/pay-level-wages-worker-productivity -labor-ee3c5728-7e56-4496-8bc6-212895a9840d.html.

29. James Briggs, "In Gary, Memories of Donald Trump's Casino Promises," *Indianapolis Star*, April 24, 2016, https://www.indystar.com/story
/money/2016/04/24/gary-memories-donald-trumps-casino-promises
/82886050/; Russ Buettner and Charles V. Bagli, "How Donald Trump
Bankrupted His Atlantic City Casinos, but Still Earned Millions," *New
York Times*, June 11, 2016, https://www.nytimes.com/2016/06/12/nyregion
/donald-trump-atlantic-city.html.

30. Hans-Wilhelm Saure, "Czech Stasi Spied on the Trumps," *Bild*, December 15, 2016, https://www.bild.de/news/ausland/donald-trump/czech
-stasi-spied-on-the-trumps-49326256.bild.html; "Czech secret agents
spied on Trump: He's 'completely tax-exempt for the next 30 years.'"
Business Insider, December 15, 2016, https://www.businessinsider.com
/czech-secret-agents-spied-on-donald-trump-he-is-tax-exempt-for-30-years
-2016-12.

31. Christopher Andrew and Vasili Mitrokhin, *The Sword and the Shield:
The Mitrokhin Archive and the Secret History of the KGB* (New York:
Basic Books, 1999); Greg Myre, "'Moscow Rules': How the CIA Operated Under the Watchful Eye of the KGB," NPR, June 10, 2019,
https://www.npr.org/2019/06/10/724099134/moscow-rules-how-the
-cia-operated-under-the-watchful-eye-of-the-kgb.

32. Hans-Wilhelm Saure, "Czech secret agents spied on Trump: He's 'completely tax-exempt for the next 30 years.'"

33. Luke Harding, "Czechoslovakia Ramped Up Spying on Trump in Late
1980s, Seeking US Intel," *The Guardian*, October 29, 2018, https://
www.theguardian.com/us-news/2018/oct/29/trump-czechoslovakia
-communism-spying.

34. Adam Lusher, "Adnan Khashoggi: The 'Whoremonger' Whose Arms
Deals Funded a Playboy Life of Decadence and 'Pleasure Wives,'" *The
Independent*, June 7, 2017, https://www.independent.co.uk/news/long
_reads/adnan-khashoggi-dead-saudi-arms-dealer-playboy-pleasure
-wives-billionaire-lifestyle-wealth-profit-a7778031.html.

35. "'Credible Evidence' Links MBS to Khashoggi's Murder: UN Report," *Al Jazeera*, June 19, 2019, https://www.aljazeera.com/news
/2019/06/khashoggi-killing-credible-evidence-linking-mbs-murder
-190619100354253.html.

36. Jane Mayer, "Donald Trump's Ghostwriter Tells All," *New Yorker*,
July 18, 2016, https://www.newyorker.com/magazine/2016/07/25/donald
-trumps-ghostwriter-tells-all.

37. Donald J. Trump, Tony Schwarz, *The Art of the Deal* (New York: Bal-
lantine Books), 27.

38. TASS, "Russian Ambassador to UN Says Met Trump Twice," August 2,
2016, https://www.rbth.com/news/2016/08/02/russian-ambassador-to
-un-says-met-trump-twice_617373.

39. Aleksandr Yunashev, "Чуркин: Ни Трамп, ни Ромни—не специалисты

во внешней политике" ["Neither Trump Nor Romney Are Experts on Foreign Policy"], *RT*, November 24, 2016, https://life.ru/t/новости /936573/churkin_ni_tramp_ni_romni_—_nie_spietsialisty_vo_vnieshnei _politikie; Elise Labott, "Russia Protests Anti-Trump Comments by Top UN Official," CNN.com, October 11, 2016, ttps://edition.cnn.com /2016/10/11/politics/russia-donald-trump-united-nations-protest/index .html.

40. Thomas Tracy, "NYC Medical Examiner Won't Release Russian UN Ambassador Vitaly Churkin's Autopsy Results," *New York Daily News*, March 10, 2017, https://www.nydailynews.com/new-york/nyc-officials -won-release-russian-ambassador-autopsy-results-article-1.2994404.

41. Shannon Vavra, "Russian Diplomats Keep Dying Unexpectedly," *Axios*, August 24, 2017, https://www.axios.com/russian-diplomats-keep-dying -unexpectedly-1513303951-de0183f3-7f77-400e-b9a2-45fb8ed7dfbd .html.

42. Bryan MacDonald, "Since Trump Won US Election, Russia-Bashing Industry Has Never Had It So Good," *RT*, March 13, 2017, https://www .rt.com/op-ed/380539-trump-won-us-election-russia/.

43. Luke Harding, "The Hidden History of Trump's First Trip to Moscow," *Politico Magazine*, November 19, 2017, https://www.politico .com/magazine/story/2017/11/19/trump-first-moscow-trip-215842.

44. Paula Span, "When Trump Hoped to Meet Gorbachev in Manhattan," *Washington Post*, July 10, 2017, https://www.washingtonpost.com /lifestyle/style/from-the-archives-when-trump-hoped-to-meet-gorbachev -in-manhattan/2017/07/10/3f570b42-658c-11e7-a1d7-9a32c91c6f40 _story.html?utm_term=.fa7f26a368ee.

45. Ron Rosenbaum, "Trump's Nuclear Experience," *Slate*, March 1, 2016, http://www.slate.com/articles/news_and_politics/the_spectator/2016 /03/trump_s_nuclear_experience_advice_for_reagan_in_1987.html.

46. Ilan Ben-Meir, "That Time Trump Spent Nearly $100,000 on an Ad Criticizing U.S. Foreign Policy in 1987," *BuzzFeed News*, July 10, 2015, https://www.buzzfeednews.com/article/ilanbenmeir/that-time-trump -spent-nearly-100000-on-an-ad-criticizing-us.

47. Ibid.

48. Rick Jervis, "Trump Confidant Roger Stone Gets the President He's Wanted Since 1988," *USA Today*, May 21, 2017, https://www.usatoday .com/story/opinion/voices/2017/05/21/roger-stone-donald-trump -documentary/101909014/.

49. "The Other Time Trump Was Huge," *Newsweek*, July 30, 2015, https:// www.newsweek.com/rise-trump-357533.

50. Michael Kruse, "The True Story of Donald Trump's First Campaign Speech—in 1987," *Politico Magazine*, February 5, 2016, https://www .politico.com/magazine/story/2016/02/donald-trump-first-campaign -speech-new-hampshire-1987-213595?o=1.

51. Claude Brodesser-Akner, "Watch: Did Trump Blame A.C. Casino Failures on Executives Killed in N.J. Copter Crash?," NJ Advance Media, August 12, 2016, https://www.nj.com/politics/2016/08/watch_did _trump_blame_ac_casino_failures_on_dead_e.html.

52. William D. Cohan, "Can Donald Jr. and Eric Trump Really Run the Family Business?" *Vanity Fair*, February 2017, https://www.vanityfair .com/news/2016/12/can-donald-jr-and-eric-trump-run-the-family -business.

53. Harry Hurt, *Lost Tycoon: The Many Lives of Donald J. Trump* (Brattleboro, VT: Echo Point Books, 1993), Kindle edition.

54. Jane Mayer, "Documenting Trump's Abuse of Women," *New Yorker*, October 17, 2016, https://www.newyorker.com/magazine/2016/10/24 /documenting-trumps-abuse-of-women.

55. John Santucci, "Donald Trump's Ex-Wife Ivana Disavows Old 'Rape' Allegation," *ABC News*, July 28, 2015, https://abcnews.go.com/Politics /donald-trumps-wife-ivana-disavows-rape-allegation/story?id=3273 2204.

56. Betsy Woodruff, "Cohen Is Prepared to Say Who Signed His Stormy Daniels 'Cover-up' Checks," *Daily Beast*, February 26, 2019, https:// www.thedailybeast.com/michael-cohen-is-prepared-to-say-who-signed -his-stormy-daniels-cover-up-checks.

57. Doina Chiacu and Sarah N. Lynch, "Cohen: Trump Ordered Him to Make 500 Threats over 10 Years," Reuters, February 27, 2019, https:// www.reuters.com/article/us-usa-trump-russia-threats-idUSKCN1 QG2MM.

58. Mark Hertsgaard, "Donald Trump's Favorite Drug Trafficker and Other Unsung Scandals of the Presidency From Hell," *The Nation*, March 13, 2018, https://www.thenation.com/article/donald-trumps-favorite-drug -trafficker-and-other-unsung-scandals-of-the-presidency-from-hell/.

59. George Orwell, *Nineteen Eighty-Four* (New York: Alfred A. Knopf, 1949), 222.

3. The 1990s: Elite Exploits of the New World Order

1. Thomas L. Friedman, "Foreign Affairs Big Mac I," *New York Times*, December 8, 1996, https://www.nytimes.com/1996/12/08/opinion /foreign-affairs-big-mac-i.html.

2. Peter Schwartz and Peter Leyden, "The Long Boom," *Wired*, July 1, 1997, https://www.wired.com/1997/07/longboom/.

3. Jane Meyer, "The Making of the Fox News White House," *New Yorker*, March 4, 2019, https://www.newyorker.com/magazine/2019/03/11/the -making-of-the-fox-news-white-house.

4. Wayne Barrett, *Trump: The Greatest Show on Earth* (New York: Regan Arts, 2016), 125.

5. Landon Thomas, "Jeffrey Epstein: International Moneyman of Mystery," *New York*, October 28, 2002, http://nymag.com/nymetro/news /people/n_7912/#.

6. Shane Croucher, "Jeffrey Epstein Autopsy Finds Hyoid Neck Bone Break, Expert Says It Raises Questions About Strangulation: Report," *Newsweek*, August 15, 2019, https://www.newsweek.com/jeffrey -epstein-autopsy-neck-hyoid-bone-broken-suicide-homicide-1454457.

7. Katie Benner and Danielle Ivory, "Jeffrey Epstein Death: 2 Guards Slept Through Checks and Falsified Records," *New York Times*, August 13, 2019, https://www.nytimes.com/2019/08/13/nyregion/jeffrey -epstein-jail-officers.html.

8. Julie K. Brown, "How a Future Trump Cabinet Member Gave a Serial Sex Abuser the Deal of a Lifetime," *Miami Herald*, November 28, 2018, https://www.miamiherald.com/news/local/article220097825.html.

9. Cockburn, "AG Barr's Father Warns of 'Dictatorship' . . . in Outer Space," *Spectator*, April 3, 2019, https://spectator.us/donald-barr-science -fiction/.

10. Rebecca Klein, "Jeffrey Epstein Was Their Teacher. He Became a Monster," *Huffington Post*, July 12, 2019, https://www.yahoo.com/huffpost /jeffrey-epstein-math-science-students-memories-194803928.html.

11. Norman Vanamee, "Who is Les Wexner, the Billionaire Former Client of Jeffrey Epstein?," *Town & Country*, July 10, 2019, https://www .townandcountrymag.com/society/money-and-power/a28350600 /jeffrey-epstein-les-wexner-connection-money/.

12. "Wexner Analysis: Israeli Communication Priorities 2003," Harvard University, http://wilsonweb.physics.harvard.edu/HUMANRIGHTS /PALESTINE/luntzwexneranalysis.pdf; Lisa Miller, "Titans of Industry Join Forces to Work for Jewish Philanthropy," *Wall Street Journal*, May 4, 1998, https://www.wsj.com/articles/SB894240270899870000.

13. Rachel Sandler, "Report: Leslie Wexner Says Jeffrey Epstein 'Misappropriated' At Least $46 Million from Him," *Forbes*, August 7, 2019, https://www.forbes.com/sites/rachelsandler/2019/08/07/leslie-wexner -says-jeffery-epstein-misappropriated-at-least-46-million-from-him /#5cdd46c26e80.

14. Ibid.

15. Bess Levin, "Of Course Jeffrey Epstein Moved His Dirty Money Through Deutsche Bank," *Vanity Fair*, July 23, 2019, https://www .vanityfair.com/news/2019/07/jeffrey-epstein-deutsche-bank.

16. Julie K. Brown, "For years, Jeffrey Epstein Abused Teen Girls, Police Say. A Timeline of His Case," *Miami Herald*, November 28, 2018, https://www.miamiherald.com/news/local/article221404845.html; Julie K. Brown and David Smiley, "New Victims Come Forward As Epstein Asks to Be Released from Jail to His Manhattan Mansion,"

Miami Herald, July 11, 2019, https://www.miamiherald.com/news
/local/crime/article232551882.html.

17. Paul Lewis and Jon Swaine, "Jeffrey Epstein: Inside the Decade of
Scandal Entangling Prince Andrew," *The Guardian*, January 10,
2015, https://www.theguardian.com/world/2015/jan/10/jeffrey-epstein
-decade-scandal-prince-andrew.

18. Stephen Rex Brown, "Jeffrey Epstein Accuser Sues Alan Dershowitz as
New Sex Trafficking Victim Reveals Herself," *Boston Herald*, April 17,
2019, https://www.bostonherald.com/2019/04/17/jeffrey-epstein-accuser
-sues-alan-dershowitz-as-new-sex-trafficking-victim-reveals-herself/.

19. Bridget Read, "Epstein Lawyer Alan Dershowitz Insists He Has a 'Perfect, Perfect' Sex Life," *New York,* July 19, 2019, https://www.thecut
.com/2019/07/epstein-lawyer-alan-dershowitz-says-he-has-perfect-sex
-life.html; John Amato, "Dershowitz: 'I Kept My Underwear On' During Massage at Epstein's Mansion," *Crooks and Liars* (blog), July 10,
2019, https://crooksandliars.com/2019/07/alan-dershowitz-i-kept-my
-underwear-during.

20. Lewis and Swaine, "Jeffrey Epstein: Inside the Decade of Scandal";
Brown, "How a Future Trump Cabinet Member."

21. Brown, "How a Future Trump Cabinet Member."

22. Landon Thomas Jr., "Financier Starts Sentence in Prostitution Case,"
New York Times, July 1, 2008, https://www.nytimes.com/2008/07/01
/business/01epstein.html.

23. Alexandra Wolfe, "Katie Couric, Woody Allen: Jeffrey Epstein's Society Friends Close Ranks," *Daily Beast*, April 1, 2011, https://www
.thedailybeast.com/katie-couric-woody-allen-jeffrey-epsteins-society
-friends-close-ranks.

24. Philip Weiss, "The Fantasist," *New York*, December 7, 2007, nymag
.com/news/features/41826/.

25. "Doe v. Trump et al. refiled complaint 9/30/16," https://www.scribd
.com/document/326055870/Doe-v-Trump-et-al-refiled-complaint-9
-30-16?campaign=SkimbitLtd&ad_group=66960X1516588Xf17583
373eb900fb6c523b3c5a53d8c3&keyword=660149026&source=hp
_affiliate&medium=affiliate.

26. Lisa Bloom, "Why the New Child Rape Case Filed Against Donald Trump Should Not Be Ignored," *Huffington Post*, June 29, 2016,
https://www.huffpost.com/entry/why-the-new-child-rape-ca_b_1061
9944.

27. Nancy Dillon and Leonard Greene, "California Woman Accusing Donald Trump of Raping Her When She Was 13 Cancels Press Conference
Amid Threats," *New York Daily News*, November 2, 2016, https://
www.nydailynews.com/news/national/calif-woman-accusing-trump
-child-rape-break-silence-article-1.2855631.

28. Clive Irving, "Ghislaine Maxwell's Father Was a Dark and Mysterious Figure, Just Like Jeffrey Epstein," *Daily Beast*, July 13, 2019, https://www.thedailybeast.com/ghislaine-maxwells-father-was-a-dark-and-mysterious-figure-just-like-jeffrey-epstein?ref=scroll.

29. Robert Verkaik, "The Mystery of Maxwell's Death," *The Independent*, March 10, 2006, https://www.independent.co.uk/news/uk/crime/the-mystery-of-maxwells-death-6107041.html.

30. Emily Hourican, "Robert Maxwell: Legacy of 'The Bouncing Czech,'" *The Independent*, October 17, 2016, https://www.independent.ie/entertainment/robert-maxwell-legacy-of-the-bouncing-czech-35131452.html.

31. Verkaik, "Mystery of Maxwell's Death."

32. Steven Prokesch, "Maxwell's Mirror Group Has $727.5 Million Loss," *New York Times*, June 24, 1992, https://www.nytimes.com/1992/06/24/business/maxwell-s-mirror-group-has-727.5-million-loss.html.

33. "Publisher Maxwell Buried in Jerusalem: Investigation: Hands Aboard the Tycoon's Yacht Are Told Not to Leave The Canary Islands as a Probe into the British Publisher's Mysterious Death Continues," *Los Angeles Times*, November 11, 1991, https://www.latimes.com/archives/la-xpm-1991-11-11-fi-1038-story.html.

34. Verkaik, "Mystery of Maxwell's Death."

35. Prokesch, "Maxwell's Mirror Group Has $727.5 Million Loss."

36. Gordon Thomas and Martin Dillon, *Robert Maxwell, Israel's Superspy* (New York: Carroll & Graf Publishers, 2003), 37–45.

37. Thomas and Dillon, *Robert Maxwell, Israel's Superspy*, 36.

38. Thomas and Dillon, *Robert Maxwell, Israel's Superspy*, 174.

39. "Jeffrey Epstein v. Bradley Edwards et al.," https://www.documentcloud.org/documents/1509483-exhibits-stm-undisputed-facts-part1.html#document/p606 percent20//.

40. Ben Schreckinger and Daniel Lippmann, "Meet the Woman Who Ties Jeffrey Epstein to Trump and the Clintons," *Politico Magazine*, July 21, 2019, https://www.politico.com/story/2019/07/21/jeffrey-epstein-trump-clinton-1424120.

41. Rosie Perper, "The Mysterious Foreign Passport Found in Jeffrey Epstein's Mansion Was Used to Enter at Least 4 Countries in the 1980s, Prosecutors Say," *Business Insider*, July 18, 2019, https://www.businessinsider.com/jeffrey-epstein-saudi-austria-foreign-passport-1980s-2019-7.

42. Vicky Ward, "Jeffrey Epstein's Sick Story Played Out for Years in Plain Sight," *Daily Beast*, July 9, 2019, https://www.thedailybeast.com/jeffrey-epsteins-sick-story-played-out-for-years-in-plain-sight.

43. Erik Larson, "Epstein Saga Enters New Phase. Will Anyone Else Be Ensnared?," *Bloomberg*, July 21, 2019, https://www.bloomberg.com/news/articles/2019-07-21/epstein-saga-enters-new-phase-will-anyone-else-be-ensnared.

44. "Ghislaine Maxwell: Profile," *The Telegraph*, March 7, 2011, https:// www.telegraph.co.uk/news/uknews/theroyalfamily/8365015/Ghislaine -Maxwell-profile.html.

45. Josh Saul, "Ex-Teen Prostitute Files Suit in Billionaire Sex-Slave Case," *New York Post*, September 21, 2015, https://pagesix.com/2015/09/21 /ex-teen-prostitute-files-suit-in-billionaire-sex-slave-case/.

46. "Ghislaine Maxwell: Profile," *The Telegraph*.

47. Marc Fisher, "Epstein's Accusers Call Her His Protector and Pro-curer. Is Ghislaine Maxwell Now Prosecutors' Target?," *Washington Post*, August 11, 2019, https://www.washingtonpost.com/politics /epsteins-accusers-call-her-his-protector-and-procurer-is-ghislaine-max well-now-prosecutors-target/2019/08/11/7af5968a-bbbd-11e9-a091 -6a96e67d9cce_story.html.

48. Leah Simpson, "Jeffrey Epstein's ex Ghislaine Maxwell gave elementary children a presentation about the ocean in January but the Massachu-setts school had 'no knowledge' of her connection to the pedophile," *Daily Mail*, August 17, 2019, https://www.dailymail.co.uk/news /article-7366333/Ghislaine-Maxwell-guest-speaker-elementary-school -January-gave-presentation-ocean.html; Yaron Steinbuch, "Jeffrey Ep-stein's Gal Pal Ghislaine Maxwell Lying Low at Massachusetts Man-sion," *New York Post*, August 14, 2019, https://nypost.com/2019/08/14 /jeffrey-epsteins-gal-pal-ghislaine-maxwell-laying-low-at-massachusetts -mansion/.

49. Vanessa Grigoriadis, "They're Nothing, These Girls," *Vanity Fair*, Au-gust 12, 2019, https://www.vanityfair.com/news/2019/08/the-mystery -of-ghislaine-maxwell-epstein-enabler.

50. Ibid.

51. Public prosecutor Yusuf Khaki Dogan, "Bill of Indictment to the Criminal Court of Antalya City, Supreme Republican Public Prosecutor's Office," Turkey, December 11, 2010 http://trump-russia.com/wp-content/ uploads/2019/07/Tevfik-Arif-Child-Prostitution-Indictment.pdf; Daily Mail Reporter, "New York Real Estate Mogul Arrested in Turkey on Suspi-cion of Running Prostitute Ring on $60m Luxury Yacht," *Daily Mail*, Oc-tober 1, 2010, https://www.dailymail.co.uk/news/article-1316831/NY-real -estate-mogul-Tevfik-Arif-arrested-suspicion-running-prostitute-ring.html.

52. Horacio Silva, "The Man Who Invented Supermodels Also Took Advantage of Them," *W Magazine*, January 12, 2017, https://www .wmagazine.com/story/john-casablancas-models-documentary-netflix.

53. Veronica Stracqualursi and Marshall Cohen, "Key Mueller Witness George Nader Hit with Underage Sex Trafficking, Child Porn Charges," CNN.com, July 19, 2019, https://www.cnn.com/2019/07/19/politics /george-nader-child-porn-sex-charges/.

54. Robert I. Friedman, *Red Mafiya: How the Russian Mob Has Invaded America* (New York: Little, Brown, 2002).

55. "Clinton Announces New Initiative Against Global Drug Trafficking Syndicates at U.N. Conference, Signs Order Barring Individuals and Companies from Trade and Commerce," National Drug Strategy Network, December 1995, http://www.ndsn.org/dec95/unconf.html.
56. Friedman, *Red Mafiya*, 266.
57. Martin Longman, "Trump Shouldn't Feel Vindicated by Phone Records," *Washington Monthly*, February 1, 2019, https://washingtonmonthly.com/2019/02/01/trump-shouldnt-feel-vindicated-by-phone-records/.
58. Tina Nguyen, "The Mystery of Donald Jr.'s Blocked Calls—Revealed?," *Vanity Fair*, February 1, 2019, https://www.vanityfair.com/news/2019/02/donald-trump-jr-howard-lorber-trump-tower-call.
59. Thomas Frank, "Secret Money: How Trump Made Millions Selling Condos to Unknown Buyers," *BuzzFeed News*, January 12, 2018, https://www.buzzfeednews.com/article/thomasfrank/secret-money-how-trump-made-millions-selling-condos-to.
60. Ibid.
61. Ibid.
62. Jesse Eisinger and Justin Elliott, "Ivanka and Donald Trump Jr. Were Close to Being Charged with Felony Fraud," ProPublica, October 4, 2017, https://www.propublica.org/article/ivanka-donald-trump-jr-close-to-being-charged-felony-fraud.
63. Michael Kruse, "Roger Stone's Last Dirty Trick," *Politico Magazine*, January 25, 2019, https://www.politico.com/magazine/story/2019/01/25/roger-stone-last-dirty-trick-224217.
64. Adam Nagourney, "President? Why Not? Says a Man at the Top," *New York Times*, September 25, 1999, https://www.nytimes.com/1999/09/25/nyregion/president-why-not-says-a-man-at-the-top.html?.
65. David Smith, "Trump, 'Blackmail' and a Pecker: Bezos Delivers Scandal with Something for Everyone," *The Guardian*, February 9, 2019, https://www.theguardian.com/technology/2019/feb/09/jeff-bezos-trump-national-enquirer-amazon-david-pecker.
66. Sue Curry Jansen, "How Western PR Firms Quietly Push Putin's Agenda," *Fast Company*, July 1, 2017, https://www.fastcompany.com/40437170/russia-quiet-public-relations-war.
67. Lachlan Markey, "Ex-Trump Aide Michael Caputo Scrambles to Scrub Russia from Bio," *Daily Beast*, November 6, 2017, https://www.thedailybeast.com/ex-trump-aide-frantically-scrambles-to-scrub-russia-from-bio.
68. Bill Carter, "Survival of the Pushiest," *New York Times*, January 28, 2001, https://www.nytimes.com/2001/01/28/magazine/survival-of-the-pushiest.html?mtrref=www.bing.com&gwh=558B7761298E9FDC4B18FCE2E78ACA30&gwt=pay.
69. Lacey Rose, "Mark Burnett Pursuing Vladimir Putin as Next Reality

TV Star," *Hollywood Reporter,* June 24, 2015, https://www.holly
woodreporter.com/news/mark-burnett-pursuing-vladimir-putin-80
4454.

70. Andrew Prokop, "The Investigation into Trump's Inauguration Money
Looks Quite Serious," *Vox,* February 5, 2019, https://www.vox.com
/2019/2/5/18211600/trump-inauguration-investigation-subpoena
-sdny.

4. The Early 2000s: Reality TV Terror

1. Wayne Barrett, "Peas in a Pod: The Long and Twisted Relationship Between Donald Trump and Rudy Giuliani," *New York Daily News,* September 4, 2016, https://www.nydailynews.com/opinion/wayne-barrett
-donald-trump-rudy-giuliani-peas-pod-article-1.2776357.

2. Brett Samuels, "Trump Ramps Up Rhetoric on Media, Calls Press 'the
Enemy of the People,'" *The Hill,* April 5, 2019, https://thehill.com
/homenews/administration/437610-trump-calls-press-the-enemy-of
-the-people.

3. Marina Fang, "A History of Donald Trump's Tasteless Comments About
9/11," *Huffington Post,* September 11, 2017, https://www.huffpost.com
/entry/donald-trump-911-anniversary_n_59b67625e4b0354e4413182b.

4. Alexandra Jaffe, "Trump in 2007: 'I'm Excited' for Housing Market Crash," *NBC News,* May 23, 2016, https://www.nbcnews.com
/politics/2016-election/trump-2007-i-m-excited-housing-market-crash
-n578761.

5. Michal Kranz, "'Why Did You Wait?': Trump Reportedly Asked the
CIA Why It Paused for Target to Walk Away from His Family Before
Striking," *Business Insider,* April 6, 2018, https://www.businessinsider
.com/trump-cia-drone-strike-terrorist-families-2018-4.

6. Yamiche Alcindor and Julie Hirschfeld Davis, "Soldier's Widow Says
Trump Struggled to Remember Sgt. La David Johnson's Name," *New
York Times,* October 23, 2017, https://www.nytimes.com/2017/10/23
/us/politics/soldiers-widow-says-trump-struggled-to-remember-sgt-la
-david-johnsons-name.html.

7. Donald J. Trump(@RealDonaldTrump), "I predicted the 9/11 attack on
America . . . ," Twitter, December 29, 2011, 11:49 A.M., https://twitter
.com/realDonaldTrump/status/152431014742986752.

8. Rebecca Kaplan, "Fact Check: Did Donald Trump Predict the 9/11 Attacks?," *CBS News,* November 26, 2015, https://www.cbsnews.com
/news/fact-check-did-donald-trump-predict-the-911-attacks/.

9. Dave Shiflett, "Another Time, Another Trump," *Wall Street Journal,*
December 21, 2015, https://www.wsj.com/articles/another-time-another
-trump-1450742675.

10. Andrew Kaczynski, "Trump Co-Author: I Won't Vote for 'No Class' Trump," *BuzzFeed News*, December 30, 2015, https://www.buzzfeednews.com/article/andrewkaczynski/trump-co-author-i-wont-vote-for-no-class-trump#.crA2gQ1o2.

11. Fang, "History of Donald Trump's Tasteless Comments."

12. Ron Suskind, "Faith, Certainty and the Presidency of George W. Bush," *New York Times*, October 17, 2004, https://www.nytimes.com/2004/10/17/magazine/faith-certainty-and-the-presidency-of-george-w-bush.html.

13. Hannah Arendt, "Lying in Politics," in *Crises of the Republic* (New York: Harcourt Brace Jovanovich, 1972).

14. Mike McIntire, "Donald Trump Settled a Real Estate Lawsuit, and a Criminal Case Was Closed," *New York Times*, April 6, 2016, https://www.nytimes.com/2016/04/06/us/politics/donald-trump-soho-settlement.html.

15. Kavitha George, "Ivanka Trump's Role on 'The Apprentice' Was Bigger Than You Might Remember," *Bustle*, February 23, 2019, https://www.bustle.com/p/ivanka-trumps-role-on-the-apprentice-was-bigger-than-you-might-remember-13077839.

16. Michael Wilner, "Will Cohen Probe Shed Light on Port Washington Role in Russia Probe?" *Jerusalem Post*, December 19, 2018, https://www.jpost.com/American-Politics/Will-Cohen-cooperation-deepen-Chabad-Port-Washington-role-in-Russia-probe-574849.

17. Christian Bautista and Will Parker, "Tamir Sapir Failed to Report $194M from Partial Sale of 11 Madison: IRS," *Real Deal*, September 12, 2018, https://therealdeal.com/2018/09/12/tamir-sapir-failed-to-report-194m-from-partial-sale-of-11-madison-irs/.

18. Darren Dahl, "My Story: Sean Yazbeck of Wavsys," *Inc.* magazine, September 2011, https://www.inc.com/magazine/201109/inc-500-sean-yazbeck-wavsys.html.

19. Asawin Suebsaeng and Gideon Resnick, "Mark Burnett Clamps Down on 'The Apprentice' Staff over Donald Trump Leaks," *Daily Beast*, November 2, 2011, https://www.thedailybeast.com/mark-burnett-clamps-down-on-the-apprentice-staff-over-donald-trump-leaks.

20. Jesse Eisinger and Justin Elliott, "Ivanka and Donald Trump Jr. Were Close to Being Charged With Felony Fraud," ProPublica, October 4, 2017, https://www.propublica.org/article/ivanka-donald-trump-jr-close-to-being-charged-felony-fraud.

21. Ibid.

22. Jim Zarolli, "Trump Denies Links To Russian-American Businessman," NPR, March 1, 2019, https://www.npr.org/2017/03/01/517988044/trump-denies-links-to-russian-american-businessman.

23. Greg Price, "Ivanka Trump sat in Vladimir Putin's Chair and Spun

Around, President's Former Associate Says," *Newsweek*, May 17, 2018, https://www.newsweek.com/ivanka-putin-chair-spun-kremlin-931754.

24. Michael Weiss, Catherine A. Fitzpatrick, and James Miller, "Trump's Russia Towers: He Just Can't Get Them Up," *Daily Beast*, June 11, 2016, https://www.thedailybeast.com/trumps-russia-towers-he-just-cant -get-them-up.

25. Andrew Rice, "The Original Russian Connection," *New York*, August 7, 2017, http://nymag.com/intelligencer/2017/08/felix-sater-donald-trump -russia-investigation.html?gtm=top.

26. Judicial Watch, "Who Is Felix Sater?," March 1, 2017, https://www .judicialwatch.org/bulletins/who-is-felix-sater/.

27. New America Foundation, "Part IV. What Is the Threat to the United States Today?," in *Terrorism in America After 9/11*, https://www .newamerica.org/in-depth/terrorism-in-america/what-threat-united -states-today/.

28. Anthony Cormier and Jason Leopold, "The Asset," *BuzzFeed News*, March 12, 2018, https://www.buzzfeednews.com/article/anthonycormier /felix-sater-trump-russia-undercover-us-spy.

29. Matt Apuzzo and Maggie Haberman, "Trump Associate Boasted That Moscow Business Deal 'Will Get Donald Elected,'" *New York Times*, August 28, 2017, https://www.nytimes.com/2017/08/28/us/politics /trump-tower-putin-felix-sater.html.

30. Matthew Mosk and Brian Ross, "Memory Lapse? Trump Seeks Distance From 'Advisor' with Past Ties to Mafia," *ABC News*, December 10, 2015, https://abcnews.go.com/Politics/memory-lapse-trump-seeks-distance -advisor-past-ties/story?id=34600826.

31. Wilner, "Will Cohen Probe Shed Light on Port Washington."

32. Joseph Tanfani and David S. Cloud, "Trump Business Associate Led Double Life As FBI Informant—and More, He Says," *Los Angeles Times*, March 2, 2017, https://www.latimes.com/politics/la-na-pol-sater -trump-20170223-story.html.

33. Flora Drury, "Litvinenko's Revenge from Beyond the Grave: Spy's Voice Recording Reveals Links Between Putin and Terrorist-As 'Proof' Emerges That Russia DID Kill Him in 'State Execution,'" *Daily Mail*, January 23, 2015, https://www.dailymail.co.uk/news/article-2923856 /Litvinenko-links-Putin-Semion-Mogilevich-terrorist-crime-boss.html.

34. Andrew G. McCabe, "Every Day Is a New Low in Trump's White House," *The Atlantic*, February 14, 2019, https://www.theatlantic.com /politics/archive/2019/02/andrew-mccabe-fbi-book-excerpt-the-threat /582748/.

35. Salena Zito, "Taking Trump Seriously, Not Literally," *The Atlantic*, September 23, 2016, https://www.theatlantic.com/politics/archive/2016/09 /trump-makes-his-case-in-pittsburgh/501335/.

36. Anita Kumar, "Buyers Tied to Russia, Former Soviet Republics Paid $109 Million Cash for Trump Properties," McClatchy, June 19, 2018, https://www.mcclatchydc.com/news/politics-government/white-house /article210477439.html.

37. Ibid.

38. Jason Leopold and Anthony Cormier, "Russian Agents Sought Secret US Treasury Records On Clinton Backers During 2016 Campaign," *BuzzFeed News*, December 20, 2018, https://www.buzzfeednews.com /article/anthonycormier/russian-agents-sought-us-treasury-records-on -clinton-backers.

39. Ibid.

40. Senator Mark Warner, press release, "Senate Vice Intel Chair Warner Presses Mnuchin on Deripaska Sanctions," January 29, 2019, https:// www.warner.senate.gov/public/index.cfm/2019/1/senate-intel-vice -chair-warner-presses-mnuchin-on-deripaska-sanctions.

41. Brennan Weiss, "Trump's Oldest Son Said a Decade Ago That a Lot of the Family's Assets Came from Russia," *Business Insider*, February 21, 2018, https://www.businessinsider.com/donald-trump-jr-said-money -pouring-in-from-russia-2018-2.

5. The Late 2000s: Heirs to the Crash

1. https://www.insidehighered.com/quicktakes/2018/11/02/new-data -adjunct-instructors; https://www.washingtonpost.com/local/education /it-keeps-you-nice-and-disposable-the-plight-of-adjunct-professors /2019/02/14/6cd5cbe4-024d-11e9-b5df-5d3874f1ac36_story.html.

2. Andre Spicer, "Donald Trump's 'Kakistocracy' Is Not the First, But It's Revived an Old Word," *The Guardian*, April 18 2018, https:// www.theguardian.com/commentisfree/2018/apr/18/donald-trump -kakistocracy-john-brennan-us-twitter.

3. Sam Petulla and Jennifer Hansler, "There Is a Wave of Republicans Leaving Congress, Updated Again," CNN.com, November 10, 2017, https://www.cnn.com/2017/11/10/politics/house-retirement-tracker /index.html.

4. Colby Hall, "'It's Blackmail': Joe and Mika Reveal How White House Threatened Them with National Enquirer," *Mediaite*, June 30, 2017, https://www.mediaite.com/tv/its-blackmail-joe-and-mika-reveal-how -white-house-threatened-them-with-national-enquirer/.

5. Alex Gibney, "Meet the Leader of Eliot Spitzer's Smear Campaign," *The Atlantic*, October 13, 2010, https://www.theatlantic.com/politics /archive/2010/10/meet-the-leader-of-eliot-spitzers-smear-campaign /64361/.

6. Denis Slattery, "'Manhattan Madam' Kristin Davis Subpoenaed in Mueller

Probe," *New York Daily News*, July 20, 2018, https://www.nydailynews
.com/news/politics/ny-pol-manhattan-madam-mueller-davis-stone
-20180720-story.html.

7. Matt Zapotosky, "Why Jared Kushner Had to Update His Disclosure of
Foreign Contacts More Than Once," *Washington Post*, July 17, 2017,
https://www.washingtonpost.com/world/national-security/why-jared
-kushner-has-had-to-update-his-disclosure-of-foreign-contacts-more
-than-once/2017/07/17/b04e8158-6b05-11e7-96ab-5f38140b38cc
_story.html?utm_term=.21f497930166.

8. David D. Kirkpatrick, Ben Hubbard, Mark Landler, and Mark Maz-
zetti, "The Wooing of Jared Kushner," *New York Times*, December 8,
2018, https://www.nytimes.com/2018/12/08/world/middlecast/saudi
-mbs-jared-kushner.html.

9. Simon Tisdall, "Trump's Cronies Are in Secret Talks to Sell Nuclear
Tech to Saudi. The Risks Are Clear," *The Guardian*, February 23, 2019,
https://www.theguardian.com/us-news/2019/feb/23/trump-cronies
-secret-talks-nuclear-tech-saudi-arabia.

10. Asawin Suebsaeng, Maxwell Tani, and Lloyd Grove, "Jared Kushner
Replaced Michael Cohen as Trump's National Enquirer Connection,"
Daily Beast, December 14, 2018, https://www.thedailybeast.com/how
-jared-kushner-replaced-michael-cohen-as-trumps-national-enquirer
-connection.

11. Andrew Prokop, "Jared Kushner's Many, Many Scandals, Explained,"
Vox, March 2, 2018, https://www.vox.com/policy-and-politics/2018/3
/1/17053398/jared-kushner-scandals-russia-clearance-loans.

12. Daniel Golden, "The Story Behind Jared Kushner's Curious Acceptance Into Harvard," *ProPublica*, November 18, 2016, https://www
.propublica.org/article/the-story-behind-jared-kushners-curious
-acceptance-into-harvard.

13. Michael D'Antonio, "Ike Didn't Like Donald Trump's Dad at All,"
Daily Beast, April 24, 2017, https://www.thedailybeast.com/ike-didnt
-like-donald-trumps-dad-at-all; Josh Gerstein, "FBI Releases Thin File
on Donald Trump's Father, Fred," *Politico*, October 8, 2016, https://
www.politico.com/blogs/under-the-radar/2016/10/fbi-releases-thin-file
-on-fred-trump-229361.

14. David Barstow, Susanne Craig, and Russ Buettner, "Trump Engaged
in Suspect Tax Schemes as He Reaped Riches from His Father," *New
York Times*, October 2, 2018, https://www.nytimes.com/interactive
/2018/10/02/us/politics/donald-trump-tax-schemes-fred-trump.html.

15. Christina Zhao, "Chris Christie Shreds Jared Kushner's Father," *Newsweek*, January 29, 2019, https://www.newsweek.com/chris-christie
-shreds-jared-kushners-father-one-most-loathsome-disgusting
-1310842.

16. Katherine Clarke, "Jared Kushner, the Accidental CEO," *Real Deal*, February 1, 2014, https://therealdeal.com/issues_articles/jared-kushner -the-accidental-ceo/.

17. Steve Cuozzo, "The Scandalous History Behind Kushner's Ritzy Midtown Building," *New York Post*, April 18, 2017, https://nypost.com /2017/04/18/the-scandalous-history-behind-kushners-ritzy-midtown -building/.

18. Clive Irving, "The Curse of 666 Fifth Avenue, the Skyscraper That Could Sink the Kushners," *Daily Beast*, March 11, 2018, https://www .thedailybeast.com/the-curse-of-666-fifth-avenue-the-skyscraper-that -could-sink-the-kushners.

19. "Ron Lauder Praises Trump As 'Man of Intelligence,'" *Times of Israel*, January 9, 2018, https://www.timesofisrael.com/ron-lauder-praises -trump-as-man-of-intelligence/.

20. Rosalind S. Helderman and Tom Hamburger, "How Manafort's 2016 Meeting with a Russian Employee at New York Cigar Club Goes to 'The Heart' of Mueller's Probe," *Washington Post*, February 12, 2019, https:// www.washingtonpost.com/politics/how-manaforts-2016-meeting-with -a-russian-employee-at-new-york-cigar-club-goes-to-the-heart-of-muellers -probe/2019/02/12/655f84dc-2d67-11e9-8ad3-9a5b113ecd3c_story.html ?utm_term=.b801662cf596.

21. Julia Horowitz and Cristina Alesci, "Kushner Companies Offloads Troubled 666 Fifth Avenue Flagship," CNN.com, August 3, 2018, https://money.cnn.com/2018/08/03/news/companies/kushner-666-fifth -avenue-brookfield/index.html.

22. Ryan Beene, "Jared Kushner Has Paid Almost No Federal Income Tax in Years: Report," *Time*, October 13, 2018, http://time.com/5424109 /jared-kushner-taxes-new-york-times/.

23. Ibid.

24. Jacob Passy, "Jared Kushner hasn't paid federal income taxes in years: New York Times," *MarketWatch*, October 13, 2018, https://www .marketwatch.com/story/jared-kushner-hasnt-paid-federal-income -taxes-in-years-new-york-times-2018-10-13.

25. Naomi Zeveloff, "When Bibi Slept in Jared Kushner's Bed," *The Forward*, February 12, 2017, https://forward.com/fast-forward/362898 /when-bibi-slept-in-jared-kushners-bed/.

26. Judy Maltz, "Kushner Foundation Gives $342K to Chabad—Still Surprised About Jared and Ivanka's Synagogue?" *The Forward*, January 9, 2017, https://forward.com/news/359482/kushner-foundation-gives -342k-to-chabad-still-surprised-about-jared-and-iva/; Chabad.org, "The Light of Truth at the UN: Excerpt of Prime Minister Netanyahu at the General Assembly, Sept 23, 2011," https://www.chabad.org/multimedia /media_cdo/aid/1632210/jewish/The-Light-of-Truth-at-the-UN.htm.

27. Ben Schreckinger, "The Happy-Go-Lucky Jewish Group That Connects Trump and Putin," *Politico Magazine*, April 9, 2017, https://www.politico.com/magazine/story/2017/04/the-happy-go-lucky-jewish-group-that-connects-trump-and-putin-215007.

28. Oliver Holmes and Kevin Rawlinson, "Roman Abramovich Granted Israeli Citizenship," *The Guardian*, May 28, 2018, https://www.theguardian.com/world/2018/may/28/roman-abramovich-granted-israeli-citizenship-tel-aviv-chelsea.

29. Schreckinger, "The Happy-Go-Lucky Jewish Group That Connects Trump and Putin."

30. Ibid.

31. Craig Unger, *House of Trump, House of Putin* (New York: Dutton, 2018), 116.

32. Chris Riotta, "Jared Kushner Failed to Disclose He Led a Foundation Funding Illegal Israeli Settlements Before U.N. Vote," *Newsweek*, December 3, 2017, https://www.newsweek.com/jared-kushner-disclosure-form-west-bank-settlements-israel-white-house-729290.

33. Aiden Pink, "Jared and Ivanka Blessed by Israeli Rabbi Who Compared Black People to Monkeys," *The Forward*, May 13, 2018, https://forward.com/fast-forward/400996/jared-and-ivanka-blessed-by-israeli-rabbi-who-compared-black-people-to/.

34. Talia Lavin, "Trump Sees All Us Jews As Israelis Because His Christian Zionist Allies Do Too," *Washington Post*, August 22, 2019, https://www.washingtonpost.com/outlook/2019/08/22/trump-sees-all-us-jews-israelis-because-his-christian-zionist-allies-do-too/; Rachel Tabachnick, "Meet Bibi's New Tribulation-Courting, Jew-Converting, Demon-Exorcising American Allies," *Daily Beast*, April 14, 2017, https://www.thedailybeast.com/meet-bibis-new-tribulation-courting-jew-converting-demon-exorcising-american-allies.

35. Charles V. Bagli and Jesse Drucker, "Kushners Near Deal With Qatar-Linked Company for Troubled Tower," *New York Times*, May 17, 2018, https://www.nytimes.com/2018/05/17/nyregion/kushner-deal-qatar-666-5th.html.

36. Michelle Nichols, "Flynn, Kushner Targeted Several States in Failed U.N. Lobbying: Diplomats," Reuters, December 1, 2017, https://www.reuters.com/article/us-usa-trump-russia-un-idUSKBN1DW015.

37. Vicky Ward, *Kushner, Inc.: Greed. Ambition. Corruption. The Extraordinary Story of Jared Kushner and Ivanka Trump* (New York: St. Martin's Press, 2019), 117.

38. Lizzie Widdicombe, "Ivanka and Jared's Power Play," *New Yorker*, August 22, 2016, https://www.newyorker.com/magazine/2016/08/22/ivanka-trump-and-jared-kushners-power-play.

39. Ibid.

40. Emily Jane Fox, "Could It Be That Vladimir Putin and Wendi Deng Are in Love?" *Vanity Fair*, March 31, 2016, https://www.vanityfair.com /news/2016/03/vladimir-putin-wendi-deng-couple; Emily Jane Fox, "Ivanka Trump Is Vacationing with Wendi Deng," *Vanity Fair*, August 15, 2016, https://www.vanityfair.com/news/2016/08/ivanka-trump -wendi-deng-vacation.

41. James Warren, "Is Rupert Murdoch's Ex a Chinese Spy?," *Vanity Fair*, January 16, 2018, Jhttps://www.vanityfair.com/news/2018/01/wendi -deng-rubert-murdoch-chinese-spy-jared-kushner.

42. Jewish Telegraphic Agency, "Trump Denies Seeking Security Clearance for Ivanka, Kushner and Other Children," November 16, 2016, https://www .jta.org/2016/11/16/politics/trump-denies-seeking-security-clearance-for -ivanka-kushner-and-other-children.

43. Michael Sainato, "Electoral College Delusions Still Plague Clinton Partisans," *The Observer*, November 21, 2016, https://observer.com/2016 /11/electoral-college-delusions-still-plague-clinton-partisans/.

44. Kyle Pope, "The Jared Bubble," *Columbia Journalism Review*, Fall 2017, https://www.cjr.org/special_report/cjr-kyle-pope-jared-kushner -observer.php.

45. Helin Jung, "Get That Life: How I Became a Political Journalist Working in the Middle of the Country," *Cosmopolitan*, January 30, 2017, https://www.cosmopolitan.com/career/a8578596/sarah-kendzior -political-journalist-get-that-life/.

46. Ibid.

6. 2010–2016: Revolution Shakedown

1. Sarah Kendzior, "Inventing Akromiya: The Role of Uzbek Propagandists in the Andijon Massacre," *Demokratizatsiya: The Journal of Post-Soviet Democratization* 14, no. 4 (Fall 2006): 545–562, https://www .academia.edu/170210/Inventing_Akromiya_The_Role_of_Uzbek _Propagandists_in_the_Andijon_Massacre.

2. Darya Korsunskaya, "Putin Says Russia Must Prevent 'Color Revolution,'" Reuters, November 20, 2014, https://news.yahoo.com/putin -says-russia-must-guard-against-color-revolutions-135807378.html.

3. Rebecca MacKinnon, "China's 'Networked Authoritarianism,'" *Journal of Democracy* 22, no. 2 (April 2011): 32–46, https://muse.jhu.edu /article/427159.

4. Katy E. Pearce and Sarah Kendzior, "Networked Authoritarianism and Social Media in Azerbaijan," *Journal of Communication* 62, no. 2 (2012), https://onlinelibrary.wiley.com/doi/abs/10.1111/j.1460-2466 .2012.01633.x.

5. Amnesty International, "Journalist Khadija Freed in Azerbaijan, After Being Blackmailed and Unjustly Imprisoned by Her Government,"

January 12, 2018, https://www.amnesty.org.uk/journalist-khadija
-ismayilova-free-azerbaijan-imprisoned-blackmailed-government
-corruption.

6. Alexey Kovalev, "Russia's Blogging Revolution," *The Guardian*, September 24, 2010, https://www.theguardian.com/commentisfree/2010
/sep/24/russia-blogging-revolution.

7. Peter Pomerantzev, *Nothing Is True and Everything Is Possible: The Surreal Heart of the New Russia* (Philadelphia: PublicAffairs, 2015).

8. Sarah Kendzior, "The Strange Saga of a Made-Up Activist and Her Life—and Death—as a Hoax," *The Atlantic*, December 20, 2011, https://www.theatlantic.com/international/archive/2011/12/the
-strange-saga-of-a-made-up-activist-and-her-life-and-death-as-a-hoax
/250203/.

9. Jaron Lanier, "The Hazards of Nerd Supremacy: The Case of WikiLeaks," *The Atlantic*, December 20, 2010, https://www.theatlantic
.com/technology/archive/2010/12/the-hazards-of-nerd-supremacy-the
-case-of-WikiLeaks/68217/.

10. Malcolm Nance, *The Plot to Destroy Democracy: How Putin and his Spies Are Undermining America and Dismantling the West* (New York: Hachette Books, 2018).

11. Ivan Sigal, Public Radio International, "Syria's war may be the most documented ever. And yet, we know so little," December 19, 2016, https://www.pri.org/stories/2016-12-19/syrias-war-may-be-most
-documented-ever-and-yet-we-know-so-little.

12. Ashley Gold, "Wylie to House Dems: Bannon Ordered Putin Messaging Tests," *Politico*, April 25, 2018, https://www.politico.com/story
/2018/04/25/wylie-bannon-putin-messages-553738.

13. Ryan Broderick, "Christchurch: This Will Keep Happening," *BuzzFeed News*, March 15, 2019, https://www.buzzfeednews.com/article
/ryanhatesthis/murder-as-a-meme-white-male-violence-is-being
-distributed.

14. Kathy Sierra, "Trouble at the Kool-Aid Point," *Serious Pony* (blog), October 7, 2014, http://seriouspony.com/trouble-at-the-koolaid-point.

15. Noreen Malone, "Zoe and the Trolls," *New York*, July 24, 2017, http://
nymag.com/intelligencer/2017/07/zoe-quinn-surviving-gamergate
.html.

16. Ryan Broderick, "Activists Are Outing Hundreds of Twitter Users Believed to Be 4chan Trolls Posing As Feminists," *BuzzFeed News*, June 17, 2014, https://www.buzzfeednews.com/article/ryanhatesthis/your-slip-is
-showing-4chan-trolls-operation-lollipop.

17. Sarah Kendzior, "Russia's Social Media Propaganda Was Hiding in Plain Sight," *NBC News*, November 2, 2017, https://www.nbcnews
.com/think/opinion/russia-s-social-media-propaganda-was-hiding
-plain-sight-ncna816886.

18. Gold, "Wylie to House Dems."
19. Sarah Kendzior, "The Minimum Wage Worker Strikes Back," Medium, April 14, 2014, https://medium.com/@sarahkendzior/the-minimum-wage-worker-strikes-back-fa4c36eb306b.
20. Pamela Engel, "Missouri State Senator Tells Police Chief She Was Tear Gassed While Protesting Peacefully in Ferguson," Business Insider, August 13, 2014, https://www.businessinsider.com/missouri-state-senator-gassed-while-protesting-in-ferguson-2014-8.
21. Nicholas Pistor and Joe Holleman, "St. Louis Prosecutor Has Faced Controversy for Decades," St. Louis Post-Dispatch, August 16, 2014, https://www.stltoday.com/news/local/metro/st-louis-prosecutor-has-faced-controversy-for-decades/article_cdd4c104-6086-506e-9ee8-aa957a31fee5.html.
22. Sarah Kendzior, "Meet Darren Seals. Then Tell Me Black Death Is Not a Business," De Correspondent, October 1, 2016, https://thecorrespondent.com/5349/meet-darren-seals-then-tell-me-black-death-is-not-a-business/1512965275833-fe73c5b1.
23. Bruce Franks Jr., "If I Don't Make This Move, St. Louis Is Going to Kill Me," St. Louis American, July 19, 2019, http://www.stlamerican.com/news/columnists/guest_columnists/if-i-don-t-make-this-move-st-louis-is/article_b6dbe594-aa4e-11e9-af76-bf4ee9e9def4.html.
24. Kim Bell, "Trump Blames Gangs of Illegal Immigrants for Woes in Ferguson, St. Louis," St. Louis Post-Dispatch, August 25, 2016, https://www.stltoday.com/news/local/govt-and-politics/trump-blames-gangs-of-illegal-immigrants-for-woes-in-ferguson/article_ab07521a-1426-5799-9908-00e3eeb5398b.html.
25. Jamil Smith, "The Central Park Five Told Us Who Donald Trump Really Is," MTV News, August 23, 2016, http://www.mtv.com/news/2922644/the-central-park-five-ad-told-us-who-donald-trump-really-is/.
26. Associated Press, "National Enquirer hid Trump secrets in a safe, removed them before inauguration," NBC News, August 23, 2018, https://www.nbcnews.com/politics/donald-trump/national-enquirer-hid-trump-secrets-safe-removed-them-inauguration-n903356.
27. Larry Solov, "Breitbart News Network: Born in the USA, Conceived in Israel," Breitbart, November 17, 2015, https://www.breitbart.com/the-media/2015/11/17/breitbart-news-network-born-in-the-usa-conceived-in-israel/.
28. Business Insider, "Donald Trump's Ex-Wife Once Said Trump Kept a Book of Hitler's Speeches by His Bed," September 1, 2015, https://www.businessinsider.com/donald-trumps-ex-wife-once-said-he-kept-a-book-of-hitlers-speeches-by-his-bed-2015-8.
29. Adolf Hitler, Mein Kampf (New York: Reynal, 1939), 212.
30. Ari Berman, "Rigged: How Voter Suppression Threw Wisconsin to Trump," Mother Jones, November/December 2017, https://www

.motherjones.com/politics/2017/10/voter-suppression-wisconsin
-election-2016/.

31. Bill Browder, *Red Notice: A True Story of High Finance, Murder, and One Man's Fight for Justice* (New York: Simon & Schuster, 2015), 329.

32. *The Week*, "The Final Presidential Debate: Obama Attacks Early and Often," October 22, 2012, https://theweek.com/articles/471162/final -presidential-debate-obama-attacks-early-often.

33. Shaun Walker, "The Trumps of Russia? How Billionaire Agalarov Family Ended Up in the Spotlight," *The Guardian*, July 15, 2017, https://www.theguardian.com/world/2017/jul/14/who-are-aras-emin -agalarov-donald-trump-jr-emails.

34. *Hollywood Reporter*, "Donald Trump's Tweet About 'Best Friend' Putin Is Most Retweeted From Final Debate," October 19, 2016, https:// www.hollywoodreporter.com/news/donald-trumps-tweet-best-friend -939986.

35. Dan Mangan, "Natalya Veselnitskaya, Russian attorney at Trump Tower meeting, charged with obstruction of justice in unrelated money laundering case," *CNBC*, January 8, 2019, https://www.cnbc.com /2019/01/08/natalya-veselnitskaya-attorney-at-trump-tower-meeting -charged.html.

36. David Filipov, "What is the Russian Order of Friendship, and why does Rex Tillerson have one?" *Washington Post*, December 13, 2016, https://www.washingtonpost.com/news/worldviews/wp/2016/12/13 /what-is-the-russian-order-of-friendship-and-why-does-trumps-pick -for-secretary-of-state-have-one/.

37. Casey Michel, "The DOJ Won't Say Why Rudy Giuliani Hasn't Registered As a Foreign Agent Under FARA Law," *Think Progress*, May 14, 2019, https://thinkprogress.org/why-isnt-rudy-giuliani-registered-as-a -foreign-agent-fara-lobbying-in-ukraine-a9289f19677e/.

38. Cristina Maza, "Should William Barr Recuse Himself From Mueller Report? Legal Experts Say Attorney General's Ties to Russia Are Troubling," *Newsweek*, April 15, 2019, https://www.newsweek.com/so -many-conflicts-so-little-time-1396435.

39. *Daily Beast*, "Dems Raise Concerns Over Mnuchin's Russia Investor Connection," January 29, 2019, https://www.thedailybeast.com/dems -raise-concerns-over-mnuchins-russia-investor-connection.

40. Betsy Woodruff, "Indicted Oligarch Dmytro Firtash Praises Paul Manafort, Says Trump Has Third-Grade Smarts," *Daily Beast*, March 20, 2019, https://www.thedailybeast.com/indicted-oligarch-dmytro-firtash-praises -paul-manafort-says-trump-has-third-grade-smarts; The Moscow Project, "Everything You Need to Know About Michael Cohen, Contextualized," May 30, 2018, https://themoscowproject.org/explainers/everything -you-need-to-know-about-michael-cohen-contextualized/.

41. Natasha Bertrand, "Former FBI Director Represented Russian Firm at

Center of Major Money-Laundering Probe," *Business Insider*, November 16, 2017, https://www.businessinsider.com/fbi-director-louis-freeh-russia-prevezon-money-laundering-2017-11.

42. Jennifer Gould Keil, "Chaos at Conservative Think Tank After Donor Revealed As Ukrainian-Born 'Oligarch,'" *New York Post*, November 14, 2018, https://nypost.com/2018/12/04/chaos-at-conservative-think-tank-after-donor-revealed-as-ukrainian-born-oligarch/.

43. Christopher Miller, "Ukraine Shows Evidence of Secret Payments Allegedly Made to Trump Aide," Radio Free Europe, August 19, 2016, https://www.rferl.org/a/ukraine-secret-payments-evidents-manafort/27933901.html.

44. *Larry King Live*, "Interview with 'The Apprentice' Host Donald Trump," February 27, 2004, http://transcripts.cnn.com/TRANSCRIPTS/0402/27/lkl.00.html.

7. 2016–2019: "A Threat More Extensive Than Is Widely Known"

1. "Trump: 'I Have Nothing to Do With Russia, Folks,'" *NBC News*, October 24, 2016, https://www.nbcnews.com/video/trump-i-have-nothing-to-do-with-russia-folks-792709187907.

2. Gwynn Guilford and Hanna Kozlowska, "Trump's GOP Platform Voiced Strong Support for Ukraine–Until It Didn't," *Quartz*, July 19, 2016, https://qz.com/736394/trumps-gop-platform-voiced-strong-support-for-ukraine-until-it-didnt/.

3. David E. Sanger, "Harry Reid Cites Evidence of Russian Tampering in U.S. Vote, and Seeks F.B.I. Inquiry," *New York Times*, August 29, 2016, https://www.nytimes.com/2016/08/30/us/politics/harry-reid-russia-tampering-election-fbi.html.

4. Amber Phillips, "The emerging timeline of Obama and Russia that is giving Democrats heartburn," *Washington Post*, June 23, 2017, https://www.washingtonpost.com/news/the-fix/wp/2017/06/23/even-democrats-wanted-obama-to-speak-out-much-sooner-about-russia/?utm_term=.e849e0d519d1.

5. Abigail Tracy, "Harry Reid Accuses the FBI of Withholding 'Explosive' Information About Trump," *Vanity Fair*, October 31, 2016, https://www.vanityfair.com/news/2016/10/harry-reid-james-comey-letter.

6. Caroline Kenny, "Harry Reid: Comey may have violated the Hatch Act," CNN.com, October 31, 2016, https://www.cnn.com/2016/10/30/politics/harry-reid-letter-hatch-act/index.html.

7. David Corn, "A Veteran Spy Has Given the FBI Information Alleging a Russian Operation to Cultivate Donald Trump," *Mother Jones*, October 31, 2016, https://www.motherjones.com/politics/2016/10/veteran-spy-gave-fbi-info-alleging-russian-operation-cultivate-donald-trump/.

8. Ibid.

9. Jeremy Stahl, "Glenn Simpson Testified that the FBI Had a Source Inside the Trump Campaign Corroborating Collusion Claims," *Slate*, January 9, 2018, https://slate.com/news-and-politics/2018/01/glenn-simpson -testified-that-the-fbi-had-a-source-inside-the-trump-campaign -corroborating-collusion-claims.html.

10. Dexter Filkins, "Was There a Connection Between a Russian Bank and the Trump Campaign?" *New Yorker*, October 15, 2018, https:// www.newyorker.com/magazine/2018/10/15/was-there-a-connection -between-a-russian-bank-and-the-trump-campaign.

11. Liz Spayd, "Trump, Russia, and the News Story That Wasn't," *New York Times*, January 20, 2017, https://www.nytimes.com/2017/01/20 /public-editor/trump-russia-fbi-liz-spayd-public-editor.html.

12. Erik Wemple, "NYT's Dean Baquet rips 'fairly ridiculous conclusion' in public editor's column on Russia coverage," *Washington Post*, January 21, 2017, https://www.washingtonpost.com/blogs/erik-wemple /wp/2017/01/21/nyts-dean-baquet-rips-fairly-ridiculous-conclusion-in -public-editors-column-on-russia-coverage/.

13. Hadas Gold and Joe Pompeo, "New York Times Eliminates Its Public Editor," *Politico*, May 31, 2017, https://www.politico.com/story/2017 /05/31/new-york-times-public-editor-239000.

14. Margaret Hartmann, "Final 'October Surprises' Reveal FBI Is Probing Trump's Alleged Russia Ties," *New York*, November 1, 2016, http:// nymag.com/intelligencer/2016/11/final-october-surprises-fbi-probing -trumps-russia-ties.html.

15. Katelyn Polantz, "Paul Manafort faces 305 years," CNN.com, March 13, 2018, https://www.cnn.com/2018/03/13/politics/paul-manafort-faces -305-years/index.html.

16. Dan Mangan and Kevin Breuninger, "Judge in Paul Manafort Trial Says He Has Been Threatened and Is Now Under US Marshal Protection," *CNBC*, August 17, 2018, https://www.cnbc.com/2018/08/17 /judge-in-paul-manafort-trial-said-hes-been-threatened.html.

17. Sabrina Siddiqui, "Paul Manafort Trial: Judge Won't Release Jurors' Names Over Safety Concern," *The Guardian*, August 17, 2018, https:// www.theguardian.com/us-news/2018/aug/17/trump-manafort-pardon -trial-jury-latest-news.

18. Zoe Tillman, "Paul Manafort's Judge Won't Face Disciplinary Action For How He Treated Mueller's Office," *BuzzFeed News*, April 1, 2019, https://www.buzzfeednews.com/article/zoetillman/paul-manafort -judge-no-disciplinary-action-mueller.

19. *Gaslit Nation* (blog), Interview with Alexandra Chalupa, Transcript, June 22, 2019, https://www.gaslitnationpod.com/episodes-transcripts -20/2019/6/22/the-alexandra-chalupa-interview.

20. Murray Weiss, "Exclusive: Paul Manafort Advised White House on How to Attack and Discredit Investigation of President Trump," *Vox*, December 14, 2018, https://www.vox.com/2018/12/14/18140744/paul -manafort-trump-russia-mueller-investigation.

21. OakTown Unfiltered (@hrtablaze), "Breaking: Twitter Friendly Version: A soft coup has been launched by the FBI . . . ," Twitter, November 1, 2016, 8:15 P.M., https://twitter.com/hrtablaze/status/793607310920720385.

22. Richard Hofstadter, *The Paranoid Style in American Politics* (New York: Random House, 1964), 65.

23. Sean Gallagher, "DHS, FBI Say Election Systems in All 50 States Were Targeted in 2016," *Ars Technica*, April 10, 2019, https://arstechnica .com/information-technology/2019/04/dhs-fbi-say-election-systems-in -50-states-were-targeted-in-2016/.

24. Jake Swearingen, "Did the Intercept Betray Its NSA Source?," *New York*, June 6, 2017, http://nymag.com/intelligencer/2017/06/intercept -nsa-leaker-reality-winner.html.

25. Dave Phillips, "Reality Winner, Former N.S.A. Translator, Gets More Than 5 Years in Leak of Russian Hacking Report," *New York Times*, August 23, 2018, https://www.nytimes.com/2018/08/23/us/reality-winner -nsa-sentence.html.

26. *Gaslit Nation* (blog), Interview with Billie Winner-Davis, June 14, 2019, https://gaslitnation.libsyn.com/reality-winner-is-in-prison-while-the -traitors-walk-free.

27. Laura Strickler, Peter Alexander, and Rich Schapiro, "White House Whistleblower Says She Felt Humiliated After Retaliation from Boss," *NBC News*, April 2, 2019, https://www.nbcnews.com/politics/white -house/white-house-whistleblower-says-she-felt-humiliated-after -retaliation-boss-n990171.

28. Paul Manafort (@PaulManafort), "Battleground states moving to Trump en masse . . . ," Twitter, November 4, 2016, 10:54 A.M., https:// twitter.com/PaulManafort/status/794553482330210304.

29. Cristina Maza, "Paul Manafort Briefed Russian Intelligence Member on 'Battleground States' that Nearly All Voted for Trump: Mueller Report," *Newsweek*, April 18, 2019, https://www.newsweek.com/paul-manafort -russian-intelligence-kilimnik-collusion-trump-campaign-1400826.

30. Charles Davis, "Jill Stein's Recount Cash Pays for Her Russia Legal Defense," *Daily Beast*, July 13, 2018, https://www.thedailybeast.com /jill-steins-recount-cash-pays-for-her-russia-legal-defense.

31. "Sarah Kendzior Responds to Breitbart," https://youtube.com/watch?v= 1ZsJlLfGkkQ.

32. Carole Cadwalladr, "Cambridge Analytica a Year On: 'A Lesson in Institutional Failure,'" *The Guardian*, March 17, 2019, https://www .theguardian.com/uk-news/2019/mar/17/cambridge-analytica-year-on -lesson-in-institutional-failure-christopher-wylie.

33. *BBC News*, "Salisbury Novichok Poisoning: Russian Nationals Named As Suspects," September 5, 2018, https://www.bbc.com/news/uk -45421445.

34. Ashifa Kassam, "Refugees Crossing into Canada from US on Foot Despite Freezing Temperatures," *The Guardian*, February 7, 2017, https:// www.theguardian.com/world/2017/feb/07/us-refugees-canada-border -trump-travel-ban.

35. The Associated Press, "Trump Aide Dismisses Statue of Liberty 'Huddled Masses' Poem," August 3, 2017, https://www.cbsnews.com/news /trump-aide-dismisses-statue-of-liberty-huddled-masses-poem/.

36. Howard Blum, "Exclusive: What Trump Really Told Kislyak After Comey Was Canned," *Vanity Fair*, November 22, 2017, https://www .vanityfair.com/news/2017/11/trump-intel-slip.

37. Lennart Meri Conference, "Dealing with the White House: The Limits of Transactional Foreign Policy," Tallinn, Estonia, May 31, 2017, https://youtube.com/watch?v=7J7G-bF2zlI.

38. Sarah Kendzior, "Speech at the March for Truth in St. Louis," June 3, 2017, https://sarahkendzior.com/2017/06/03/my-speech-at-the-march -for-truth-in-st-louis/.

39. "Donald Trump Rally Speech in Denver, Colorado July 29, 2016," https:// www.youtube.com/watch?time_continue=2096&v=5Mg7UPLEX4I.

40. Thom Hartmann, "Bill Barr—Cover-Up Artist," *Salon*, January 20, 2019, https://www.salon.com/2019/01/20/bill-barr-cover-up-artist _partner/.

41. Timothy B. Lee, "How Manafort's Inability to Convert a PDF File to Word Helped Prosecutors," *Ars Technica*, February 23, 2018, https:// arstechnica.com/tech-policy/2018/02/how-manaforts-inability-to -convert-a-word-doc-to-pdf-helped-prosecutors/.

42. Natasha Bertrand, "New Court Filings Show Manafort Made Substantial Edits to Ukraine Op-Ed He Denied Ghost-Writing," *Business Insider*, December 8, 2017, https://www.businessinsider.com/new-court -documents-show-paul-manafort-edited-ukraine-op-ed-2017-12.

43. "Rick Gates Pleads Guilty, Asks Judge for Spring Break Trip to Boston," *CBS News*, February 23, 2018, https://boston.cbslocal.com/2018 /02/23/rick-gates-guilty-plea-boston-trip/.

44. Josh Gerstein, "Rick Gates Nixes Family Trip to Boston After Threats," *Politico*, March 1, 2018, https://www.politico.com/story/2018/03/01 /rick-gates-vacation-boston-threats-432624.

45. Howard Blum, "How Scared Should Trump Be of Mueller?," *Vanity Fair*, December 1, 2017, https://www.vanityfair.com/news/2017/12 /how-scared-should-trump-be-of-mueller-ask-john-gotti-or-sammy-the -bull.

46. Kevin Johnson and Bart Jansen, "Michael Flynn's Sentencing Collapses Amid a Judge's 'Disgust' Over Former National Security Adviser's

Conduct," *USA Today*, December 18, 2018, https://www.usatoday.com /story/news/politics/2018/12/18/michael-flynn-sentencing-collapses -judge-disgust-former-trump-aide/2352912002/; Alex Pappas, "Michael Flynn's Sentencing Delayed by Judge After Dramatic Hearing for Ex-National Security Adviser," *Fox News*, December 18, 2018, https:// www.foxnews.com/politics/former-national-security-adviser-michael -flynn-sentenced.

47. Adam Rawnsley, "Mueller Goes Easy on Michael Flynn for Spilling the Beans," *Daily Beast*, December 5, 2018, https://www.thedailybeast .com/mueller-recommends-lenient-sentence-for-michael-flynn.

48. David Gilmour, "The Gateway Pundit Conference Was a Who's Who of Conspiracy Theorists," *Daily Dot*, September 18, 2018, https://www .dailydot.com/layer8/gateway-pundit-conference/.

49. Rebecca Morin, "These Are All the Trump Associates Targeted in House Judiciary's Wide-Ranging Probe," *Politico*, March 4, 2019, https://www.politico.com/story/2019/03/04/jarry-nadler-trump-house -probe-1201126. Note to readers: My book is not a comprehensive work on every Trump associate implicated in this criminal probe. Such a work would be encyclopedic. The eighty-one people and organizations on this list should all be investigated; unfortunately, that list itself is also the tip of the iceberg.

50. Andrew Prokop, "Brett Kavanaugh Wrote That Presidents Shouldn't Be 'Distracted' by Criminal Investigations," *Vox*, July 9, 2018, https:// www.vox.com/2018/7/9/17551584/brett-kavanaugh-president -criminal-investigation.

51. Katelyn Polantz and Caroline Kelly, "Mueller's Office Disputes BuzzFeed Report That Trump Directed Michael Cohen to Lie to Congress," CNN .com, January 19, 2019, https://www.cnn.com/2019/01/18/politics /mueller-statement-buzzfeed/index.html.

Epilogue: End Times Road Trip

1. Sarah Kendzior, "Trump's America, Where Even Park Employees Have Become Enemies of the State," *The Guardian*, January 28, 2017, https://www.theguardian.com/commentisfree/2017/jan/29/trump -america-parks-employees-enemies-of-state.

Index

Q&A with Anand Giridharadas

Sep. 29, 2020

ANAND GIRIDHARADAS: To start at the end, you've been warning about the authoritarian threat of Donald Trump for years now. Given the president's comments in recent days, where do you think we stand?

SARAH KENDZIOR: We've been living through what I've called a "deja news" cycle, where the same stories appear again and again but they are stripped of the context that reveals their full horror or impact. The latest iteration of this is Trump saying that he may not accept the election results and stoke violence if he doesn't win. This is literally the same thing that Trump—and Roger Stone—threatened in 2016, but the media is calling it "unprecedented" and making no reference to Trump's 2016 statements, despite that one of them was said at a debate and was widely covered at the time.

This bizarre selective amnesia is tremendously damaging. The American people need chronology and context to understand the threat. Also, the fact that he threatened this in 2016 should have made officials prepared with a response should he threaten it again in 2020. They should have assumed he'd do it, this time with the backing of the state, and should have come up with a plan to combat it. Instead, they feign shock to avoid accountability. So we stand at a dangerous precipice, but it's made far more dangerous by the refusal of so many people to admit how we got here.

ANAND: The new disclosures about Trump's tax evasion and faux success are, on one level, same old, same old. And on another level, potentially a big deal. How do you understand them in the context of this moment? And do you worry that the more likely criminal prosecution gets in his post-presidency, the more desperate we can expect to see him, the more willing he will be to steal the election or incite violence, to avoid jail?

SARAH: We knew Trump hadn't paid taxes. Hillary Clinton said this during one of the debates, but there was little follow-up to her claim. There was also little follow-up on a series of documents from the Czechoslovakian security services revealed in 2016, which stated that in 1977 Trump had entered a bizarre agreement with the federal government to not pay taxes until 2007. We do not know the terms of this arrangement, but the documents are indeed real. UK journalist Luke Harding investigated them, and I wrote about them and their ramifications in *Hiding in Plain Sight*. It's a big untold part of this story, especially when you connect Trump to his four decades of dealing with transnational organized crime and corrupt U.S. government officials, which is what I did in my book.

As for the debt and other information revealed in the *New York Times* piece, none of this is surprising, but people need to learn how to interpret it. People should review his mentor Roy Cohn— Trump's tax-dodging, mobbed-up, media-savvy lawyer who was the biggest influence in his life. Cohn dreamed of dying owing the US government an enormous amount of money, and in 1986, he did. Acquisition of wealth is not the goal for either Trump or Cohn; debt is not a problem for them. A luxurious lifestyle, powered by fraud and threat and untouchable by law, is the goal. People need to examine not only Cohn and Trump's crimes but the complicit actors that enabled them, which in this case includes the IRS, the Department of the Treasury and other broken US institutions. Trump and Cohn are symptoms of a broader disease.

Trump will continue to try to steal the election. That was always the goal, and the tax stories don't change that. The revelations about his taxes also won't affect his base in the way some pundits claim. Trump doesn't care if they know that he doesn't pay taxes, because he thinks taxes are for suckers. His base will also see it this way. What I do wish his base (and everyone else) would understand is that the reason Trump doesn't pay taxes is because he is a key part of the so-called "deep state" and "DC swamp" and "NYC elites" that his base claims to despise.

But in terms of the election, the focus should be on the mechanisms of rigging—domestic voter suppression, foreign interference, insecure machines, the destruction of the US Postal Service, and so on—and what to do if he cheats and is caught or refuses to concede, both of which are likely. No one should ever compromise in holding him and his crime cult accountable.

ANAND: Now, to go back to the beginning, what was the training and thinking you'd done that shaped your way of seeing Trump when he arrived on the presidential scene?

SARAH: I have a Ph.D. in anthropology. My research was on authoritarian politics in post-Soviet independent states, particularly Uzbekistan. When Trump began campaigning in 2015, I immediately saw parallels between him and the flamboyant Central Asian kleptocrats I had long studied. The deeper I looked into Trump's past, I found that his connection to corrupt actors from the former Soviet Union was not only metaphorical but distressingly literal. This became particularly clear when he appointed Paul Manafort, longtime oligarch and Kremlin lackey, as his campaign manager.

I was also alarmed by how easy it would be for his campaign to exploit social media. As a graduate student studying Uzbekistan at a time when the internet was relatively new, I was interested in how digital media affected trust, and what I found was that it increased paranoia and fractured the fledgling bonds among Uzbek exiles scattered across the world who were, thanks to the internet, able to communicate regularly for the first time. This was a controversial observation when I was in grad school—between 2006 and 2011—because conventional wisdom was that the internet was an inherently liberating technology that would further the spread of democracy. To say otherwise made you a heretic, but I've gotten used to being that. A heretic is just a person who tells the truth too early.

I was also watching how authoritarian rulers like Vladimir Putin or Ilham Aliyev were purposefully leaving the internet open *just enough* to bombard the population with propaganda instead of censoring it all together. This approach, which Rebecca MacKinnon called "networked authoritarianism," became the model not only for authoritarian states but for crumbling democracies over the past decade.

Trump's savvy use of digital media was aided by his skill at manipulating print and cable media, which he has successfully done for four decades, whether through tabloids, reality TV, or Twitter. My first job out of college was at the New York *Daily News*. I worked there from 2000 to 2003, so I got an inside view of how the media is made and what kind of narratives New York journalists swallow and spit out. I knew Trump's real backstory, and I knew how he would rewrite it.

I also had another unique vantage point: I live in St. Louis, a city that never recovered from the economic crash of 2008. This region was and remains in tremendous economic pain, and Trump was skilled at exploiting that pain in 2016, though, of course, he had no interest in remedying it. Many journalists missed this because they live in wealthy coastal enclaves and believed that the "recovery" was real. I strongly oppose the "real America" vs. "false America" dichotomy—or the "red state" vs. "blue state" dichotomy for that matter—because it's bullshit. Like I wrote in my book, America is purple—purple like a bruise. But it's true that media is an insular profession dominated by people who tend to be out of touch with everyday American life. However, they're just as out of touch with everyday people in New York City or D.C. as they are with everyday people in Missouri. The gulf isn't about geography so much as it is about wealth and networks, though obviously where you live reflects that somewhat. Anyway, I have no interest in being part of that world, and I think my aversion to it helped me tell the story of Trump honestly.

ANAND: There were obviously a lot of boorish and racist and pseudo-tyrant comments as far back as 2015. But when would you say you first sat up and felt that Trump represented a real, as opposed to a rhetorical, authoritarian threat?

SARAH: Immediately. Every country that becomes a dictatorship started with a chorus of people saying, "It can't happen here." It can happen anywhere. And in 2015, the US was extremely vulnerable to autocracy. We had experienced fourteen years of eroded institutional trust due to 9/11 and the illegal wars in its aftermath, we had endured unremedied economic hardship, and we were also contending with hyperpartisanship, a rise in racist violence, and the upheaval of digital technology. Those are the conditions where demagogues emerge, and Trump launched his campaign by calling Mexicans rapists and murderers. It was obvious he was going to campaign as a demagogue to rule as an autocrat.

The history of the US is the history of selective autocracy— Native American genocide, slavery, Jim Crow laws, internment camps, and so on. Not only could it happen here, it already had happened here, and Trump is an open racist who ran on an openly racist, xenophobic, hateful platform. That is deeply threatening to the body politic whether he wins or loses, but Trump had the full force of the GOP and its goal of destroying government—which dates back to the Reagan era—behind him, in addition to having led a life immersed in organized crime, business, media, and entertainment. He was trained by Roy Cohn in blackmail, bribery, and other mobster tactics. He also was backed by sophisticated foreign autocrats and oligarchs who were using him as a vehicle for their own agendas. That adds up to an incredible threat.

And on top of that, you had Trump literally telling you what he was going to do. In 2014, he said he wanted economic collapse, riots, and everything to be a total disaster to make America great again. That kind of rhetoric from him is very consistent; it goes back to the mid-1980s. It reflects the corporate raider–mafia mind-set he was raised in but is exacerbated by the sadism and fatalism that is unique to his personality. And, again, none of this was hidden. Officials and media didn't want to call it what it was, either because of their own tolerance for racism and xenophobia or because they didn't want to admit how rotted and vulnerable the institutions they led had become.

ANAND: Alarmism is underrated. Discuss.

SARAH: It is bizarre to me that people critique "alarmism" without defining it. If you describe a threat and give evidence to support why you believe there is a threat, you are not an alarmist in a pejorative sense. You are a realist sounding the alarm. If you keep insisting that everything is fine or that things will magically work out in the face of evidence that it is not fine and it will likely not work out, you are not a realist, and you are not rational. You are a fool.

ANAND: Can you talk about how you were portrayed by people who felt you were being alarmist or extrapolating too much? Have any of them come around and told you you were right?

SARAH: I've gotten some apology letters, but no apologies or retractions for the hit pieces that ran on me in major publications, some of which fabricated things I said or wrote. It was harder for people to label me "alarmist"—or the misogynist version of that, "hysterical"—than to label others because of my credentials and my track record, but they tried anyway. And they failed. I don't care much about how I'm portrayed because my work speaks for itself, and I speak for myself. I've never had to retract anything or apologize for a bad prediction. I'm a careful researcher, and I only present information or hypotheses when I'm reasonably confident that I'm right.

I think the fact that I got every major thing right is less interesting than the question of why all the people who got nearly everything wrong still have jobs.

I encourage people to simply stop watching those people or reading them, because they're giving out bad information, and there are so many good scholars and analysts who got it right from the start and continue to get it right now. I was not at all alone in seeing the threat of Trump and the demise of democracy coming. Your time is better spent reading them or reading history books.

But it's important for some people to pretend my work doesn't exist because, as I said before, they need to feign shock to dodge accountability. And I destroy the plausibility of shock. They can never say "no one could have seen this coming," because I saw it coming and documented it ceaselessly.

And, again, I was not alone—other people did the same thing, often approaching it from different angles reflecting their expertise. It's important to note that most people who predicted our political direction accurately were women and/or not white, which played a major role in why their theories were dismissed. As much hell as I've had to go through, I did not have to face what journalists who aren't white face. Media as an institution is very racist, and they are now uncomfortable that black and brown people were much better at anticipating what Trump would do than white people. And media racism kills—their failure to portray Trump and those around him—Stephen Miller, Jared Kushner, and others—as a threat helped streamline brutal policies predominantly aimed at black and brown Americans. White elitist journalists need to reckon with their role in causing mass death and suffering.

ANAND: I think one of the things that has been challenging in persuading people of the immediacy of the Trumpist authoritarian threat is how incapable and laughable and buffoonish he is. Despite all the historical examples of dangerous leaders who were, or were seen, that way, it has seemed hard for many people to process the idea that a man so incompetent could ever achieve something like authoritarian rule. Can you talk about that perception as you see it and the relationship between authoritarianism and (in)competence?

SARAH: The Trump administration covers crime with scandal and covers malice with incompetence. I describe this tactic in depth in *Hiding in Plain Sight*, but it's one that you see throughout Trump's whole life, from his days as a protégé of Roy Cohn up to today. It's intertwined with his ability to manipulate the media. He has no shame, so he doesn't care if people are mocking him or if he's mired in a scandal that has no legal consequences. He cares about three things: money, power, and immunity from prosecution. If you threaten any of those things, you have leverage. But people would rather talk about how he wrote "covfefe" in a tweet.

I don't think Trump is some geopolitical mastermind; he only learns what he needs to know and leaves the rest to the lawyers. But he's skilled at spin and propaganda. He played a fictional version of himself on television for over a decade and spent decades before that playing "Donald Trump" in tabloid media. This is part of what made him such an appealing target for the Kremlin and transnational criminal actors: he is an ideal front man.

But to sum up: When people say that Trump is incompetent, the follow-up question needs to be "incompetent at what?" Is he incompetent at governing, navigating bureaucracy, and strengthening America's position in the world? Yeah, he probably would be, if he ever tried to do those things. But that's not why he's there. He's in office to destroy this country and enrich himself, and he's very good at that. He's very skilled at that, and he's spent his life building up those skills. The problem is that the US political establishment insists on seeing everything through a lens that dismisses the idea that Trump genuinely has no interest in serving this country and, in fact, enjoys hurting this country. With COVID-19, for example, they kept insisting he was unqualified, he was making errors, and that's why he let the virus spread. Whereas I saw the situation and said he's doing this intentionally—he wants to kill people and make money off the crisis. He is absolutely willing to let Americans die; he gets off on it. And I was right.

Trump also doesn't mind if people know this about him. He likes to get caught; he doesn't want to be punished. And since no one will punish him, since no one will set boundaries and contain him for the sake of this republic and its people, we are in a lot of trouble.

ANAND: If Trump is indeed trying to straight-up steal the election, what do other countries' experiences reveal to be the most effective checks on that before, during, and after?

SARAH: Telling the truth is the most important thing. No matter how horrifying the truth is, you have to tell it, and not worry about being labeled an alarmist. You will probably have to worry about threats to your life, but that's unfortunately what happens when your country is becoming a mafia state. The full story of this operation and its goals need to be documented and exposed. I did my part with *Hiding in Plain Sight*, and on *Gaslit Nation*, and there are many other scholars and analysts who did their part by following the money, looking at the culture of corruption around him, analyzing intelligence and criminal operations, and so forth.

The US is in a different situation than a typical country that is transforming from democracy to autocracy, at least historically speaking. We may not be in a unique situation now because other countries, like the UK, are subject to the same forces, but it is different from the fascist takeovers of the past. First, let me say that I am fine with Trump being called a fascist because he is using fascist tactics, and it's a word that resonates with the public. We need a wide, inclusive, and resolute American opposition movement, and this word conveys the necessary urgency.

But I've largely called him an authoritarian or autocrat instead of a fascist because "fascist" implies loyalty to the state. A fascist wants to embody and expand the state and usually has imperial ambitions. Whereas Trump wants to destroy the US: he wants to strip it down and sell it off for parts to both domestic and foreign backers. His cohort's ambitions are similar to what oligarchs and other hypercapitalists did to the USSR after its collapse—which is not surprising because the Kremlin and an associated network of plutocrats and oligarchs are the prime backers of this operation.

You also see Israeli Prime Minister Benjamin Netanyahu's influence, the head of an apartheid state, on Kushner, who is far more influential at devising policy than Trump. Looking at what has happened to Russia and Israel under their brutal leaders is a good guide for predicting what may happen to America, at least in terms of policies. But the difference is that Trump truly doesn't care if the US survives. This makes him different from dictators like Hitler or Stalin, who wanted to conquer, and who were deeply wedded to the idea of the nation-state. It makes him different from Netanyahu and Putin as well, because they want to expand their territory and preserve their nations. The Trump administration is simply a transnational crime syndicate masquerading as a government.

That is why those who seek to keep our democracy and sovereignty need to understand that Trump does not even respect the traditional limitations of fascism: he doesn't care if the country itself is defeated, as long as *he* is not defeated. So Americans who are standing up for our country need to assess their leverage in that context. We are dealing with a new kind of threat, and we need to come up with new measures to combat it. I encourage people to be very creative in their approach. Open your mind to the darkest possibilities of what they would do and then consider what mechanisms you would need to stop them. Don't be hesitant or shy. Know that you're not fighting alone and that there is not one simple solution to this, because we are not just battling Trump, we are battling a coalition of corruption amidst deeply broken institutions. Be resolute and flexible and strategic.

That may sound like vague advice, but that's because this a long-haul fight, and your mind-set going into this fight matters. If you expect a quick win, you will be disappointed. Americans tend to blame themselves for systemic problems. They do that with the economy, and now they're doing that with protest. But the problem is not them—it's this disgusting, broken system. Your job is to fight back and stand up for others, but, understandably, it's not an easy process when you're contending with this level of rot.

ANAND: Which of our institutions—media, courts, civil service, universities, and everything else—have held up well to the authoritarian threat in your view, and which have not?

SARAH: That's a tough question to answer because, first, all of those institutions were already rotting before Trump got in—that's, in part, how he got in—but also because COVID-19 has accelerated the damage so profoundly. I would say it's more a matter of the individuals within those institutions. Some have done a very good job despite their industries themselves being corrupt. The saddest thing to see is what has happened to the courts, because they are usually the last bulwark against autocracy. That's why the GOP has tried for so many decades to control them and take us from a representative democracy to an autocracy run by the decrees of lackeys. People need to look more deeply at why the courts have failed. There have been so many threats against judges, juries, lawyers, and others in this system—the issue is not just complicity and incompetence, but fear of threats. We are living in a mafia state.

ANAND: In a country this high on the idea of how free it is, I think it's hard for people to visualize what authoritarianism even means in the American context. Let's say Trump steals the election and goes full-blown tyrant in the second term, but within the kind of systemic constraints you'd still expect to hold, can you help me visualize what you think that would look like?

SARAH: Domestically, we will lose many of our constitutional rights, especially since Trump will have the Supreme Court backing him. Protest will increasingly be criminalized, and we will likely lose our freedom of speech and media to some degree. I don't think this will be done in a straightforward way, like a repeal of the First Amendment, but through excessive litigation and increasing government control over social media monopolies.

We will continue to see racist and xenophobic policies and extreme abuse of migrants. The economy will continue to deteriorate, and Trump and his lackeys will see this as an opportunity to strip the country for parts, buy up public lands and landmarks, and privatize and destroy them. I'm also worried about public education, which they have long sought to destroy, and which is already suffering during the COVID-19 crisis. The Trump crime cult will see this as an opportunity to finish public education off. They also will do nothing to the climate crisis. They believe in climate change, but they are accelerationists—they see a depopulated earth as easier to control. Those are just some of the nightmares we will face on a domestic level.

I'm concerned that term two of Trump will involve his cohort fulfilling long-held violent ambitions abroad. I'm particularly worried about the potential genocide of Palestinians and the deals that Netanyahu's Israel is making with autocratic [Persian] Gulf states. Kushner is a lifelong friend of Netanyahu, subservient to him; the US will aid him in these endeavors, no matter how corrupt. Kushner also is close to Saudi Crown Prince Mohammed bin Salman, who is also incredibly dangerous, and his relationships should be monitored closely. I am worried that the US will go to war with Iran, which is a long-held goal of many Trump advisers both in the US and abroad. Meanwhile, Putin has his own imperialist ambitions, which is one of the main reasons he wanted Trump in office. He wanted to ease sanctions and destroy the Western alliance that stood as a bulwark against him doing things like invading Ukraine and other former Soviet states. That Western alliance is much weaker now, and Trump is his willing accomplice along with other dictators and mafiosos, so we should expect more invasions from Russia.

ANAND: In a post-Trump era, how do you think we should deal with those who were complicit in the Trumpist nightmare? Answer with regard to different levels of complicity: merely voting for him, giving him significant money, working for him, enabling him in Congress. How do you think about creating accountability for what happened versus healing and giving people a face-saving way out if they genuinely want one?

SARAH: I believe in redemption, but redemption needs to be earned. Right now, we have corrupt actors working for this administration, or Trump's crime syndicate being rewarded by the publishing or media industries with lucrative deals. The officials who failed to stop Trump are similarly rewarded. Meanwhile, you have people like whistleblower Reality Winner in prison banned from telling her own story. So we need to reverse these incentives. I encourage people to boycott books from confirmed bad actors, the same way I encourage people to stop reading the publications of the journalists who downplayed the threat and lied about what was really happening.

The people who committed crimes in this administration need to be prosecuted. Some of the crimes are so severe that they are violations of the Geneva Convention. They are crimes against humanity. We need Nuremberg-style trials. We also need the US government to come clean about the transnational crime syndicate that has existed since the 1980s (albeit with precursors beforehand), featuring Semion Mogilevich, Jeffrey Epstein, Ghislaine Maxwell, and other extremely dangerous criminals. We need answers as to why these extremely dangerous criminals were not only allowed to remain free by officials but were feted by elites and whitewashed by the media. There is a giant, largely buried story here. I tell a great deal of it in *Hiding in Plain Sight* and other authors, like Craig Unger and Julie K. Brown, have told parts of it as well. No one should be let off the hook here; no institution or individual should be viewed as beyond reproach.

In terms of ordinary Americans, I think minds may change if

people learn the full truth about what's been done to this country. I have heard from Trump supporters who read my work and changed their minds because they learned about ties to Epstein, Mogilevich, and other parts of his criminal history. Some of the things they were most surprised about were direct quotes from Trump himself. They had never heard them because most media won't cover them—not just Fox, but "liberal" outlets like *The New York Times*.

In most cases, these former Trump supporters were given a copy of my book by a relative or friend who disliked Trump and wanted them to understand the full story. Personal trust relationships play a big role in changing perception; it's not like my book is some magic bullet. But I think everyone appreciates knowing that they are not hallucinating this level of institutional failure, which crosses party lines. It is corruption so vast and horrifying that it's difficult to process. It has structured the last forty years of American life, which means it has structured my entire life and the lives of many people who are feeling lost and hurt and abandoned.

I don't excuse people who back bigots. Everyone who voted for Trump was, at the least, willing to overlook overt racism and cruelty, and they should reckon with that. But I think getting the truth goes a long way to changing perception. This is not to say that people are not responsible for their terrible decisions, and I consider voting for Trump to be a terrible, hurtful decision. But I am curious what will happen if we fully confront all these broken institutions and their sins—corruption, systemic racism, exploitation, and so on—instead of keeping up a façade of pride or normality or even of ignorance, which is a façade that officials cling to so they can avoid having to remedy these crises.

People are always asking me where I find hope, and I tell them I don't think of things that way—I don't believe in hope, but I don't believe in hopelessness. I believe in the truth and in doing the right thing because it's the right thing to do; let the chips fall where they may.